DIACHRONIC DIALECTOLOGY

Publications of the Philological Society, 53

WILEY

DIACHRONIC DIALECTOLOGY

New Methods and Case Studies
in Medieval Norwegian

Tamsin Blaxter
Gonville & Caius College,
University of Cambridge

Publications of the Philological Society, 53

WILEY

CONTENTS

LIST OF FIGURES

LIST OF TABLES

ABBREVIATIONS

Main text abbreviations

CRE	Constant Rate Effect
CRH	Constant Rate Hypothesis
DN	Diplomatarium Norvegcium
du.	dual
GIS	geographical information system
GWR	Geographically Weighted Regression
L1	first language
L2	second language
MLG	Middle Low German
nom.	nominative
NP	noun phrase
pl	plural
sg.	singular
SV	subject-verb
VS	verb-subject

Glossing abbreviations

ACC	accusative
DAT	dative
DU	dual
GEN	genitive
INF	infinitive
PL	plural
PRET	preterite
PRS	present
SG	singular

ACKNOWLEDGEMENTS

Writing this book has been a much longer, rockier road than expected – or at least, longer and rockier than I planned. Perhaps that's true of all books. As is also true of all books, this work could not have been written without help and counsel from many people around me along the way. My thanks to my PhD supervisor, David Willis, who offered vital guidance in the early years of this project; to my PhD examiners, Peter Trudgill and George Walkden, for their helpful feedback and encouragement; to Thomas Marge, whose insights into the problems of parameter setting were invaluable; to Francis Nolan and an anonymous reader who reviewed the proposal and manuscript for the Philological Society and offered essential advice in reshaping my initial plan; and to Susan Fitzmaurice and Melanie Green at the Philological Society, who gave the project their blessing and guided me through the publication process. All of this help was gratefully received and without it the book would have had a quite different – and much inferior – form. Needless to say, all remaining errors of fact, analysis or judgement are my own.

INTRODUCTION

1.1. *Foreword*

Early in the work on my PhD research project I came across the *Diplomatarium Norvegicum*: a sprawling, chaotic corpus of Late Medieval texts from or about Norway, a majority of them in Norwegian. This was a body of texts quite unlike most corpora developed for historical linguistics. It was comprised of a great many separate texts most of which were very short, were transcriptions of original manuscripts, and about which we could identify a date and place of publication relatively easily. I was immediately deeply excited about the possibilities it offered for dialectology.

I had previously been working on language change and gender in the texts of the medieval *Íslendingasögur*. These are a fascinating and unique source for historical linguistic study in their own right: they are long, intended as realistic narratives, and feature a lot of dialogue in direct speech from a diverse set of characters. However, they share a number of deficits with many other corpora used for historical linguistic work. As a small number of long texts, they are a poor dataset for studying intertextual variation. If each text is just one datum then, beyond a certain point, it doesn't matter how big your corpus is in tokens – with just forty to sixty texts, there is only so much you can ever say about what determines the differences between them. As long, high-status literary texts, the *Íslendingasögur* are all known only from copies (descending from chains of copying of unknowable length), many of them are known in multiple recensions, and we have limited information about their authorship. Even a piece of metadata as simple as what decade such a text should be dated to is uncertain, subject to debate, and probably has multiple true answers in different senses. Doing dialectology with these was quite impossible (trust me!)

The documents in the *Diplomatarium Norvegicum* were right at the other end of the spectrum of what is possible for a corpus of medieval documents, and seemed the perfect source for historical dialectology. However, the corpus was not in a good state to undertake this work. It was in a custom format that modern software could not read, and the date and place information for each document was given in the form of free-text strings: not machine-readable, and therefore useless for doing large-scale work. I set to work transforming these into numeric dates and co-ordinates and quickly discovered that the situation was worse than I had realised. There was so much variation in the quality of the placenames given, and many of them were so extremely ambiguous, that the work was not simply to transform the localisations as given into a set of co-ordinates, but to localise each document from other modern sources and from the medieval text itself.

This job turned out to be by far the longest single piece of work I did during my PhD (indeed, it isn't as fully complete as I would like even now), and I had not made a huge amount of progress before I realised the scale of the gamble I was making. As a PhD student your most valuable resource is your time. By pouring months (and eventually years) of work into localising these texts, I was putting myself in a position where a lot was riding on the hope that they would be a good source for historical dialectological work. If I could find no spatial patterns in language use between the texts, I would have sunk a great chunk of my PhD into a single task with nothing much of use to show for it.

I stopped the work and started trying to explore dialect variation in the texts I had localised so far, hoping to find confirmation that I was on the right track. To my horror, I was faced with what seemed to be maps of random noise. When I mapped linguistic features of individual texts I could see no patterns. If I grouped the texts together into regions – municipalities, counties, k-means clusters – I could convince myself that there were patterns, but they were subtle and far from confidence-inspiring. I almost gave up, and started trying to think of other directions I could take the work, or ideas for other projects entirely. But, all the while, I was bothered by niggling doubts about the crudeness of the tools I was using to explore my data. I could not find any well-established and agreed-upon way of exploring language variation in time *and* space together in the historical linguistics literature, and the obvious approaches I was taking all had equally obvious deficits. I was far from sure that there were any dialectological patterns to find in my data, but I was sure that there were many ways in which I could be missing such patterns if they were there. What I needed, I thought, was some algorithm for determining the most relevant subset of the data to answer the question of real usage at any particular point in space and time. This thought was the beginning of my journey towards choosing and refining the approach to historical dialectology which I present in this book.

I am not a statistician or a geographer by training, but I do believe that important steps forward in our field can often come about through dialogue with neighbouring disciplines like these. New methods informed by cross-disciplinary engagement can expand what we are able to say about our data manifold and in so doing expand the boundaries of the knowable. Looking back, it is striking to me that my first view of the texts which I explore in this book suggested that there might be no meaningful spatial variation between them. By contrast, I would now take a view much more consonant with my initial optimism about the *Diplomatarium Norvegicum*: that it is hard to find better-structured sources for doing medieval dialectology. I hope the reader will be convinced of this from the findings I present here. The point, however, is that without the right tools, I could not even see with confidence that my sources contained any patterns worth pursuing. The right analytical instrument can make the difference between histories we can describe in some detail and confidence, and mysterious events irrevocably lost to time.

I do not wish to insinuate that there are no other good approaches out there in the historical linguistics literature or that no-one else has arrived at similar methods to those which I advocate here. What is clearly the case, however, is that there is no widely agreed-upon set of approaches for dealing with spatial data in historical linguistics, and as a result most possible historical dialectology remains undone. The historical corpora we have constructed are often optimised for exploring intratextual variation in complex or rare grammatical features. They are built from the texts which other disciplines (literature, history) have deemed most important and worthy of dissemination. Many of the sources which would be most suited for historical dialectology are under-explored for any kind of linguistic work, and even where historical linguists have investigated them, space is rarely in focus. Where there exists consensus wisdom concerning the dialectology of historical languages, these ideas are often based on impressionistic, qualitative work undertaken long before digital methods were available. In this book I hope to impress upon the reader the wealth of detailed spatial information that may be hidden in such sources, and inspire them to try these methods on their own data.

What is more, I hope to convince the reader of the *value* in understanding spatial variation in our data. Dialectology may seem to researchers in other sub-disciplines a little like linguistic stamp-collecting. We find patterns – words or grammatical features associated with particular places and times – purely for the sake of cataloguing them in atlases, with no deeper theoretical goals in mind. This view, however, would be to disastrously underestimate the potential of spatial evidence about language use. All speakers exist in space, are born in particular places, live in particular settlements, make journeys to others. All speech occurs at some location. If it is the case that all languages spoken in more than one settlement must vary over space – and this does seem to be true to a first approximation, especially when we look to the pre-modern period – then any theory about how a language changes, how its speakers use it for social purposes or how it influences and is influenced by other languages, must interact in some way with spatial variation. If we can draw inferences from a theory to the dialectology of a language, then spatial evidence can be used to test that theory. Thus the evidence of dialectology – properly analysed and visualised so that it relates to the questions at hand – may turn out to be of use to researchers in almost any sub-field of historical linguistics.

It is with this proselytising mission that I have approached this book: not just with the goal of presenting my research on the historical dialectology of Norwegian and what it can tell us about wider questions in historical linguistics, but aiming also to provide the reader with a new set of tools with which to explore their own languages of interest and convince them that that exploration may be well worth the effort. In this way, I hope to offer something for everyone. For those already interested in statistical methods in dialectology I offer a discussion of some problems and possible solutions. To those with no such background I offer a (hopefully) approachable guide that makes no assumptions about existing skills. And even for those with no intention of carrying out their own historical dialectological investigations, I hope to offer an informative set of investigations into Norwegian language history. Whether I have achieved any of these goals must remain, of course, up to the reader.

1.2. *Structure*

Chapter 2 presents the statistical methods to be used, arranged roughly to recount the processes by which I arrived at them. Chapters 3 and 4 present background information on the corpus I used to investigate the dialectology of medieval Norwegian, how I built on the existing corpus to develop it, and how the data was collected for each variable. Chapters 5, 6 and 7 present investigations into these data, each structured around a different research question with a different scope: a question about specific grammatical phenomena in the history of Norwegian; another about the history of the language as a whole and its place in our understanding of sociolinguistic typology more broadly; and a final question concerning how language change operates in space. Chapter 8 summarises conclusions from these chapters. Finally, chapter 9 offers a step-by-step guide to undertaking your own investigations in historical dialectology using the R package I developed for this project, kernelPhil

2

THE STATISTICS OF SPACE IN HISTORICAL LINGUISTICS

2.1. *Introduction*

Getting an understanding of the distribution of language features in space from historical datasets is far from easy, and we have long lacked sufficiently powerful tools to do it well. Describing the spatial distributions of noisy datasets is a relatively difficult problem in and of itself, and much of the methodological history of dialectology concerns the development of different ways of idealising or summarising the messy realities of speech data. However, in historical linguistics we are faced with extra challenges. Our data is typically noisier than the data of the linguistics of contemporary languages and, because we have no control over what has been preserved, we have far less capacity to design our datasets to suit the analytical tools we have available to us. We are usually dealing with written language data and are faced with a host of questions about the quality of that data and the unknown set of biases that may have shaped it: these problems may interfere with spatial distributions. The most serious issue of all, however, is the fact that where contemporary linguistic data is distributed in two-dimensional space, ours is distributed in three-dimensional space: we also have to deal with time. In this chapter, I will discuss these methodological challenges: how these sorts of data have been dealt with in previous scholarship, how the methods which I advocate here work, and why they are especially suited to our problems. Readers who are primarily interested in the linguistics and not the statistics may find this chapter relatively dense, and might wish to skip ahead to chapter 3.

2.1.1. *Visualising time and space: problems and solutions*

The data of historical linguistics are very bad. This may come as a shock to the student when they first graduate from primers, textbooks and standard editions to the unpolished evidence of historical manuscripts and inscriptions. The texts themselves seem messy and inconsistent, with constant lacunae, variation in orthography, and so on. Statements about provenance are often revealed to be much more nuanced and subject to disagreement than they might first appear. Widely accepted views about when and where a language underwent certain changes may be based on very tenuous pieces of evidence, and an understanding of the history of the field often reveals how much our best guesses at language history are contingent on particular accidents of textual survival.

At the root of many of the issues with the data of historical linguistics is the fact that our sources are usually only indirect evidence for the phenomena in which we are interested: we are generally asking questions about language as *spoken* in particular times and places; what we have are written data, often from different times and places. Because – except in a handful of cases in very recent language history – we have no access to any contemporaneous spoken data to compare to, we cannot know for sure what effect the written medium has on the linguistic features we are interested in. We must simply think of it as a source of unquantifiable statistical noise – in effect, an unidentifiable, random proportion of our data are 'wrong' as measures of the phenomena we are investigating. Three other factors add more noise to our data:

- dating of texts is often uncertain and therefore must often be in error;
- our knowledge of where the people who produced texts were from is often incomplete and uncertain, and our best guesses must therefore often be wrong; and
- many texts are known only through copies, often with a chain of copyists of unknown length: this multiplies the aforementioned two problems many-fold.

Given this context, it is unsurprising if we find that our data seems chaotic and complex. Consider Figure 1, which shows the word found in medieval Norwegian charters for 'become': native *verða* (pale blue) or borrowed *blífa* (dark red); overlapping points have been subject to random scattering. These are, as historical linguistic data go, extremely simple: texts uniformly have either *verða* or *blífa*, not both; there are only two variants. Yet it is far from easy to describe the distribution. Perhaps we get an impression of greater use of *verða* in rural areas, more *blífa* in the densely-populate clusters around the coasts – but this is far from obvious, and hard to quantify by looking. What is more, no attempt has been made here to visualise text date. Perhaps, even if we are right about the spatial distribution we have identified, this distribution is a product of change over time, with texts from some regions tending to be later than others?

Given such noisy data, then, our main problem is one of how to visualise it to best enable us to spot patterns. Over the years, there have been various approaches to the problem of creating readable visualisations of historical linguistic data in space and time. Perhaps the most common approach is simply not to create visualisations at all. The author's impression of spatial and temporal distributions can be given in prose ('*verða* tends to occur more often in early texts and texts from rural areas', '*blífa* is particularly common in charters from Bergen' and so on). Features may even be assigned to named dialects and the spatial distributions of these dialect areas never precisely defined, putting us a step further from the textual evidence itself (consider, for example, labels like 'Mercian', 'Anglian' and 'West Saxon' in the dialectology of Old English). The deficits of these ways of doing things are numerous: the reader must already be familiar with the geography of the region in order to imagine the distribution described, and even so, complex distributions may be relatively difficult to picture from a description; it is completely unaccountable, since it is impossible or very difficult to check the author's claims; it is very imprecise.

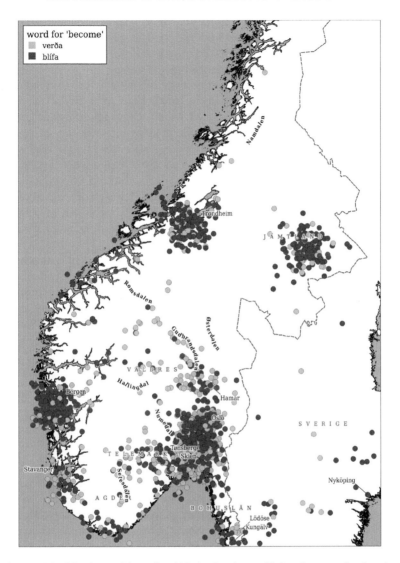

Figure 1. Word for 'become' in medieval Norwegian charters [Colour figure can be viewed at wileyonlinelibrary.com]

A variant of this approach might be to segment the data into regions and then give counts and relative proportions of the different variants in each region in a table. Such regions might be the cells of a regular grid, or an author might borrow from another domain and use externally-defined political or economic regions. This is an improvement in some respects – certainly, it has a greater degree of numerical specificity. One could go further and map the values from the table, colouring regions by proportion or by majority variant, or simply writing the values in the centre of each region. This allows a reader unfamiliar with the geography to understand the distribution. However, these approaches – and any approach that imposes predefined spatial groups onto the data – suffers from the problem that the regions are necessarily arbitrary. The distributions of linguistic features are not automatically predictable from any other spatial features – isoglosses are not compelled to run along political boundaries or geographical features; dialect regions need not all be the same size, or a regular shape. Accordingly, whatever spatial groupings we impose on the data will be very likely to cross-cut the dialect regions we are trying to illuminate: does an apparent 50:50 region reflect non-spatial variation, or does it reflect the fact that the region is bisected by an isogloss? Furthermore, this approach in and of itself does not solve the additional problem of visualising time. It can be combined with periodisation, but this introduces the same problem of arbitrary groupings on the time axis.

Another approach is to represent every single datum – whether this be text or token – in its location on the map as some kind of symbol. Symbol shape, colour and size can then be manipulated to express multiple pieces of information simultaneously (such as length of text, identity of variant, date of text); alternatively, some of this information can be given in labels. This was the approach taken in Figure 1, and it has been taken further in Figure 2, with text date indicated by shape and variant indicated by colour. This is still not especially easy to interpret, certainly with any precision. A careful reading of the map reveals that *blífa* is more common later (there are many red triangles, few red circles). We can, perhaps, detect the signs of interaction between place and date: are there more triangles around Oslo, fewer in regions like Jämtland, Gudbrandsdal and Valdres? Such readings remain imprecise and vague.

What we need is a combined statistic and method of visualisation which is able to treat both space and time continuously and that summarises trends across both, without imposing groupings, and preferably also offers some indication of whether the differences we see are big enough to be interpreted, or whether they could well be the product of noise. Some such approaches do exist in the literature, and two will be mentioned here.

In a study of vowel reduction in West Frisian from 1300 to 1550, Versloot (2008, 2020) calculates weighted moving averages for the rates of features of interest across localised documents – this is effectively the two-dimensional iteration of the kernel smoothing method used in this book, and we could compare it to techniques used in modern synchronic dialectology (see further below). A central feature of all such methods is the 'kernel function', the way in which importance (weight) decreases with distance (these are discussed further in section 2.2). Versloot (2008: 349–50) offers two kernel functions, the inverse distance function:

$$f(d) = \frac{1}{d^n} - 1,$$

and the linear decrease function

$$f(d) = \begin{cases} 1 - d^n & \text{if } d \leq 1 \\ 0 & \text{otherwise} \end{cases},$$

where d is the distance between two points divided by a limiting bandwidth ($d = D/D_0$) and n is a scaling parameter (Versloot settles on the linear decrease function as preferable for the data of historical dialectology (personal communication)). Neither of these kernel functions are used here, although note that the inverse distance function is equivalent to a triangular kernel if $n = 1$. This method clearly answers some of the problems we have identified. It offers a method of visualising spatial patterns across the data while treating space as continuous; it estimates specific values at specific locations. However, it offers no way to answer the question of whether the differences observed are statistically significant or could be the result of noise. More crucially, it offers no continuous way to deal with time: the data can be periodised and spatial moving averages calculated for each period, but this suffers from the problems of arbitrary division of the data described above.

Willis (2017) uses geographically weighted regression (GWR) (Fotheringham et al. 2003) to infer the likely progression of a Welsh morphological innovation at different locations and in different syntactic contexts from survey data, using speaker year of birth as a proxy for date, then plots the date at which the innovation is estimated to have passed 50 per cent with dates mapped onto colour; an example figure from this paper is reproduced as Figure 3. This method clearly fulfils our criteria: it does not impose arbitrary periods or spatial groupings onto the data, produces a figure which is intuitively readable, and offers statistical tests for the presence of significant variation in space and in time. However, there are still problems. Using a parametric method like regression imposes a predefined shape and maximum complexity onto our distribution in time: in Willis's application, the change progresses in a straight line with the same slope everywhere, and only the y-intersect differs in space. This thus cannot precisely reproduce reality in which we assume the speed of change, or even the exact shape of rises and falls, can differ in space. It would be possible to build more complex regression models in this vein to partially alleviate this problem, but the possibility space for models increases hugely with any increase in model complexity, and we quickly come up against the limits of our small datasets. All but the very simplest GWR models are known to suffer from problems of collinearity which are relatively difficult to fix (Wheeler & Tiefelsdorf 2005). Furthermore, although this type of model does allow us to answer the question of whether there is *some* significant spatial and temporal variation in the data (in the sense that we can check whether the GWR provides a

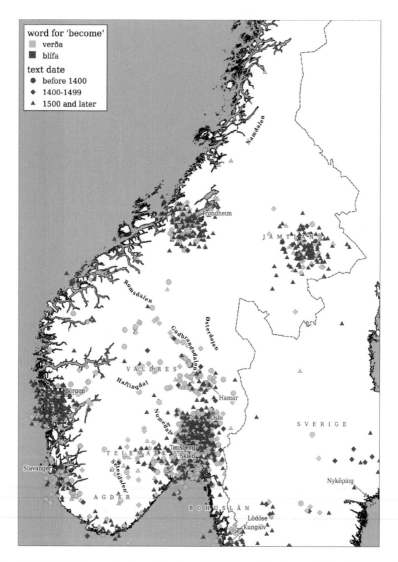

Figure 2. Word for 'become' and text date in medieval Norwegian charters [Colour figure can be viewed at wileyonlinelibrary.com]

better fit to the data than a non-spatial model, and whether including a term for date results in a better model fit than not including it), it does not allow us to ask this question of specific pairs of localities or any other specific contrasts.

2.2. Kernel smoothing

The approaches for summarising and visualising the data of historical dialectology which I advocate in this book are part of a family of methods

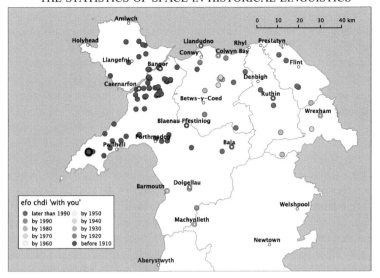

Figure 3. Estimated year at which the rise of innovative pronoun *chdi* passes 50 per cent of usage in the context of preposition *efo* 'with' on the basis of geographically weighted regression from Willis (2017) [Colour figure can be viewed at wileyonlinelibrary.com]

generally referred to as kernel smoothing; tools like kernel density estimation, *k*-nearest neighbour smoothing and weighted moving averages all fall under this umbrella, and these tools are widely used in signal processing for tasks like cleaning audio, recovering corrupted images, applying blur to images, and so on. These are all methods for estimating the value of some underlying function from sparse and noisy data; they all have the effect of interpolating between separated samples and smoothing the estimates to reduce noise. They have been used for synchronic dialectology (for example Rumpf et al. 2009; Sibler 2011) for data from various different linguistic domains.

These methods rely on a central assumption about the function we are estimating: that nearby data are more relevant for estimating the value at a point than distant data because function values will be more alike at near than at distant points. For historical dialectology we are working in geographical space and in time, so this can be unpacked to the following two assumptions:

1. all other things being equal, dialects are more similar to nearby dialects and more dissimilar to distant dialects (i.e. there is spatial autocorrelation for linguistic features); and
2. all other things being equal, varieties of the same language at different times are more similar if the time distance is smaller (i.e. there is temporal autocorrelation for linguistic features).

Assumption 1 is an important finding of dialectometry (Séguy 1973; Nerbonne 2010) but also a founding assumption of all dialectology. Indeed, by using terms like 'dialect' at all we assert that there are spatially-defined groups of speakers whose language shares properties it does not share with speakers outside their region. It can also be seen that the assumption of spatial autocorrelation must follow from any normal understanding of how language changes spread in space. Speakers must acquire new features from other speakers with whom they are in contact, and speakers exist in space. The degree of spatial autocorrelation implied might differ between models of linguistic diffusion, with models which prioritise long-distance migration and contact implying lower spatial autocorrelation, but it is still the case in these models that nearby speakers tend to be more similar (for more on such models, see chapter 7).

Similarly, Assumption 2 follows naturally from our understanding of how language change works. Generally, change is gradual: many changes happen in continuous domains and progress gradually; there are changes which happen in discrete domains and so necessarily (at least in some sense) happen abruptly, but even if multiple abrupt changes are correlated (such as in the 'catastrophic change' of Lightfoot 1979; 1991), a language at two dates is still more likely to have those features in common if the two dates are closer. What is more, since in practice the data of historical linguistics generally allow us to study only the language of the speech community and not the individual (even if sometimes the language of the individual is our theoretical object of study), even abrupt change must progress gradually through the community by the process of population death and replacement.

2.2.1. Kernel smoothing for spatial variation

We can conclude, then, that spatial and temporal autocorrelation are reasonable assumptions for the data of historical dialectology, allowing us to use kernel smoothing methods. The basic approach is very simple. For each point in n-dimensional space for which an estimate is to be calculated, a weighted average is taken of all the data, where the weights are a function of distance from this point: the further away a datum is in time and space the lower weight it is assigned in our average, reflecting the fact that we assume it offers less relevant evidence. We call the function which derives weights from distances the 'kernel function' (k) and the scale on which it operates the 'bandwidth' (b). We have a matrix of noisy observations of the rates of v variants at p points, $X_{1...v,1...p}$. We must first calculate a matrix of distances between all points $D_{1...p,1...p}$. The estimate for variant j at point i is then:

$$\hat{f}(i,\ j) = \frac{\sum_{l=1}^{p} k\left(d_{i,l},\ b\right) X_{j,l}}{\sum_{n=1}^{v} \sum_{l=1}^{p} k\left(d_{i,l},\ b\right) X_{n,l}}.$$

In other words, we take the sum of the product of kernel weights and the rate of our variant of interest at every point, and divide this by the sum of the product of kernel weights and the rates of all variants at every point. If our variant frequencies at each point are already defined as usage proportions between 0 and 1, then:

$$\hat{f}(i,\ j) = \frac{\sum_{l=1}^{p} k\left(d_{i,l},\ b\right) X_{j,l}}{\sum_{l=1}^{p} k\left(d_{i,l},\ b\right)}.$$

Having so defined the core of our method, we must determine the kernel function: the importance of points as evidence and therefore the weight assigned to them should fall off with distance, but what should the shape of this decline be? A range of functions are available to us. We could simply weight all points within a certain distance 1 and all points beyond this distance 0; this is referred to as a square kernel. We could assign weights declining on a straight line up until a certain distance, and assign all points beyond this distance 0; this is referred to as a triangular kernel. We could assign weights falling off on a Gaussian curve of some width. There are many others, but these three commonly used options are visualised in the top panel of Figure 4. The practical differences between these different kernels, for sufficiently large datasets, are often relatively small. One important difference has to do with the way very distant data are treated. The Gaussian kernel, and any other kernel function with limit 0, will always assign some non-zero weight to all data, and

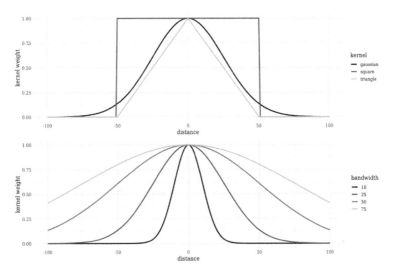

Figure 4. Kernel weights by distance for different kernel functions (top panel) and Gaussian kernel with different bandwidths (bottom panel)[1] [Colour figure can be viewed at wileyonlinelibrary.com]

[1] Throughout this book, where colour is used in figures and maps to communicate scales or categories, both lightness and hue are used together. This means that it is possible to read the figures printed in greyscale (contrasting only the differences in lightness) but much easier to read the figures in colour. The reader is advised to refer to the full colour, online edition of the book whenever a precise or detailed reading of figures is needed.

so can be useful with unevenly distributed datasets with some sparsely sampled regions. The square or triangular kernel might assign *all* data weights of 0 in such cases, making it impossible to give an estimate, whereas it will still be possible to give an estimate with a Gaussian kernel because there will still be non-zero weighted points.

All of these kernel functions have some kind of scaling parameter: the distance beyond which weight 0 is assigned for square and triangular kernels, the width (standard deviation) of the Gaussian curve for the Gaussian kernel. As mentioned above, this scaling parameter is referred to as the bandwidth, and the Gaussian kernel with different bandwidths is visualised in the bottom panel of Figure 4.

The choice of bandwidth is generally more impactful than the choice of kernel function (Rumpf et al. 2009: 287). These are smoothing methods – fundamentally, what we are doing is smoothing the data in order to reduce the salience of the noise and better perceive the signal – and the bandwidth is the parameter which controls the amount of smoothing we are applying. Consider Figure 5,[2] which demonstrates kernel smoothed estimates for our *verða>blífa* dataset with the same kernel function (a Gaussian kernel) but bandwidths of 10, 50, 100 and 500km (the kernel smoothing method has the effect of combining multiple documents at the same point and so no scattering is needed; instead, symbol size is used to indicate the size of the sample at each point). As we increase the bandwidth of the kernel, we get more smoothing. In the panel with the lowest bandwidth, we see that our estimates are still very noisy: individual outliers, points with vastly higher or lower estimates than their closest neighbours, are common. Since such a chaotic spatial distribution with so many tiny regions seems unlikely from our a priori knowledge of dialectology, we can assume that this bandwidth is probably too low. By contrast, the panel demonstrating a bandwidth of 100km is probably over-smoothed – many features have disappeared, and differences between those that remain have been minimised. Finally, the panel with bandwidth 500km demonstrates that as our bandwidth approaches infinity, estimates at all points will approach the unweighted mean. We will return to setting bandwidths in section 2.3 below.

The kernel functions we have discussed so far are static: the same relationship between distance and weight holds at all points in space. However, this need not be the case. We can instead define a kernel function such that the bandwidth

---

[2] Note that I have described these as interpolation methods as well as smoothing methods, and they do indeed allow for interpolation: we can take an estimate at any location, not only locations where we have a sample. However, for this map and others in this book, I have only made and visualised estimates at the sample points. This decision serves the goal of making effective visualisations, rather than being dictated by the statistic itself. Medieval Norway was highly unevenly populated, with large, mountainous regions with no population at all. Interpolating estimated usage into these regions would clearly be misleading – there was no dialect there to estimate. However, we have enough documents in our corpus to provide a relatively good map of where the population was located at the time, at least within southern Norway, and so simply mapping estimates at the sample points gives a reasonable representation of this interacting human and physical geography.

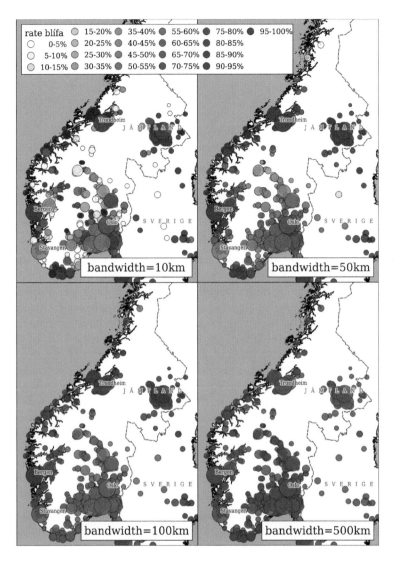

Figure 5. Estimated proportional use of *blífa* 'become' over locations in medieval Norwegian charters using kernel smoothing with a Gaussian kernel and bandwidths of 10, 50, 100 and 500km [Colour figure can be viewed at wileyonlinelibrary.com]

shrinks or expands dynamically in response to local sample density – these are referred to as dynamic kernels. The simplest version of this would be to assign a weight of 1 to the nearest k neighbours and a weight of 0 to all other points – this is effectively a square kernel with a bandwidth expanding to the radius of a circle that includes exactly k points. This form of smoothing can be referred to specifically as k-nearest neighbour smoothing. By the same logic, we could define a dynamic triangular kernel whose bandwidth was set as the distance to the kth point, or a Gaussian kernel whose width was set such that the sum of kernel weights was k. In each case, our bandwidth parameter now effectively describes a sample size on which averages are to be taken, rather than a distance in space.

Dynamic kernels have two main advantages for our purposes. More so even than static kernels which never assign 0 weights, like the Gaussian kernel, dynamic kernels can be appropriate for dealing with unevenly distributed samples. Consider the distribution of samples seen in Figure 2 and 5: regions like Romsdalen or Namdalen have very few samples, whereas in the densely-populated south-east we have many hundreds. A circle with a radius large enough to include even ten nearest neighbours in the least densely-sampled regions would cover the whole of Viken, whereas a reasonable sampling window in the south-east would include no near neighbours around many points elsewhere. Although we could use a static Gaussian kernel here, we would be faced with a trade-off: with a low bandwidth we would under-smooth sparsely sampled regions, with the estimate at each point overwhelmingly determined by the sample at that point; with a higher bandwidth we would get a reasonable estimate in under sampled regions, but smooth over potentially interesting variation in the south east. A dynamic kernel allows us to have our cake and eat it: in sparse regions, the effective sample window expands to be large enough to work with, and in dense regions it shrinks to allow us to use our data most effectively.

Secondly, setting the bandwidth in terms of effective sample size instead of in terms of distance is extremely useful for power analysis, thus allowing us to understand the specificity of our estimates. We will return to this point in section 2.3.3 below.

2.2.2. Time

We have an idea, then, of how we can use the kernel smoothing method to deal with geographical space, and generally speaking, we can deal with time with exactly the same set of methods. Figure 6 shows kernel smoothed estimates for the *verða>blífa* change in time alone, varying the kernel function (left panels) and bandwidth (right panels). As with kernel smoothing in space, the Gaussian kernel achieves smoother estimations than the other functions but the more important effect is from the choice of bandwidth. Higher bandwidths smooth out more of the noise, but also potentially obscure real features of the distribution. Notice the asymmetry between the beginning and end of the change, most obvious in the 10km Gaussian smooths (top right): because the change starts some time into the period covered by the corpus, we have a long stretch of time in which it is at 0 per cent, but it only reaches completion at the very end of our time period if at all. As a result, when we use higher bandwidths, the estimates at the end of the change probably underestimate the real value because they are

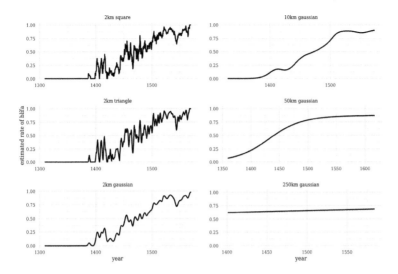

Figure 6. Estimated proportional use of *blífa* 'become' over time in medieval Norwegian charters using kernel smoothing with varying kernel functions and bandwidths

calculated on temporal windows which include more early than late data, whereas those in the early and middle stages of the change do not.

How then do we combine this method with our parallel method for geographical space? We have two options: we could treat time and geography together as a three-dimensional space, with a single kernel function weighting each datum by its distance from a place and a time; or we could have two separate kernel functions, one in space and one in time, and take the product of these two weights.

A single kernel in three-dimensional space may seem preferable on the basis of conceptual neatness, but it has certain disadvantages compared with treating the two separately. Distances in space and time are measured in different units, and it is not obvious what number of years should be equivalent to what number of kilometres. We could effectively set bandwidths for space and time independently by scaling co-ordinates and years before calculating the kernel smoothed estimates. However, applying a kernel function separately to each has the advantage that we can potentially use different kernel functions for time and space, reflecting the fact that distributions in time and space may be different and so the ideal kernel function may not be the same in each. I have done this in previous publications (Blaxter 2017b; 2019; Blaxter & Kinn 2018; Blaxter & Trudgill 2019), using a static Gaussian kernel in time and an adaptive square kernel in space. Here, I will use a static Gaussian kernel in time and an adaptive Gaussian kernel in space.

If applying two kernels, the question of ordering arises. For static kernels, ordering makes no difference since we are taking the product of the two kernel weights, but for dynamic kernels this is an important question. By applying the dynamic kernel second, we maintain control over the effective sample size, thus keeping the benefits for power analysis. The data used for the examples in this chapter and the case studies in chapters 5–7 are more unevenly distributed in space than in time, so we will use a static Gaussian kernel in time followed by an adaptive Gaussian kernel in space. Effectively, our spatial sample window expands and shrinks to ensure not just that enough data from nearby locations are included, but enough data from nearby locations *and* nearby dates.

2.3. *Parameter setting*

A remaining question regarding the use of kernel smoothing methods for historical dialectology is how to set the parameters of the functions: how do we choose the bandwidth of the temporal kernel and the bandwidth of the spatial kernel? Since different bandwidths can radically affect the impression of the distribution we get, how we arrive at different choices of bandwidth is crucial so that we can have greater confidence that our results are meaningful – but also in order to avoid adjusting our research design with a specific desired finding in mind ('*p*-hacking'). Since we can often make features of the distribution appear or disappear in our estimates by changing the bandwidth, it is important to have an approach which takes away our ability to manipulate our results.

Here we will discuss three possible approaches to this question:

1. setting bandwidths based on real-world priors;
2. setting bandwidths based on predictive accuracy; and
3. setting bandwidths based on power analysis.

Whichever approach we choose, we are dealing with two trade-offs. Firstly, higher bandwidths result in more smoothing, which means that noise is more effectively minimised. However, greater smoothing also means reduced resolution: potentially real differences are minimised at increasing distances, estimates at more widely separated points become less independent, and as a result our ability to see local patterns is reduced. Thus, there is a trade-off between resolution and noise-reduction. Secondly, if we decrease the bandwidth of the temporal kernel, we gain a greater resolution in time. However, doing so reduces the amount of data available at each point in time. With less data available at each point in time, we would need a higher spatial bandwidth to achieve the same amount of spatial smoothing, leading to a lower spatial resolution. Thus there is a trade-off between spatial and temporal resolution.

2.3.1. *Setting bandwidths based on real-world priors*

One approach to setting bandwidths is to determine them on the basis of our independent knowledge of the phenomena we are exploring. Language variation is generated by human movement and contact behaviours and so we know a priori that meaningful dialectal differences cannot exist on a scale smaller than the regions in which everyday contact takes place. Seen differently, dialect is a property of the speech community and so there is no need to explore variation at a resolution greater than the scale at which such communities exist. With enough data, we could estimate variation in usage across distances of just a few metres by setting our spatial bandwidth to an extremely small value, but this would clearly be pointless since we can be sure that any such differences must be noise.

We can think of this in terms of the distance at which estimates should be independent: if we are interested in highlighting differences between places, then estimates made for these places should be based on non-overlapping datasets; if we are definitely *not* interested in differences between places, then estimates between them *should* be made with overlapping datasets. When using a Gaussian kernel, there is a consistent relationship between these distances and bandwidth. The bandwidth in this case is the standard deviation of the Gaussian distribution. For a two-dimensional, symmetrical Gaussian distribution, the radius of a circle which will include 95 per cent of the volume under the curve (i.e. the resulting weights) is 2.2365σ, so points separated by at least 2.2365σ are close to independent. For a one-dimensional Gaussian distribution, the range centred on 0 that will include 95 per cent of the weights is -1.6448σ to 1.6448σ.

Using this, we can identify a rule-of-thumb lower bound for spatial resolutions by identifying the distance below which we believe any differences must be noise (that is, the minimum distance between distinct speech communities) and dividing this minimum distance by 2.2365. We can apply the same logic to setting the temporal bandwidth. If we believe that change takes place primarily in native acquisition then the length of a generational cohort divided by 1.6448 offers a similar lower bound on temporal bandwidth. We can identify upper bounds by identifying the minimum distances or lengths of time over which we *do* need to have distinct estimates and dividing these by 1.6448. Keeping bandwidths below this threshold will ensure that estimates at locations or points in time which we need to contrast are calculated on largely non-overlapping datasets. For spatial bandwidths, this might mean the distance between specific locations we want to compare; for temporal bandwidths, this might mean the length of time over which the change takes place.

To take the example of our medieval Norwegian data, if we assume that the smallest likely definition of a speech community was a parish, then the distance between parishes in the most densely populated regions represents the smallest possible distance at which we might be interested in linguistic differences. Rural parishes in south-eastern Norway are rarely closer than 5km from one another. At the other end of the scale, it will definitely be important to us to be able to distinguish the major cities of Oslo, Bergen, Stavanger and Trondheim, the closest pair of which are Bergen and Stavanger at about 160km apart. This suggests our spatial bandwidths should be between $\frac{5}{2.2365} = 2.24$km and $\frac{160}{2.2365} = 71.54$km. If we treat generational cohorts as spanning around a decade and a given change takes place over around 150 years, this suggests our temporal bandwidths should be between $\frac{10}{1.6449} = 6.08$ years and $\frac{150}{1.6449} = 91.19$ years.

As this demonstrates, although priors of this type do offer bounds on what reasonable bandwidths might be, those bounds are extremely wide: there is a huge difference in the amount of smoothing achieved by bandwidths of 2.24km and 6.08 years and bandwidths of 71.54km and 91.19 years. We will often find that we can determine whether given features of the dataset are visible or entirely smoothed by changing bandwidths within these ranges, raising the risk of *p*-hacking. Furthermore, we might wonder whether bandwidths should also be sensitive to properties of the dataset we have to work with and not only to the real-world phenomena in which we are interested.

2.3.2. *Setting bandwidths based on predictive accuracy*

A different approach to parameter setting is to use predictive accuracy. We can split the dataset into a training set and smaller testing set, apply our smoothing techniques only to the training set, and see how well our estimates predict the values found in the testing set. We then adjust our parameter settings, repeat the process, and see whether we have better predictions. We can continuing doing this until we have identified the pair of bandwidths which allow the most accurate prediction. This should have the result of identifying the parameters which best minimise noise and highlight the signal, since the signal should be the correlated pattern which makes prediction possible. We will not go into detail on this method of parameter setting since it was found not to be a useful method with the data under study and so will not be the method chosen for the remainder of the analyses in this monograph. However, it is worth briefly covering why it was not effective here and more generally is unlikely to be the best choice for historical dialectology.

Firstly, there are some practical problems with cross-validation. The various versions of this method are distinguished by how the data are divided into training and testing sets, the most rigorous of which is leave-one-out cross-validation. Under this approach, the testing set is a single datum and the training data are all of the sample points in the dataset except for this one. The analysis is repeated for every point, so that at the end we know what bandwidths best allow prediction of every point in the dataset on the basis of the all the others. Because of the very large number of permutations involved, this approach to parameter setting is extremely time-consuming. We can use different definitions of the training and testing sets, such as dividing the dataset into *k* partitions at random and exploring what bandwidths allow prediction of the data in each partition on the basis of the others (*k*-fold cross-validation). These non-exhaustive methods are faster – although still potentially quite slow for large datasets – but less accurate than exhaustive leave-one-out cross-validation.

Secondly and more crucially, the data of historical dialectology is not well suited to this approach. The assumption of cross-validation approaches is that the data are made up of two components: a correlated signal and random noise. Since the noise is uncorrelated it offers no useful information for prediction, and so the bandwidths that allow the most accurate predictions will be those which best smooth out the noise while minimally affecting the signal. However, this assumption is likely to be violated by the data of historical linguistics. Many of the known sources of noise in our datasets *are* likely to produce correlated errors across multiple samples:

- writers who (unbeknownst to us) are migrants from other localities produce noise in our localisations, and if those writers produce more than one document then this noise will be correlated;
- writers who work from earlier exemplar documents we are unaware of will produce noise in our textual datings, and this noise will be correlated if more than one extant document is produced from the same exemplar;
- regional variation in documentary drafting norms will produce correlated noise in the signal from specific regions;
- regional or temporal variation in degrees or distribution of literacy will produce correlated noise in the signal from specific regions or periods; and
- mismatches between the writers we can identify (for the charters explored in this monograph, the signatories) and the whole set of people involved in producing the language of a given text (scribes, writing instructors, local lawmakers, witnesses whose speech is transcribed, etc.) could render the language of multiple texts from the same region interdependent in innumerable invisible ways.

None of these are 'signal' in the sense that none of them have anything to do with the phenomenon we are interested in (spoken language variation in space and time), and yet all of them could produce spatially and temporally correlated patterns in our datasets that would be statistically indistinguishable from the signal. As some of these would tend to operate on very small scales compared with the patterns we are interested in, this should have the result that cross-validation will suggest extremely low parameter settings. With correlated noise at a small enough scale, the best way to predict any given sample is simply to look at its nearest neighbour; if this is the case, the best bandwidths for prediction will be close to zero, with almost no smoothing of estimates. This is indeed what was found for most of the datasets explored in this book.

A related approach which avoids this problem is to create idealised synthetic data with the same spatial properties as our real dataset and a simulated change starting at some realistic point of innovation and spreading outwards at a rate such that it goes to completion in a realistic amount of time. The noise we add to this dataset will be uncorrelated. We can then find the best fit parameters that allow prediction of this dataset with kernel smoothing. This was the approach used in Blaxter (2019). However, this method requires a series of pieces of a priori knowledge of the data we are investigating that are hard to justify. We have to know the time period over which the change happens, have a guess at where it was innovated and have a reasonable spatial model of its spread, and the best way to get these pieces of information is to use kernel smoothing, resulting in circularity. Much more importantly, however, we need an estimate of how much noise to add to the synthetic data. This is hard to achieve because there is no obvious way of estimating the amount of noise from the data and there are a very large number of unknowns (many mentioned in the paragraphs above) involved, making a truly a priori estimate very difficult. Yet the amount of noise synthesised is the main parameter which will control the optimum bandwidths we settle on. Clearly a method of parameter setting that itself relies on a parameter that we have no reasonable way to set is not to be preferred.

2.3.3. Setting bandwidths based on power analysis

Another reasonable approach to setting bandwidths is to do so with reference to the degree of accuracy we want our final estimates to have. We will start by considering how to do this for spatial kernel smoothing alone.

For a given confidence level (α), sample size (n) and standard deviation (σ), the estimated mean ($\hat{p}$) has confidence intervals:

$$\hat{p} \pm z_\alpha \frac{\sigma}{\sqrt{n}},$$

so to achieve a given margin of error (m), we can calculate the required sample size:

$$n \geq \left(\sigma \frac{z_\alpha}{m} \right)^2,$$

where z is determined with the quantile function of the normal distribution:

$$z_\alpha = Qnorm\left(\frac{\alpha}{2}\right).$$

In our case, we are taking a series of local samples from a known global population. As mentioned above, a core assumption of dialectology is that variable language use has positive spatial autocorrelation. As a result, it is reasonable to assume that the variance of our local samples will usually be lower than the population variance, so we can conservatively use the population standard deviation in calculating our required n. If we are dealing with a categorical variable with more than two variants (as is common for dialecto-logical data), then we can use the standard deviation of the most frequent variant: as this variant will necessarily have the highest variance, this will give us a larger sample size than necessary to achieve our desired margins of error for the other variants. We can then set the confidence level and margin of error we want to achieve, and if we are using a k-nearest neighbour kernel, our bandwidth k simply equals n.

For example, taking the *verða>blífa* dataset and first applying a Gaussian temporal kernel with a bandwidth of 100 years centred on 1490, we have a weighted population standard deviation of approximately 0.456. If we want to have 95 per cent certainty that our estimates lie within 10 per cent of the true values, then:

$$k \geq \left(0.456 \cdot \frac{z_{0.05/2}}{0.1}\right)^2,$$

$$k \geq \left(0.456 \cdot \frac{1.960}{0.1}\right)^2,$$

$$k \geq 79.88.$$

Usually we would have to round the sample size to a whole number, but since we are dealing with weighted data here and so we already have non-integer sample sizes, we can simply set $k=79.88$. This is visualised in Figure 7.

Keeping in mind that a higher value of k implies a lower spatial resolution in the resulting estimates, we are dealing with a trade-off here: the greater confidence and the smaller the desired error margins, the lower resolution can be achieved. Figure 8 shows the relationship between confidence level, margin of error and k for this dataset.

If we divide the size of the dataset (i.e. the sum of weights) by k, we get the number of separate subsets of the data of sufficient size to make an estimate: effectively, the number of cells that could be fully distinguished. Defining the resolution in this way, Figure 9 shows the relationship between confidence level, margin of error and resolution.

Thus far, we have been working with an adaptive square kernel (k-nearest neighbours). If we are instead using a Gaussian spatial kernel, an additional step is required: we must determine the bandwidth that creates samples of size k. If samples were distributed completely evenly with a density of 1, this would be the width of a symmetrical two-dimensional Gaussian curve with maximum height $= 1$ such that the volume under the curve was equal to k. If A is the maximum height, (x_0, y_0) is the centre of the curve, and σ_x, σ_y are the standard deviations of x and y, then the equation for the two-dimensional Gaussian curve is:

$$f(x, y) = A \cdot \exp\left(-\left(\frac{(x - x_0)^2}{2\sigma_x^2} + \frac{(y - y_0)^2}{2\sigma_y^2}\right)\right).$$

If our curve is centred on (0,0), $A = 1$ and $\sigma_x = \sigma_y$ (i.e. the curve is symmetrical), then:

$$f(x, y) = \exp\left(-\left(\frac{x^2 + y^2}{2\sigma^2}\right)\right).$$

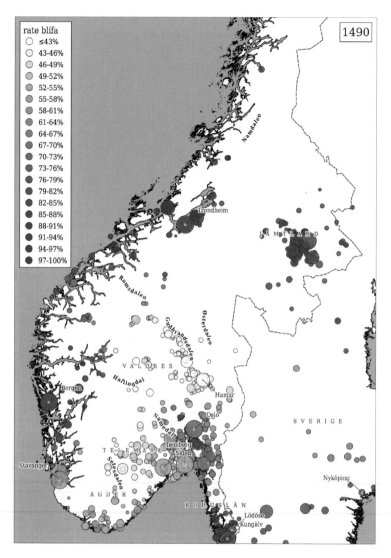

Figure 7. k-nearest neighbour estimates for *verða>blífa* with a Gaussian temporal kernel centred on 1490 and bandwidth of 100 years and k = 79.88 [Colour figure can be viewed at wileyonlinelibrary. com]

The volume under this curve is:

$$\int\limits_{-\infty}^{\infty} \int\limits_{-\infty}^{\infty} \exp\left(-\left(\frac{x^2+y^2}{2\sigma^2}\right)\right) = 2\sigma^2\pi,$$

so if we know that the volume we want to achieve is *k*, then:

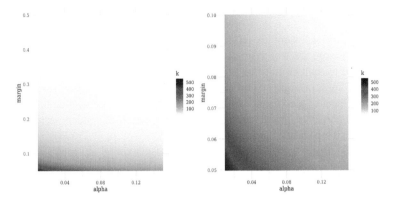

Figure 8. *k* by margin and alpha for *verða>blífa* data with a temporal kernel centred on 1490 and bandwidth of 100 years [Colour figure can be viewed at wileyonlinelibrary.com]

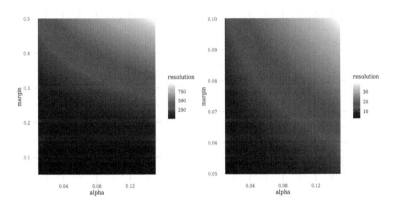

Figure 9. Spatial resolution by margin and alpha for *verða>blífa* data with a temporal kernel centred on 1490 and a bandwidth of 100 years [Colour figure can be viewed at wileyonlinelibrary.com]

$$\sigma = \sqrt{\frac{k}{2\pi}}.$$

If we know the density of the samples $d \neq 1$, then:

$$\sigma = \frac{\sqrt{k/2\pi}}{d}.$$

For many real datasets, samples will not be evenly distributed. In such cases we could use some measure of local sample density to calculate the bandwidth at each point: this can represent a good and fast approximation. However, data of the sort explored in this book are sufficiently unevenly distributed that this does not provide even an approximately accurate value. The bandwidth that achieves a sum weight of data n at a given point is highly sensitive both to the exact distribution of local samples and to features of the overall distribution such as the locations of large areas with no samples. Accordingly, an optimisation algorithm can be used at each point to identify the bandwidth which most closely achieves the sum of kernel weights equalling n. Here, the optimise function from the base R stats package is used to estimate the bandwidth at each point such that the sum of weights equals n; this function uses a combination of golden section search and successive parabolic interpolation.

For the figures in this book, an adaptive Gaussian kernel in space will be used. If we wanted a static Gaussian kernel, we must then select a single bandwidth. We could take the maximum bandwidth required for any point and use this as the global bandwidth. This has the advantage of being conservative in that it achieves the error margin and confidence level required at every point. However, for datasets with spatial outliers, this will result in far higher bandwidths than required at the vast majority of points, and so the unnecessary loss of much spatial resolution. A perhaps better approach, where a dataset has such outliers, is to use the mean bandwidth required across all points, or to use the maximum for only non-outlying points (given some definition of outliers).

We must then address question of setting temporal bandwidths. The temporal bandwidth determines the effective size of the dataset available at a given point in time, and so for a given k the temporal bandwidth determines the spatial resolution: higher temporal bandwidths allow higher spatial resolution. Since temporal bandwidth directly determines temporal resolution, with higher temporal bandwidths implying lower temporal resolution, we have the expected trade-off between spatial and temporal resolutions. Assuming that we want the best possible temporal resolution given our other specifications, we can set our temporal bandwidth to the minimum value necessary to achieve a specified spatial resolution for a given k.

Consider Figure 10, based on synthesised data. The top left panel demonstrates that our fictional change passes the 50 per cent mark roughly in the middle of the time period considered; as we can see from the bottom left panel, this means that the variance also peaks around year 50. The top right panel shows the sum of weights per year given a temporal kernel with a bandwidth of 10 years: the samples are very evenly distributed in time, far more so than any real dataset is likely to be. The bottom right panel then shows the relationship between temporal bandwidth and the spatial resolution that could be achieved given $\alpha = 0.05$, margin $= 0.1$. Generally, the higher the variance the higher k, and so the higher the temporal bandwidth must be in order to achieve a given spatial resolution. If we decide that the minimum acceptable spatial resolution is 20 (i.e. twenty distinct cells, equivalent to a 4×5 grid), then the best temporal bandwidth is 31 years; this is determined on the basis of the most restrictive point, indicated by the dotted line, which is indeed within the period when the variance is highest.

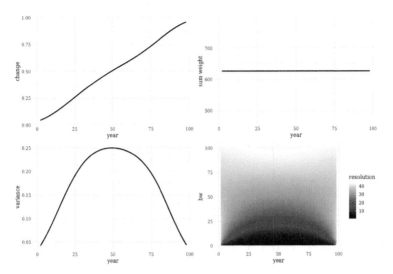

Figure 10. Relevant factors for temporal bandwidths for evenly distributed synthesised data [Colour figure can be viewed at wileyonlinelibrary.com]

Now consider Figure 11. Again, this is based on synthesised data, but this time with samples much more unevenly distributed in time: we have more than three times as much data to work with towards the beginning of the change than at the end. Here we can see that the size of the dataset available has a much bigger

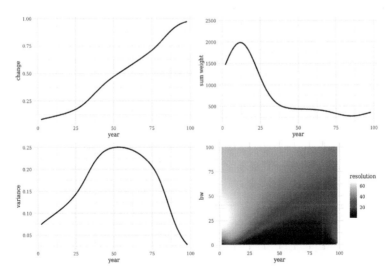

Figure 11. Relevant factors for temporal bandwidths for unevenly distributed synthesised data [Colour figure can be viewed at wileyonlinelibrary.com]

effect on the spatial resolutions possible with a given temporal bandwidth than the variance does, and so the most restrictive point which will determine our temporal bandwidth is the point in time considered with the lowest amount of data. If we set the minimum acceptable spatial resolution to 20, we determine the lowest possible temporal bandwidth is 41 years on the basis of a point around year 86.

Figure 12 visualises the same statistics for our real test dataset, the *verða>blífa* dataset. The midpoint of the change is passed around 1475 and variance peaks around the same point; sample density is quite consistent for much of the period covered but reaches a peak more than nine times higher than the overall median during the 1520s, and this huge spike in sample density has a large effect on the temporal bandwidths needed to achieve our goal spatial resolution of 20. The most restrictive point is around 1400, at the beginning of the period covered and furthest from this spike in sample density, and the minimum temporal bandwidth needed is around 217 years: a value that (following our arguments about reasonable maxima on the basis of real-world priors in section 2.3.1) is far too high. With a temporal bandwidth of 217 years for a change that largely takes place over a 100 year period, it will be very difficult to get any real sense of how the distribution changes over time. We can see this if we visualise the change in time alone with this bandwidth, which has been done in Figure 13.

Figure 14 then shows how the minimum temporal bandwidths change if we increase our acceptable error margins, thereby decreasing n. In bottom right panel of Figure 12, we specified $\alpha = 0.05$, margin $= 0.1$; in other words, we want to have 95 per cent confidence that our estimates are within 10 per cent of

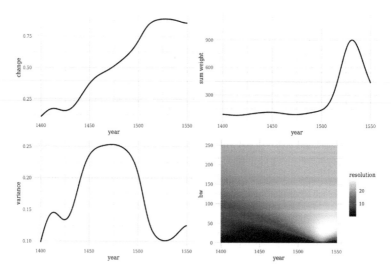

Figure 12. Relevant factors for temporal bandwidths for the *verða>blífa* dataset [Colour figure can be viewed at wileyonlinelibrary.com]

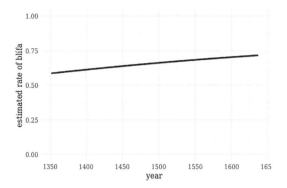

Figure 13. Kernel smoothed rate of *blífa* over time with a gaussian kernel with temporal bandwidth of 217 years

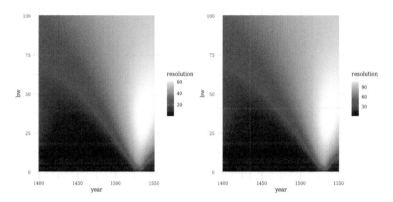

Figure 14. Spatial resolution by year and temporal bandwidth for *verða>blífa* data with error margin of 0.15 and 0.2 [Colour figure can be viewed at wileyonlinelibrary.com]

the true value. If we relax those requirements so that estimates must be within 15 per cent of the true value, as visualised in the left panel of Figure 14, we find that the temporal bandwidth needed is much lower, at 75 years; if we relax them further as visualised in the right panel of Figure 14, so that estimates need only be within 20 per cent of the true value, the temporal bandwidth needed to achieve a spatial resolution of 20 falls further to 41 years. In the case of the 0.15 margin, the 'choke point' – the point in time where variance and data availability combine to put the most stringent restrictions on temporal bandwidths, given our desired spatial resolution – is still simply the earliest point we look at, furthest from the spike in data in the 1520s and 30s. With the higher margins of 0.2, the choke point is closer to the midpoint of the change.

Comparing Figures 13 and 14, we find good evidence that this dataset might simply not be large enough to achieve error margins as narrow as 10 per cent or 15 per cent while maintaining reasonable spatial and temporal resolution. Firstly

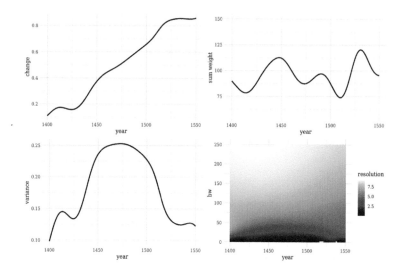

Figure 15. Relevant factors for temporal bandwidths for partially balanced subset of *verða>blífa* data [Colour figure can be viewed at wileyonlinelibrary.com]

and more obviously, the temporal resolution required to achieve the margins of 0.1 is 217 years, or 75 years for margins of 0.15. Since the main body of the change takes place over a period of only a little more than a century, this means that our temporal resolution is very poor. Estimates for 1400 and for 1510, roughly at either end of the period during which the change is progressing steadily, are 0.5169σ or 1.4667σ away from each other with these two parameter settings and so in either case are calculated on substantially overlapping datasets. This is clearly less than ideal. Put another way, we suggested in section 2.3.1 above that a rough rule for the maximum reasonable temporal bandwidth for a Gaussian kernel was the length of time taken for the main period of the change divided by 1.6449, in this case and $\frac{110}{1.6449} = 66.88$ years. Our bandwidths with 0.1 and 0.15 margins are greater than this, whereas margins of 0.2 allow us to stay below this maximum.

More subtly, in the changing location of the choke point we can see evidence that we are only able to achieve the narrower margins by taking advantage of the huge spike in the size of the dataset in the 1520s and 1530s: with the narrow margins, the choke point is simply the point in time furthest from this spike. This means that for the main period of change, we need temporal resolutions large enough to ensure that a substantial part of the sample being used for our estimates comes from this late period. This will clearly skew our estimates, making it appear that the change is closer to completion than it really was during the fifteenth century. This is confirmed by repeating the calculations for the narrow error margins ($\alpha = 0.05$, margin $= 0.1$) on a dataset including only a sample of the data from the sixteenth century such that sample size per decade is of a similar magnitude to the sample sizes available in the 15th century, as visualised in Figure 15.

It is now not possible to achieve the desired resolution of 20 distinct cells at all. Thus for this dataset, we must settle for the higher error margins. One problem with this approach has to do with our definition of the spatial resolution as the number of distinct cells that could in principle be distinguished, the sum of weights over k. Although this is the number of distinct datasets of size k that *could* be distinguished, real samples will not be distributed so as to facilitate this. Real spatial resolution will be substantially lower, and – if we are using an adaptive kernel – will vary between locations. An alternative approach is to specify individual points on the map for which it is important to us to have an estimate and identify the minimum temporal bandwidth such that estimates at these points are independent.

Define the set A of points where estimates must be independent and calculate the distance matrix $\mathbf{A}$ between these points such that $\mathbf{A}_{i,j}$ refers to the distance between points i and j. Using our earlier definition that when using a Gaussian kernel points separated by at least 2.2365σ are close to independent, this means identifying the minimum temporal bandwidth such that:

$$\sigma_i \leq \frac{\mathbf{A}_{i,j}}{2.2365},$$

for every value of i and j where $i \neq j$, and where the bandwidths at each point $\sigma_{1\ldots a}$ are determined by an optimisation algorithm such that the sum of weights at each point will equal our desired sample size k. For other spatial kernels, this will differ. For example, if using a square kernel, denoting the bandwidths at each point $b_{1\ldots a}$, then samples will overlap if the bandwidth is greater than half the distance between any two points, then we must simply ensure that:

$$b_i \leq \frac{\mathbf{A}_{i,j}}{2}.$$

To take the example of the verða>blífa dataset, it might be important to us to be able to contrast rates in the different major towns and cities of Norway at different times, so we can take the major towns of medieval Norway as the points A *for which we need independent estimates.*

The distance matrix $\mathbf{A}$ for these points is shown in Table 1.

Table 1. Distance matrix for major cities of medieval Norway

	Oslo	Stavanger	Bergen	Trondheim	Hamar
Oslo	0km				
Stavanger	305.34km	0km			
Bergen	306.48km	160.57km	0km		
Trondheim	393.77km	558.47km	431.45km	0km	
Hamar	100.49km	362.98km	317.77km	296.33km	0km

So, taking the distances to each point's nearest neighbour (see Table 2) and assuming we are using a Gaussian kernel, we must find the minimum temporal bandwidth such that there exists a spatial bandwidth at each point equal to or less than which will give a sum of weights equal to k (these spatial bandwidths are visualised with dotted red lines in Figure 16). Setting $\alpha = 0.05$, margin $= 0.2$, we find the relationships between spatial and temporal bandwidths visualised in Figure 17. The first five panels show the spatial bandwidth needed to achieve this confidence level by temporal bandwidth and year: spatial bandwidths in kilometres at each point are visualised with colours and contour lines. The dotted contour line in each case shows the maximum spatial bandwidth at this location that maintains independent estimates. The sixth panel shows only these maxima. From this we can see that we would need a temporal bandwidth of 43.28 years; the choke point is Stavanger in 1439. This is unsurprising, since there is very little data for Stavanger in the fifteenth century and very little for the surrounding area in any period. If we decide that an improved temporal resolution is more desirable than an independent estimate for Stavanger, we could look only at the other four points. In this case, we would need a temporal bandwidth of 32.52 years and the choke point would be Hamar in 1451. If we exclude Hamar as well, and want distinct estimates for just the three largest cities, we can achieve lower error margins of 0.125 with a temporal bandwidth of 36.43 years; maps with these bandwidths are given as Figure 18.

2.3.4. Conclusions

In summary, we have looked at three approaches by which we might set kernel bandwidths: using our a priori knowledge of the real-world phenomena we are interested in setting reasonable bounds; finding the bandwidths that achieve the best predictive accuracy on real or synthesised data; and using power analysis. The most useful of these has been shown to be power analysis, although we can see how bringing in priors derived from real-world knowledge for what bandwidths are reasonable helps to interpret the results of this approach. Within this approach, we have explored two ways of determining the optimal trade-off between spatial and temporal resolutions: one by using an abstracted idea of spatial resolution based on the size of the dataset, and one by identifying the bandwidths needed to keep the estimates at a prespecified set of points largely independent.

Table 2. Distances to nearest cities

Oslo	44.93km
Stavanger	71.80km
Bergen	71.80km
Trondheim	132.50km
Hamar	44.93km

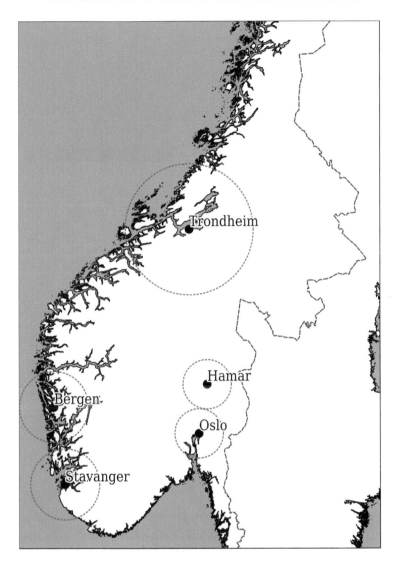

Figure 16. Points for which independent estimates are required [Colour figure can be viewed at wileyonlinelibrary.com]

How then will we put these approaches into practice here? For the remainder of the examples in this monograph, the methods described above for calculating temporal bandwidths on the basis of a set of spatial points whose estimates must be largely independent will be used. Where the research goal is to compare some specific set of points (for example, when trying to determine which of two places led a change compared to the other), these points will be used; for all other cases,

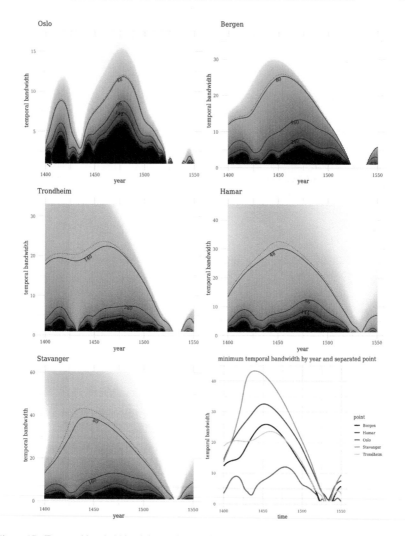

Figure 17. Temporal bandwidth minima to keep estimates at cities from overlapping for *verða>blífa* dataset with α = 0.05 and error margins 0.2 [Colour figure can be viewed at wileyonlinelibrary.com]

where a general overview is needed, the five largest cities of medieval Norway will be used. In terms of desired power, $\alpha = 0.05$ in all cases, but the desired error margins will be adjusted to identify the greatest specificity possible for the dataset whilst keeping within reasonable bounds for temporal resolution. Where the goal is to get an overview of a change over time (the usual purpose to which the kernel smoothing method is put in this book), these bounds will be set as the time taken for the change in question to progress from 15 to 85 per cent nationally divided by 1.6449 (i.e. ensuring that estimates at 15 per cent and 85

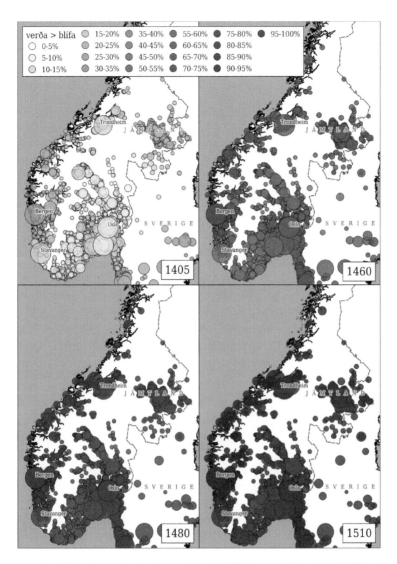

Figure 18. Spatial kernel smoothed estimates of *verða>blífa* between 1405 and 1510 [Colour figure can be viewed at wileyonlinelibrary.com]

per cent are not based on substantially overlapping samples). Where the goal is fundamentally to compare two points in space, and diachrony is largely irrelevant, a looser standard of the time taken to progress from 5 to 95 per cent over 1.6449 will be used. This will not be reported in detail in each case, but the bandwidths arrived at by this method will be given in the Appendix.

3

LANGUAGE IN MEDIEVAL NORWAY AND SOURCES OF DATA

3.1. *Introduction*

The case studies in chapters 5–7, as well as the example data already seen in chapter 2, all concern changes in Old and Middle Norwegian and are based on research in a single corpus, the *DN online* (derived from the *Diplomatarium Norvegicum*). Accordingly, some background information may be helpful for readers in contextualising the phenomena explored. In this chapter, I will first give some background on the sociolinguistic situation in Norway in the period under study (roughly 1275–1550) (section 3.2), and then describe how the corpus was constructed and the sources which comprise it (section 3.3).

3.2. *Norway and Norwegian in the late medieval period*

Norwegian is a Continental Nordic language, a group of languages descending from Old Norse comprising Norwegian, Swedish and Danish, and contrasting with the Insular Nordic languages, Faroese and Icelandic. Norwegian is also classified as a West Nordic language, along with Icelandic and Faroese, in contrast to East Nordic Swedish and Danish. At an earlier period we might also include the Nordic varieties spoken in Orkney, Shetland and Greenland in Insular Nordic and in West Nordic. The odd status of Norwegian, straddling the two possible subgroupings of the Nordic family, reflects both changing relationships among these varieties over time and the peripheral position of Norwegian in either grouping.

In what are truly the earliest written sources for Nordic, the runic inscriptions, it is hard to find clear geographical differences in language use: we read a relatively standardised single language across the entire language area, although these data are hard to interpret and often ambiguous. However, when we turn to the earliest sources for each language in the Latin alphabet we find that Old Icelandic and Old Norwegian are dialects with a great number of features in common, and that they differ in many ways from Old Swedish and Old Danish. At this point, then, it certainly makes sense to talk about West and East Nordic, and this is unsurprising, since the North Atlantic islands (including the Faroes, although there we have little early written evidence equivalent to our wealth of texts from medieval Iceland) had largely been settled from Norway. Over the following centuries these territories came under common rule to different degrees, in different combinations, and for different periods of time. Iceland, the Faroes, Shetland, Orkney and Greenland were all ruled from Norway from before the beginning of the period covered here. Norway and Sweden shared a monarch for some of the time from 1319. The Kalmar Union joined these with Denmark under a common monarch – although not entirely common rule – for much of the period 1397 to 1523. Norway and Denmark were joined under a common monarch from 1380, and continued in a closer union after Swedish independence in 1523. This union lasted long past the end of the period on which we focus here. Orkney and Shetland were annexed by Scotland in 1472.

At the same time, these polities interacted a great deal with powers further south, and in particular the Hanseatic League. The Hanseatic League was a mercantile union of guilds and trading towns primarily in the Low Countries and northern Germany, along with their outposts (*kontôr* 'office') in important cities within a number of neighbouring states. The Hanseatic League was not a state *per se*, and has been compared to a modern multinational company, but it did nevertheless wield significant military and naval power in addition to its decisive economic power. The Kalmar Union was formed partly out of a need to counterbalance this pressure from the south, and the League played a fundamental role in shaping the Norwegian economy over the period studied here.

This brief political background is given so as to facilitate understanding of the sociolinguistic situation. Norwegian was far from isolated. It was subject to contact with Swedish and Danish (which should probably be classified as dialect contact in this period) as well as extensive internal dialect contact and contact with Insular West Nordic languages. This contact was not balanced: first Swedish and later Danish had greater social prestige and institutional support than Norwegian, reflecting differentials of wealth and power across Scandinavia, with the result that writing in Norway had shifted entirely to a Danish standard by the mid sixteenth century. At the same time, there was much contact with Middle Low German, the operating language of the Hanseatic League, in urban centres throughout Scandinavia. There was also contact with Sámi in northern Sweden and Norway, although we have far less information about this from written sources. In section 3.2.2, I will give a more detailed overview of the nature of contact among these languages in the late medieval period. Much of this background is particularly relevant to the investigation in chapter 6, on the effects of different types of contact in the history of Norwegian, but it also plays a role in the investigation in chapter 7, on the different spatial patterns of diffusion of language change through the Norwegian population.

3.2.1. Sociolinguistic statuses of the languages

At the beginning of the period covered, Latin was the primary written language used for official purposes throughout Scandinavia and the Hanseatic League; there was, however, more of a tradition of vernacular writing in Norway than in Sweden, Denmark or the Low Countries. Middle Low German replaced Latin for record keeping in the Hanseatic League in the 1370s, coinciding with its expansion as a lingua franca and prestige language around the Baltic (Jahr 1999: 128; Braunmüller 2012: 101). After the political union of Norway with Sweden and Denmark, written Swedish and Danish gained prestige relative to Norwegian and Latin. Nevertheless, Latin proficiency remained high (Rambø 2012: 46); Berg

(2017) and Nesse (2002: 165) highlight examples of code-switching between written Danish-Norwegian and Latin at the very end of the period covered.

The sociolinguistic statuses of the spoken languages are harder to discover from written sources. Nevertheless, a broadly similar picture probably applied: Norwegian declined in status but retained an association with the traditional power blocs of church and state; Swedish and Danish were high-status varieties associated with the aristocracy and increasingly with church and state; Low German was a high status but foreign variety associated with trade. Hall (2013: 4, 25–6) argues that the church was also an important vector of Low German influence. Braunmüller (2012: 101–2) and Jahr (1999: 128) emphasise that there were no 'standard' languages in a modern sense and that in speech as in writing there was considerably more variation than today.

3.2.2. Contact

3.2.2.1. Periods of contact with Low German

Language contact with Sámi and dialect contact among the Nordic languages and between dialects of Norwegian can be assumed to have been constant throughout the period, but the timing of contact with Middle Low German needs to be circumscribed. Contact between Middle Low German and Norwegian began with Norwegian merchants travelling to Sweden and the Low Countries, but the main portion involved German merchants travelling to Norway. German merchants from the new Baltic towns reached eastern Norway first, with German ships arriving in Tønsberg as early as 1205 (Nedkvitne 2014: 49–50). A special relationship between Rostock and Oslo/Tønsberg developed in the early fourteenth century (Nedkvitne 2014: 48); from 1378, Hansa officials were empowered to function as a law court for Hansa merchants in the area and from at latest 1420, Rostock was their court of appeal (Nedkvitne 2012: 29–30). The Hansa period in this part of the country is thus regarded as lasting from around 1250 (or possibly earlier) until 1500 (Rambø 2012: 47).

The beginning of the Hansa period in Bergen is difficult to define. Bergen was already an important port trading with English and Low German merchants before the Hanseatic League began to play a role. Nedkvitne (2014: 50) suggests that German merchants from the Baltic towns, particularly Lübeck, reached Bergen by 1247, whereas Hammel-Kiesow (2015: 33) suggests that trade between Lübeck and Bergen (import of grain, flour and malt from Lübeck, export of North-Norwegian dried cod from Bergen) was already established by 1240. Regardless, Wendish Hansa cities succeeded in ousting English and Flemish merchants from the Norwegian market by latter half of the thirteenth century (Hammel-Kiesow 2015: 33) and Bergen became increasingly important to Hansa merchants (Nesse 2012b: 81–2). This gradually changed the nature of the German presence in Bergen, from a small number of merchants integrated in the town in the thirteenth century towards a larger and more separate group; this was accelerated by the Black Death (Nesse 2002: 82). The Hansa quarter was first described as such in 1358 (Nesse 2002: 82) and was established as a kontor in 1366 (Nedkvitne 2012: 22). The kontor declined from the seventeenth century, disappearing by around 1750, although a substantial number of German speakers remained until after 1800 and German was used in some spheres until 1866 (Nesse 2002: 82). The nature of the German presence changed again in this final period, becoming more integrated (Nesse 2002: 83). Accordingly, we can define the Hansa period in Bergen as lasting from 1250 to 1650 (as Rambø 2012: 47) or 1750 (as Nesse 2002).

In Sweden and Denmark the period during which contact with Middle Low German took place was similar, but the scale was larger. An agreement between Birgir jarl and the city of Lübeck invited German merchants to settle as Swedish citizens in 1250, a time at which cities like Stockholm were growing rapidly due to German trade (Mähl 2012: 113–14). German migration into Sweden increased and probably peaked during the reign of Albrecht von Mecklenburg (1364–1389) when many German nobility emigrated to Sweden and were favoured by the king; at this point Swedish charters in Middle Low German start to appear (Mähl 2012: 114–16).

As mentioned above, contact between Continental Scandinavian and Low German also took place in ecclesiastical contexts. This contact began and peaked earlier: the Scandinavian church was part of the archdiocese of Hamburg-Bremen until 1104, and Norway gained its own archbishop only in 1151 (Hall 2013: 4).

3.2.2.2. Scale of contact with Low German

Having defined the relevant period, we must estimate the scale of contact between Norwegian and Low German. In Norway, there is general agreement that the German population in Bergen was far larger than in Oslo and Tønsberg (Jahr 1999: 123; Rambø 2012: 47) and some scholars have pointed towards this difference as an explanation for peculiarities of Bergen dialect not shared by Oslo and Tønsberg (e.g. Enger 2011: 182–3).

Nevertheless, absolute population sizes are difficult to estimate in the medieval period. Trudgill (2011: 57) suggests that Bergen in the 1400s had a population of 7,000 of which 2,000 were Germans (29 per cent), rising to 4,000/9,000 in summer (44 per cent). These figures are cited from Rambø (2008) where they are cited from Nesse (2001). Nesse (2002: 83–4) (a reprint of Nesse 2001) cites three historians: Helle (1982: 489) estimates that the population was around 7,000 at the beginning of the fourteenth century, dropped with the Black Death, then rose again to around 8,500 by the end of the sixteenth; Fossen (1979: 761) concentrates on a later period, adding that the number of inhabitants surpassed 10,000 around 1700; Nedrebø (1990: 37) suggests these figures are too low, estimating a population as high as 15,000 by the early seventeenth century. Within this, Helle (1982: 743, 762) estimates between 900 and 1,800 resident Germans in the fifteenth century, rising to a height of around 2,000, and doubling in summer. If we assume that the town's population dropped by 40 per cent with the Black Death around 1350[3] and then grew steadily until the next estimate in 1600, then the population of Bergen in the 1400s grew from around 5,000 to 7,000 (Helle) or from around 6,000 to 11,000 (Nedrebø). If we assume that the range estimated by Helle for the number of Germans in the population in the 1400s covers the entire century, we have 900/5,000 (18 per cent) Germans in 1400 rising to 2,000/6,800 (29 per cent) Germans by the end of the century. Assuming all of these figures are for winter and that the Hansa population did indeed double in summer, we have 1,800/8,500 (31 per cent) in 1400 rising to 4,000/8,800 (45 per cent) in 1500 in summers. A slightly different estimation is given by Nedkvitne (2012: 22) of around 1,000 merchants (including servants) when the kontor was officially established in the late fourteenth century, doubling in the summers.

Nesse (2002: 84–6) emphasises that the Hansa were not the only migrants in Bergen. German craftspeople arrived in their wake and represented a significant economic and power bloc of perhaps 200 permanent residents by the end of the Middle Ages (Fossen 1979: 66 ,68; Helle 1982: 750). Conflicts between the Hansa and English and Dutch merchants suggest that these latter groups were also a significant presence in the town in the late fifteenth century (Nesse 2002: 86). The town's Nordic-speaking population also included migrants: figures from the later period covered by Nesse suggest that only around 35 per cent of Scandinavian citizens in Bergen had been born in the town, with the rest from Denmark, Sweden, North Norway and elsewhere in West Norway (Nesse 2002: 84–5). To these permanent residents should be added travellers from North Norway who visited every summer to trade with the Hansa (Nesse 2002: 85).

The Hansa are thought to have been more populous in Denmark and Sweden. Mähl (2012: 116–17) suggests they represented 30–40 per cent of the population of Stockholm from the very early history of this city; the number was so great that a legal limit of 50 per cent was placed on the number of seats they could hold on the city council. Nedkvitne (2012: 19) estimates about a third of taxpayers in Stockholm at the end of the fifteenth century were Germans, but suggests that the proportion of the whole population was lower. The same figure is given by Trudgill (2011: 57; citing Dahlbäck 1998) for Stockholm in 1460 and a higher figure of between a third and half the population for Kalmar (Trudgill 2011: 57; citing Blomkvist 1979).

3.2.2.3. Integration

Just as important as scale and chronology in our account is the level of integration of Hansa merchants in Scandinavian towns. A key theme in the

---

[3] The Black Death had a greater impact in Norway than elsewhere in Scandinavia: studies of land usage and written records suggest death rates over 40 per cent in most of Norway and nowhere less than 25 per cent, compared with more variable rates in Sweden and Denmark and rates consistently below 15 per cent in Finland (Antonson 2009:624–625). A higher estimate is given by Vahtola (2003:569) of a 60-65 per cent death rate, resulting in desertion of 56 per cent of named farms and perhaps 61-62 per cent of other holdings. For further discussion of this, see section 7.1.

history of Bergen is how little integrated the Germans were into Scandinavian life. This reflected conscious policy by both local and Hanseatic authorities: Hansa merchants were not citizens and could not take part in city administration; local courts could not deal with Hansa matters except where there was a conflict between a merchant and a local; Hansa merchants were not allowed to run companies with non-Hansa and had to have all their dealings in public places; the Germans had their own churches; Hansa merchants were not allowed to marry; no women were allowed to stay in Bryggen, the walled palisade where the Hansa lived, and the Hansa themselves were not allowed to leave this area at night (Nesse 2012b: 82; Burkhardt 2015: 133–2,142,146). Nedkvitne (2014: 33) summarises: '[t]here is no evidence of extensive social contacts between the two ethnic groups in the period 1366–1559'. By contrast, Burkhardt (2015: 132–3, 147, 151) emphasises that in spite of these policies there was some integration with the local population, noting examples of Hansa merchants having friendships with Norwegians, employing Norwegian women to do their washing, and employing local prostitutes.

The situation was not identical at all times or places: Bergen was exceptional in the degree to which the Hansa remained apart from town life (Jahr 1999: 123; Nedkvitne 2012: 30, 32). The Hansa in Oslo and Tønsberg had fewer legal privileges than those in Bergen but also fewer legal restrictions; merchants in Oslo and Tønsberg took families with them, rather than living in an entirely adult male colony; they had no separate institutions like churches; and they were scattered throughout the area, rather than living in a closed block (Rambø 2012: 47–8; Burkhardt 2015: 159).

Degree of integration also varied over time. In Bergen in the period 1247–1299 there was a positive policy of integration, in which migrants who stayed for more than a year were treated legally like citizens; this was reversed over the period 1299–1380, when it was made impossible for foreigners to become citizens. As the relative power of local authorities and the League reversed in the fourteenth century, neither the Hansa authorities nor individual merchants ever felt much incentive to align themselves with locals and so never resumed integrated life (Nedkvitne 2012: 30–2). The trend was the same in the east. Merchants who chose to become citizens of Oslo or Tønsberg were originally allowed to remain members of Hansa and use their privileges in towns like Bruges and Flanders, but this policy was reversed around 1400 and such migrants were instead expelled from the Hansa (Nedkvitne 2012: 30); nevertheless, even after this point some did choose local citizenship and were welcomed by the local authorities.

Overall, then, we find a range of situations: degree of integration lessened over time and was always lower in Bergen than in the east. Degree of integration in Swedish cities like Stockholm was probably more like that in Oslo and Tønsberg but the numbers were higher: German immigrants had local citizenship but formed a distinct class, maintaining German language and culture for generations (Mähl 2012: 117; contra Jahr 1999: 122, who suggests that Germans quickly integrated and became Swedish).

3.2.2.4. Bilingualism

There has been much debate in the scholarly literature over the nature of bilingualism with Low German in late medieval Scandinavia. Clearly there was societal bilingualism – Middle Low German speakers lived alongside Nordic speakers in many settlements, documents were produced in both languages, etc. – but how this functioned at an individual level is surprisingly difficult to demonstrate with any confidence.

In earlier literature we find the idea that an 'interlanguage', 'mixed language' or pidgin developed. This is closely linked to the proposal that imperfect adult learning of Nordic languages by Middle Low German speakers caused morphological change (for which see further chapter 6). For such morphological change to be a consequence of a stage at which a pidginised version was spoken, such a pidgin must have existed. Haugen (1976: 314) writes:

> The average urban speaker in Bergen, Oslo, Copenhagen, Kalmar, Stockholm or Visby [...] was moderately bilingual, and he submitted to a mild creolization of his language. Only so can we account for the massive adoption of replacements for native terms [...], the merger of inflections and the new analytic syntax.

Wessén (1954: 27) too suggests that German immigrants failed to correctly learn Swedish inflections and that features of their mixed language spread to native Swedish speakers. However, the idea that a mixed language or pidgin ever arose is rejected by more recent scholars (Jahr 1999: 133–4; Elmevik & Jahr 2012: 11–14) on the basis that there is simply no written evidence for such a variety.

More popular in recent years is a cluster of proposals around the idea that communication between Low German and Nordic speakers was by means of receptive bilingualism: that, broadly speaking, Scandinavians spoke their own languages, Germans spoke theirs, and each understood but did not speak the other's. This idea too has a long history in the literature, having been suggested by Seip as early as 1934 (Seip 1934: 23–4, 27–9; Seip 1993: 128), and has been defended particularly by Braunmüller (1989; 1995; Braunmüller 2007; 2012). It builds on the proposed parallel with communication among speakers of the modern Continental Nordic languages, described as 'semi-communication' – defined as poor passive bilingualism with some short-term accommodation where languages are typologically similar and genetically related (Norde 1997: 39–41; Braunmüller 2012: 95). The suggestion is that, unlike their modern counterparts, the medieval Nordic languages were close enough to Low German to allow this mode of communication and accordingly there was no need for people ever to develop productive bilingualism.

This hypothesis is reviewed by Nesse (2002: 136–8) who concludes it is plausible but emphasises that conditions were less conducive than among the modern Nordic languages and so some degree of long-term accommodation would be needed. She argues that contact between Middle Norwegian and Middle Low German in Bergen was never intense: each group used their own language and had little motivation to learn the other (Nesse 2002: 148; 2012b: 82). The receptive bilingualism hypothesis is also reviewed by Berg (2016) who is more tentative in his support, suggesting (agreeing with Braunmüller 2007: 34–8) that receptive bilingualism became less widespread later in the period and was always an acquired skill requiring substantial exposure to the other language. Berg also presents evidence that the situation was asymmetric: more Norwegians understood Low German than vice versa, and indeed some were active bilinguals (Berg 2016: 207–8). Overall, he remains agnostic on whether bilingualism was usually productive or receptive: 'semi-communication was no automatic process, as there are several written statements from the early sixteenth century pointing to lack of understanding. It is also very hard to keep this phenomenon apart from bilingualism in the written records. Irrespective of the exact nature of the language contact, the preserved texts show at least that Low German was read and understood among Scandinavians' (Berg 2017: 91). Rambø (2012: 48) disagrees slightly, emphasising that some Norwegians in Bergen would have used Middle Low German, whilst suggesting that the situation was reversed in Oslo and Tønsberg: better integrated Germans, including children, would have spoken Norwegian, whilst Norwegians had little motive or opportunity to learn German even passively.

For my own part, I reviewed the evidence adduced by other scholars for the nature of bilingual practices in Norway in this period in Blaxter (2017a: 51–6) and came away a little more sceptical than Berg (2017) about the hypothesis that bilingualism was largely receptive; I will summarise this review more briefly here. Although there is no truly conclusive evidence that Middle Low German and Middle Norwegian were mutually incomprehensible of the sort found for other languages at some outposts of the Hanseatic League (such as instructional materials in the local language for Hansa merchants new to the region; Jahr 1995: 20), there is evidence of communication difficulties. We have at least four examples of Low German speakers expressing difficulty understanding Nordic languages (Brattegard 1932: 302; Jahr 1999: 130; Hall 2013; Berg 2016: 195–6), two instances of Norwegians reportedly not being able to speak Low German (Hall 2013; Berg 2016: 198)[4] and one instance in which this is, at the very least, strongly implied (DN I.961). We have at least two instances of Scandinavians reporting that they *do* understand Low German, in one of which this point is emphasised repeatedly (Berg 2016: 197–8). We have at least one example of a document by a Norwegian issued in Low German, and one of the reverse (Berg 2016: 205–6). We have translations from Danish-Norwegian into Low German in the sixteenth century (Nesse 2012b: 84–5) and references to translation

---

[4] Note that the example discussed in Hall (2013) is from a text recording events which were already history when it was written, and the historicity of individual episodes in it might be cast in doubt. However, this should not undermine its value as evidence here: the plot of the episode in question hinges on the fact that the characters cannot understand one another and so its effectiveness as a narrative relies on the audience finding it believable that Norwegians would not be able to understand Low German, irrespective of whether the specific events were real.

elsewhere (Berg 2013: 186–7; 2016: 199–200). There are also examples of code-switching between Latin, Danish-Norwegian and Low German in more informal documents (Nesse 2012b: 87, 89–90; 2012a; Berg 2016: 201–303).

All of this paints a picture in which the ability of Low German and Norwegian speakers to understand one another's languages was far from automatic and passive; rather, it was a distinct skill which might be commented upon in some instances or identified as lacking in others. Either the ability (DN I.961) or its absence (many of the examples above) could be problematised and politicised. This strongly suggests a language contact situation involving a meaningful level of individual bilingualism, not a dialect contact situation in which only some accommodation and no language learning *per se* was needed.

3.2.2.5. Latin

Latin competence was common: all members of the clergy as well as many secular officials and scribes had their education in Latin. As Berg (2016; 2017) shows, code-switching between productively composed Latin and Danish-Norwegian can be found in lower status texts, suggesting an active productive competence in the language was common. It is difficult to assess the relevance of this contact. It was probably more concentrated in larger towns with cathedrals (Oslo, Bergen, Stavanger, Trondheim and Hamar), but nevertheless compared with other types of contact must have been very evenly distributed. There were Latin-educated clergy everywhere, not only in Norway but throughout medieval Europe (including Iceland and the Faroes), yet there were no native speakers. Thus it is not obvious how we can use this contact as an explanatory factor in accounts of language change in European languages of the period, since there are no places in which it was absent to which to compare. Nevertheless, it should be borne in mind as part of the linguistic context.

3.2.2.6. Dialect contact

Dialect contact with Swedish and Danish was a major influence in the history of Norwegian. As mentioned under section 3.2 above, Norway came under common rule with Sweden and Denmark from the fourteenth century, and the state began to place Swedish and Danish (and German) officials into ecclesiastical and secular offices from the 1370s onwards (a Dane was first appointed bishop of Bergen in 1370) (Nesse 2002: 85; Nedkvitne 2012: 32–5). Written Swedish and Danish were prestige varieties: we see increased influence from Swedish written norms in the latter half of the fourteenth and early fifteenth centuries, and steadily increasing influence from written Danish in the fifteenth century until all texts in Norway can be said to have been written in Danish (although often with some Norwegian features) from the early sixteenth century onwards.[5] There was also substantial contact between the spoken languages, as

---

[5] For an excellent account of the shift from written Norwegian to Danish, arguing convincingly that it should be seen not as language shift at all but as standardisation, see Berg (2018).

the aristocracies of the three countries were largely the same. This contact thus took place in three settings: in the upper classes, especially among those in state offices; in commercial contexts, particular through Danish merchants; and through the dialect continuum with Swedish dialects along the Swedish border, particularly (for the region we cover here) in Østfold, Hedmark and Trøndelag. Contact among the upper classes, those in state offices and in commercial contexts, like the contact with Middle Low German, was probably focused on larger towns, but state offices and the seats of the upper classes were not specifically limited to the trading towns of Bergen, Oslo and Tønsberg.

Dialect contact among Norwegian dialects cannot be discounted as an important factor in language change in this period. The Norwegian population seems to have had a high degree of geographical mobility in the medieval period. The higher social classes went on religious pilgrimages abroad from the early years of Christian Scandinavia. This practice extended to the lower social classes to some extent, even including peasants: places of pilgrimage emerged in northern Germany in the fourteenth century and internal places of pilgrimage were frequented by visitors of the lowest social strata from very early (Orrman 2003a: 458). The economic stability and wealth contributed by Hansa trade drove economic specialisation, with the result that technological developments spread very quickly (Nedkvitne 2012: 19). All clergy had to travel to centres of ecclesiastical education such as monasteries and cathedrals for training (Orrman 2003a: 461) and remained formal members of cathedrals. To highlight the scale of this travel, consider that parish priests as far north as Þróndarnes parish in Hálogaland (modern Trondenes in Harstad municipality) would have had to travel to the cathedral in Trondheim for their education, a journey of 917km on modern roads. The Black Death in the mid-fourteenth century caused a drastic depopulation (see above and further under section 7.1) and at least Bergen was largely repopulated by migration (Dahlbäck 2003: 616). Perhaps most importantly, the Hansa trade in Bergen entailed a huge amount of movement between Bergen and North Norway. Fisheries in North Norway produced dried cod which was transported between the North and Bergen every year by the 'Norderfahrer'. These northern travellers often financed their journeys with loans from the Hansa merchants to whom they sold the stockfish, and transported grain back to North Norway. This became so large a part of the economy that farming was abandoned in large parts of North Norway, which relied entirely on imported grain (Burkhardt 2015: 143–4). Thus we can assume that Norwegian dialect contact was significant everywhere, but particularly so in Bergen, North Norway, and the cathedral cities.

3.2.2.7. Sámi

We must also consider contact with Sámi. Sámi settlement may have reached as far south as Valdres in the late Viking and early medieval eras (Bull 2010: 176). Certainly it included all of Trøndelag, Jämtland and Härjedalen, and everywhere north of there. Many features in Norwegian and Swedish have been associated with Finno-Ugric contact; in the period under consideration here, Kusmenko (2008) proposes that consonant lengthening, vowel assimilations and the rise of complex prepositions in northern Norwegian and Swedish dialects should be ascribed to Sámi contact; these arguments are reiterated by Bull (2011: 16–19), who suggests that Sámi, Finnish and Swedish-Norwegian constitute a Sprachbund (Bull 2011: 24). Particularly relevant for this work, a large-scale language shift from South Sámi to Norwegian happened in the southernmost parts of the Sámi area in the medieval period. Writing about the present, Bull (1995; 2011: 19–23) highlights phonological and morphological simplifications in North Norwegian dialects related to ongoing language shift from Sámi to Norwegian – we might guess that a similar phenomenon took place further south in earlier centuries. Sámi contact is much harder to work with than the other sources of contact we have discussed here, since medieval written sources offer us little evidence for the nature of Sámi settlement and interaction with Nordic speakers, in contrast to the wealth of evidence we find concerning Hansa. Nevertheless, it must be borne in mind as a relevant factor.

3.2.3. A note on Jämtland

Jämtland (Norwegian Jemtland/Jamtaland) was a largely self-governing region which came under Norwegian rule in 1223 (Njåstad 2003: 152; Slungård 2015: 9). In terms of governance it remained peculiar: it was formally part of Norway but retained much autonomy and its own internal governing practices (Njåstad 2003: 149); ecclesiastically, it was part of the archdiocese of Uppsala (Njåstad 2003: 152). Thus at the beginning of our period, Jämtland fell at the overlap between the Norwegian and Swedish spheres of influence. Over time, it gradually turned towards Sweden. From 1340, charters from Jämtland show influence from the Old Swedish written standard, and Swedish influence is detectable in the legal procedures described (Larsson 2012: 50). Swedish influence, both ecclesiastical and political, increased again at the beginning of the fifteenth century (Njåstad 2003: 150). From the end of the fifteenth century, the bishop in Uppsala exerted closer control over the clergy in Jämtland and Swedish political influence continued to grow after the end of the Kalmar Union (Njåstad 2003: 150; Slungård 2015: 9).

As a result, the interpretation of linguistic evidence from Jämtland is difficult. The Swedish ecclesiastical connection means that charters from Jämtland show far more influence from the Swedish written standard than those from elsewhere in Norway which might lead us to doubt their value for revealing properties of speech, but for the same reasons this was also a region where contact between spoken Norwegian and Swedish was at its most intense. Thus when a change happened earlier in Swedish than Norwegian and earlier in Jämtland than the rest of Norway, it is unclear whether this indicates that Jämtland was the point of contact through which the change diffused into Norway or whether we are seeing the influence of written Swedish on documentary language.

3.3. *The Diplomatarium Norvegicum and the DN online*

The sources for the investigations into language change in Old and Middle Norwegian in the remainder of this book come from one specific set of publications, the *Diplomatarium Norvegicum*. Document-level annotations for signatory names, titles and likely social class, for date, and for localisation have been added to these texts; the resulting resource, the *DN online* (Blaxter 2017a), is the corpus used throughout. It will be necessary to give some background both on the texts and their publication history, and on the additions that have been made to them for this work.

3.3.1. *The Diplomatarium Norvegicum*

The *Diplomatarium Norvegicum* (Langer & Unger 1847–1861; Unger & Huitfeldt-Kaas 1863–1900; Huitfeldt-Kaas 1901–1903; Huitfeldt-Kaas et al. 1902–1919; Huitfeldt-Kaas et al. 1910–1915; Magerøy 1970–1976; Næshagen 1990–1995) is a major source of Old Norwegian and almost the only source of Middle Norwegian. The DN consists of 23 volumes of transcribed medieval documents, although only the first 22 are included here: the original texts are dated between 991 (DN XIX.1) and 1727 (DN XIV.567), but 99 per cent of the texts date between 1220 and 1565, 90 per cent between 1325 and 1535. The documents are referred to as 'charters' (*diplom*) in the Norwegian literature, and indeed a great number of them are charters in the sense used more generally outside Norway (that of legal documents conferring [usually property] rights). However, there are also many legal documents of other types (testaments, records of witness testimonies [*vitnebrev*] and trials, legal summons, etc.). A great many documents were added to the *Diplomatarium Norvegicum* from the personal archives of two figures who were exiled from Norway during the Reformation and whose archives were therefore preserved independently in their entirety, King Christian II and Archbishop Olav Engelbrektsson (Berg 2017: 89–90). Among these documents are a still wider range of text types, including accounts, drafts, and (somewhat) more informal notes. As a result, the documents that make up the *Diplomatarium Norvegicum* are often referred to collectively simply as 'letters' (*brev*). Volumes I–XXII of the *Diplomatarium Norvegicum* were digitised in the 1990s as part of *Dokumentasjonsprojektet*, a government-funded project at the Universities of Oslo, Bergen, Trondheim and Tromsø to digitise material concerning Norwegian language and history (Dokumentasjonsprosjektet 1997a; Dokumentasjonsprosjektet 1997b). This digital edition is in a format resembling XML, but with various differences; importantly from the point of view of compatibility, most tags are not matched with end tags.

In total, the corpus numbers more than 18,000 such documents, although only 13,152 contain Nordic-language text (most of the remainder are in Latin or Middle Low German, with a few in Dutch, High German, French and English).

The corpus these charters comprise is invaluable for diachronic studies because, unusually among medieval documents, the majority of documents include explicit information about provenance. The texts generally specify date and place of issue as well as the names and titles of signatories (Mørck 1999: 264–66). Such information is key for research into relationships between linguistic structures and external factors.

The form of these documents also allows us to distinguish originals from copies in the vast majority of cases. In order to produce a copy of a document with legal force, it was necessary to have witnesses attest to its veracity, confirmed with their seals, and this information had to be given first. Thus, where documents are copies, we normally effectively have an older document quoted within a larger framing document, making it extremely clear where the original text ends and the copied text begins. An example of this type is shown in Figure 19. As a whole, this is a transcription of a single manuscript from the Arnamagnæan collection, itself a witnessed transcription of a (lost) earlier document. However, in the *Diplomatarium Norvegicum* it has two entries: the copied document DN IV.295, dated to the 7th of December 1345, and the framing document DN IV.304, dated to the 9th of July 1346. Thus these can easily be treated as separate documents in our corpus. For all of the investigations described in this book, only original texts have been used as evidence (so in this case, DN IV.304 would be included but DN IV.295 would not).

framing text (DN IV.304)

Ollum monnum þæim sem þetta bref sea æder hœyra senda Þorgeir Berþorsson Siguater Aluersson korsbrœder j **Stawanghre** Ormer prester a **Þimini** ok Ormer prester j **Vikadale** q. g. ok sina, kunnigt gerande at mer saam ok ifuir lasom bref meder heilum ok hangandum inciglum vspil t ok vskrapad sua vattande ord fra orde sem her seggir...

To all those people who see or hear this charter[.] Þorgeir Bergþórssonr and Sigvatr Alfrssonr[,] choristers in **Stavanger**[,] Ormr[,] priest at **Þimin**[,] and Ormr[,] priest at **Vikadalr**[,] send g[od's] g[reetings] and their own, making known that we saw and read through [a] charter with whole and hanging seal uncorrupted and unscratched thus attesting word after word as [it] says here...

copied text (DN IV.295)

Ollum monnum þæim sem þetta bref sea æder hœyra senda Peter Niculasson prester a **Jalsa** ok Gutþormr Ogmundarson kællaramader j biscups garde j **Stawangre** q. g. ok sina kunnigt gerande at mit varom þer j hia j lopteno œfra firir ofuan ported j Simunar garde j **Stawangre** in vigilia concepcionis beate virginis vm kuelded anno domini mo. ccco. xlo. quinto er Pal Onondarson talade sua til sira Ogmundar Þoraldarsonar korsbrodor j Stawangre sem her fylger. þu hifuir gert sem ein heiriansson ok þu ert halfuer skalker ok þu skalt ei vita fyr en ek hifuir vppi iliannar a þer ok ek skal setia gudstiordina a halsen a þer firir þæt sem þu hifuir gort ok þat skal kosta þit lif ok sua þit saghde han til brodor meistara Ogmundar Olafs(sonar) ok til sannenda her vm setto mit okor incigli firir þetta bref er gort var j **Stawangre** in festo concepcionis beate virginis are sem fyr seggir.

To all those people who see or hear this charter[,] Pétr Nikulássonr[,] priest at **Jalsi**[,] and Guðþormr Ogmundarsonr[,] cellar-servant in [the] bishop's estate in **Stavanger**[,] send g[od's] g[reetings] and their own[,] making known that we two were then present in the upper chamber above the door in Simun's estate in **Stavanger** *in vigilia concepcionis beate virginis* in the evening *anno domini* 1345 when Pál Onundarsonr spoke thus to rvd. Ogmundr Þórvaldarsonr[,] chorister in Stavanger[,] as here follows: You have acted like a son of Herjan [Odin] and you are half [a] rogue and you will not know [it] until I have [come] up to the soles [of your feet] and I will put god's [?] around your neck because of what you have done and it will cost [you] your life and so for that[,] he said to brother master Ogmundr Ólafssonr in affirmation hereof we two set our seals on this charter which was made in **Stavanger** *in festo concepcionis beate virginis* in [the] year which [it] says before.

framing text (DN IV.304)

...Ok til sannenda her vm setto mer var incigli firir þetta transkriptum er gort var j **Stawangre** in crastino sanctorum in Selio anno domini mo. ccco. xlo. sexto.

...And in affirmation hereof we set our seals on this transcript which was made in **Stavanger** *in crastino sanctorum in Selio anno domini* 1346.

• signatories   • **possible localisations**

Figure 19. Example charter(s) DN IV.304 and IV.295 [Colour figure can be viewed at wileyonlinelibrary.com]

3.3.1.1. Abbreviation

The texts in the *Diplomatarium Norvegicum* are nominally diplomatic transcriptions of the medieval manuscripts on which they are based, but in practice the level and quality of transcription has varied over time. Volumes I–XX were published relatively regularly between 1847 and 1915, followed by a long break before volume XXI starting in 1970. Accordingly, volumes XXI and XXII (and volume XXIII, although that is not included in this project) have different transcription practices to the first twenty volumes. In addition to comparing volumes XXI and XXII to the earlier volumes, a selection of the documents in the earlier volumes have also been published elsewhere with independent transcriptions, allowing us to make direct comparisons of specific texts. Particularly useful are Hødnebø (1960, 1966). Consider the two transcriptions of the same manuscript given below; the first line is DN II.61, the second is Hødnebø (1960) nr. 78 (figure 20)

Some features of the manuscript which Hødnebø's transcription reproduces but Langer & Unger do not are unimportant for our purposes. The use of *r* rotunda, tall *s*, or insular *f* were never linguistically meaningful but purely letter-shape variants: <joʒundar> was effectively the same spelling as <jorundar>, and so losing this information makes no difference to an investigation into any linguistic variable. Likewise the choice of a modern *oe*-digraph <œ> vs. a hooked *o* <œ> is unlikely

Ollom	monnom	þeim	sem	þetta	bref	sia	æða	hœyra
Ollom	monnom	þeim	sem	þetta	bʒeꝛ	sia	æða	hoyꝛa
all.DAT.PL	man.DAT.PL	M.DAT.PL	REL	this.N.ACC.SG	letter.ACC.SG	see.PRS.3PL	or	hear. PRS.3PL

sendir	(Andres)		Pals	son	q.		g.	
sendir	´[yngre hand: Andres]´		pals	ſon	ǀ	queðiu.	guðs.	
send.PRS.3SG	Andres.NOM.SG		Pálsson.NOM.SG		greeting.ACC.SG	god.GEN.SG	

ok	sina.		ek	gerir	ydr	kunnight	at	ek
ok	sína.		ek	gerir	ydr	kunnight	at	ek
and	POS.REF.F.ACC.SG.		1SG.NOM	make.PRS.3SG	2PL.DAT	known	COMP	1SG.NOM

hæfir	fengit	Arna	Jorundar	syni	fullt	vmboð	ok
hæꝛir	ꝛengit	arna	joꝛundar ǀ syni	ꝛullt	vmboð	ok
have.PRS.1SG	given	Arni.DAT.SG	Jorundarson.DAT.SG	full.N.ACC.SG.	charge.ACC.SG	and

loglight	at	sælia	ok	rað	firir	gæra	þui	tuæggia
loglight	at	sælia	ok	rað	ꝛirir	gæra	þui	tuæggia
legal.N.ACC.SG	INF	sell.INF	and	advice.N.SG	for	do.INF	N.DAT.SG	two.GEN

manaðar	mata	bole	i	Sauði	er	Hilldigunnr
manaðar	mata	bole	i	sauði	er	hilldigunnr
month's food.GEN.PL	cultivated land.DAT.SG	in	Sauðr.DAT.SG	REL	Hildigunnr.NOM.SG

husprœyia	væðsetti	mer.	ok	til	sannz	vitnis	burðar
huspꝛoyia	væðſetti	mer	ǀ ok	til	sannz	vitnis	burðar
mistress.NOM.SG	pawn.PRET.3SG	1SG.DAT	and	in	true.M.GEN.SG	witness testimony.GEN.SG

sætti	ek	mitt	insigli	firir	þetta	bref.
sætti	ek	mitt	insigli	ꝛirir	þetta	bꝛeꝛ.
set.PRET.1SG	1SG.NOM	POS.1SG.N.ACC.SG	seal.ACC.SG	on	this.N.ACC.SG	letter.ACC.SG

To all those people see or hear this charter[,] (Andres) Pálssonr sends g[od's] g[reetings] and his own. I make known to you that I have given Arni Jorundarsonr full and legal charge to sell and take care of the two *mánaðarmata* of cultivated land in Sauðr which Mrs. Hildigunnr pawned to me. And in true witness testimony I set my seal on this charter.

Figure 20. Transcriptions of DN II.61 and Hødnebø (1960) nr.78

ever to erase linguistically meaningful variation. Langer & Unger add modern capitalisation to the text – clearly inconsistent with a current understanding of 'diplomatic transcription', but actually relatively helpful for our purposes, in the sense that it facilitates reading of the texts without interfering with anything we might be interested in – and in a similar vein ignore manuscript lineation. Hødnebø is rather more informative about the nature of the word <Andres>, and this is useful, but Langer & Unger do at least indicate to us that this word was an insert of some sort, allowing us to avoid including it in any analysis.

Where there is an obvious problem is in the treatment of abbreviations: comparison with other transcriptions such as Hødnebø's, or with facsimiles of the original documents, shows that these are expanded silently in volumes I–XX of the *Diplomatarium Norvegicum*. Old and Middle Norwegian writing made heavy use of both phonological and lexically-specific abbreviations, and silent expansion of abbreviations presents a problem when examining phonological and orthographic variables, and, to a lesser extent, morphological variables in these texts. In principle, editors expanded abbreviated forms by comparison with unabbreviated forms of the same word in the same text. From a statistical perspective this practice would have the effect of lowering intratextual variation without affecting intertextual variation. However, comparison of some of the texts to independent transcriptions casts doubt on the idea that all editors followed this practice, and in short texts such exemplars would often be lacking anyway. How, then, can we be sure that patterns we find in data which include an unknown set of abbreviated forms are really properties of the original texts (and therefore potentially of the spoken language) and not something introduced by modern editors?

The principled answer is that we cannot. However, the realities of the phenomena we are investigating should give us some confidence. The vast majority of the work presented in this book focuses on the relationships between linguistic variables and external variables: place, time, and potentially the identity of signatories. There is no obvious mechanism by which editors could have introduced systematic patterns relating orthography and location given that when most of these volumes were transcribed, a great many of the places in them had not been identified. Likewise since there were no published hypotheses about relationships between linguistic variables and the identities of signatories at the time that most of these documents were transcribed, it is difficult to see what biases the editors could have introduced through their transcription practices. They could, in principle, have introduced biases relating to document date. Working with such documents for any period of time, a scholar inevitably develops a sense of what is 'normal' in the orthographies of different periods, and this set of expectations could have been expressed whenever there was some optionality in the transcription. This might conceivably have affected the distribution of certain linguistic features over time in these texts, although it is not obvious precisely what effect to expect it to have had.

In practice, for any given variable we can estimate the proportion of our data which might have been influenced by this kind of editorial intervention by comparing a sample of the data to independent transcriptions of the same documents such as Hødnebø's. Most abbreviations were of a handful of high-frequency words (like *ok* 'and'), vowels or coda /m n r/, and so the possible effects on our data are mostly limited to phonological variables concerning vowels and coda consonants, or morphological variables that could be distinguished only by a vowel or coda consonant. Among the case studies in this book, the loss of the voiced dental fricative and the rise of svarabhakti vowels are the two major examples. In each case, an attempt has been made to estimate the proportion of the data likely to have been abbreviated: this can largely be thought of as an estimate of an amount of additional noise added by transcription practices, rather than of a specific bias in the data.

3.3.2. *Annotation*

The digital editions of the *Diplomatarium Norvegicum* were a good starting point, but needed some further development to create a corpus suited to modern historical linguistic work. The corpus had to be converted from its ad hoc encoding into something readable by modern software, and machine-readable annotations had to be added to the texts for the various external variables relevant to this research. The resulting annotated, searchable corpus is available online (Blaxter 2017a) and will be referred as the *DN online* to distinguish it from the unmodified *Diplomatarium Norvegicum*. For more detail on the work done on this corpus, the reader is referred to Blaxter (2017b: 61–99).

3.3.2.1. *Dating, background on signatories*

The texts in the *Diplomatarium Norvegicum* were each dated by the editors, but these dates were free text and were in a variety of formats and spelling systems, reflecting the long period of time over which the volumes were published. These were transformed into Unix timestamp ranges (i.e. offsets in seconds from midnight of the 1st of January 1970). In most cases, the documents are dated to the day, but in some cases, usually where there is no explicit date given in the text itself, the editors have given a larger range of possible dates. In practice, the midpoint of ranges is used for all calculations in this book.

Each text was also tagged for the names and titles of its first signatory and for whether any of the signatories was a woman. This was done to allow the exploration of sociolinguistic variation in these texts. To take the example of DN IV.304 given in Figure 19, the signatories are two members of the cathedral at Stavanger, <Þorgeir Berþorsson> and <Siguater Aluersson>, and two parish priests, both called <Ormer>, but in the database only the first of these four is recorded. This exclusive focus on the first signatory follows the general tradition in sociolinguistic work on the charters, and is rationalised on the basis that the first signatory was almost always the highest ranked and can be assumed to have had the greatest influence over the language of the text (Grøtvedt 1949: 9–10; Mørck 1980: 17; 1999: 272; Schimmelpfennig 1985: 19; Farstad 1991: 8–10).[6] These social annotations are not used in the case studies in this book, but have been used in conjunction with the spatial methods described here for historical sociolinguistic investigations in Blaxter (2017b) and Blaxter & Kinn (2018) and are available for future researchers to take advantage of.

3.3.2.2. Localisation

More important for the work presented here are text localisations. The texts in the *Diplomatarium Norvegicum* are already localised, but not in a way which is sufficient for this kind of work. For each text, the editors supplied a written localisation, most often in the form of a single placename; these will be referred to as the editorial localisations.

Many editorial localisations are only slightly adapted from placenames which appear in the texts. DN IV.296 and IV.304 (Figure 19) are both localised as 'Stavanger'. Here, the placename which appears in the text is unambiguous and the editors have simply given the modern form. This is also done with placenames whose form has changed more substantially between Middle and Modern Norwegian; for example, many texts are localised as 'Bergen', reflecting textual forms like <Biorghwin>, <Biargvinn>, <biørguin>, etc.

However, not of all the editorial localisations reflect current or even real modern forms. Sometimes, differences between the modern placename and the form given by the editors reflect changes between nineteenth-century norms of written Riksmål Norwegian, which was closer to Danish, and modern Norwegian; at other times, it is simply a modified transcription of a placename in the text. For example, DN II.748 is labelled 'Hvalbein' reflecting textual <Hvalbeinom>. The modern form is *Kvalbein*, but this sound change would not usually have been represented in nineteenth-century written Norwegian. Accordingly, we cannot tell whether the form given by the editors was intended as the modernised form in 1852, or a simple transcription of the form in the text. To take a different example, DN XI.204 is localised as 'Hirtathveit', reflecting <Hyrthatwetom> in the text itself (the modern Norwegian form is *Hørtvet*). Here, we see that the editors have made only slight changes to the form of the name: guessing (incorrectly) that the <y> in the text represents /i/; normalising <-twet-> to '-thveit' (representing the element -*þveit*); normalising the first <th> to 't'; and removing the case ending. This is clearly simply a representation of the form found in the text and not a reference to a modern placename known to them. There is no absolute rule determining which forms are modernised or normalised by modern editors and which are not. Generally speaking, larger, well-known modern places are more likely to be modernised. It seems likely these differences basically reflect the information available to editors:

---

[6] As discussed in section 3.3.2.2 concerning localisation, there is good reason to be suspicious of this reductive assumption, and it would be desirable work in future to expand annotations to include other signatories and even non-signatories mentioned in the text.

where they recognised placenames, they gave these in their modern form to aid readers in identifying them; where they did not, they reproduced the forms in the texts with varying degrees of faithfulness.

This differential difficulty in recognising textual placenames is also reflected in the amount of detail given in editorial localisations. For some texts, a placename is followed by a bracketed larger placename to help disambiguation. An example is 'Nes (Kvindhered)' for DN XI.111 reflecting modernday *Nes* in *Kvinnherad kommune*. These too are often taken directly from the texts: in this case <Nes j Kuinherad>. There is a tendency to add this extra information for common placenames (like *Nes*), although the practice is by no means consistent: there are twenty one charters whose editorial localisation is just 'Nes', in spite of the fact that there are more than eighty localities called *Nes* in Norway (even excluding those which were called *Nes* in the medieval period but have changed today or the more than 300 compounded placenames beginning with *Nes-*).

The second inconsistency in editorial localisations regards where in the texts the information was taken from. There are four main sources of localisation information used by the editors of the DN:

1. indication in the eschatocol of where the charter was issued, typically in the formula *þetta bréf er gjǫrt var í* 'this charter which was made in [placename]';

2. indication at the beginning of the body of where the legal meeting described took place, in one of various formulae such as *vér várum í* [placename] *á* [date] *ságum ok heyrðum* 'we were in [placename] on [date], saw and heard';

3. placenames introduced in association with individual signatories, of which we find two types:

   • we find preposition + placename phrases acting as surnames, typically for untitled individuals who are not given any other names in the same text – these placenames are usually individual estates or farms, presumably the property of the signatories;

   • and we find preposition+placename phrases following certain titles such as *(sóknar)prestr* '(parish) priest', *biskup* 'bishop', *lǫgmaðr* 'lawyer' and *syslumaðr* 'sheriff' – these placenames indicate the jurisdiction or domain of the offices; and

4. placenames in the content of the charter itself, such as the land sold or the settings of events reported in witness depositions.

These four sources of information appear to have been used in that order of preference: the editorial localisation most typically assigns the text to its place of issue; where this is not given, it falls back on the location of the meeting; and so on. If the localisation is uncertain, typically meaning that only the third or fourth of these types is available, it is (inconsistently) given in square brackets; for example, DN II.64 (Figure 20) is localised as '[Voss.]' on the basis of the farm name <Sauði> (modern *Saue* in Voss). Where the charter cannot be localised by its text, it is marked 'uten sted' ('without place') or similar (this is sometimes done even if there are some placenames mentioned in the body of the text). Approximately 330 original charters in a Nordic language are marked as unlocalisable in this way.

A new layer of machine-readable localisations have been added for the *DN online*. In significant part these are based on Rygh's *Norske Gaardnavne*, an encyclopaedic series of books which attempt to record all Norwegian farms known from the medieval period (Rygh et al. 1898–1936). However, Rygh was just a starting point: some farms not identified in Rygh were identified in these localisations, and indeed by no means all the localisations are farms. The new localisations are different to the editorial localisations in the DN in several ways:

- all placenames are fully expanded and identifiable: where the editorial localisation for DN XI.204 reads just 'Hirtathveit', the localisation in the *DN online* specifies parish, nineteenth and twentieth century municipalities, traditional region, and county ('Hørtvet, Efteløt sokn, Sandsvær herad/Kongsberg kommune, Numedal, Buskeruds amt/Buskerud fylke');[7]
- all placenames are associated with latitude-longitude co-ordinates; and
- where there are multiple locations mentioned in a text, it can be given multiple localisations.

This work has been undertaken in two stages of which the second is not yet complete. The first stage was to identify the single best localisation for each text (using the same order of priority among types of place mentioned as that used for the editorial localisations); this has been completed for all original, Nordic-language texts in the corpus. The second was to identify all other possible localisations from each text. This is extremely time-consuming and is complete only for a subset of texts. However, in principle, it should be preferred. There are obvious practical difficulties with localising texts to multiple places with many traditional ways of visualising text localisations, and with such methods we might have to just plot a single localisation per text, or to plot a single centre point of all possible localisations. With our kernel smoothing methods, however, these difficulties are easily overcome: we can simply include at a text at *all* the points to which it is localised, but weight it at $1/x$ at each location (where x is the number of localisations).

The rationale among the editors of the *Diplomatarium Norvegicum* and previous researchers for preferring the place of issue of the text is that this is the single most likely 'true' localisation for the language. The exact nature of text production in Norway in this period is surprisingly difficult to ascertain from the

---

[7] Note that these were recorded before the changes in administrative structures in 2020 and so do not reflect the numerous mergers of counties and municipalities carried out then.

sources, but many scholars assume that a great proportion of texts were written by professional scribes (even though these are explicitly mentioned only in a tiny subset of texts), and that such a scribe was most likely to be someone from the text's place of issue – thus the single person most directly responsible for the language of the text would be likely to be someone from the place of issue. However, since the exact contributions that different people made to the production of most texts is obscure, there are many ways in which other locations mentioned in a text *could* instead be the best localisation for the text's language. Indeed, it is easy to find instances where distinctive linguistic features may be associated with an identifiable individual. To continue with the examples in Figure 19, DN IV.295 has present singular of *hafa* 'have' with a raised vowel <hifuir>. This form occurs in just two other texts, one of which is DN IV.344, dated to the 15th of March 1349, and also with the editorial localisation of Stavanger. DN IV.295 and IV.344 mention a single individual in common: *Ormr*, parish priest at Vikedal, is a signatory to DN IV.304, the framing text in which IV.295 appears, and the beneficiary of the legal judgement in DN IV.344. It is possible that the form <hifuir> should be attributed to some unknown scribe in the bishop's estate at Stavanger who worked on both manuscripts, but given that we have a *known* individual who had some involvement in the production of both texts, it is also possible that the form should be attributed to him. In that case, it would be more correct to localise this linguistic peculiarity to Vikedal than to Stavanger. For these reasons, for those texts which have been localised to multiple places, all localisations are used in the case studies in this book.

An additional complication concerns regions. Many placenames used in the texts identify single settlements – indeed, by far the most common type of placenames we find in the text are farm names. However, there are also many placenames which refer to larger locations, i.e. locations which can *contain* other locations: parishes, legal and ecclesiastical domains, traditional regions of various sizes, valleys, islands and so on. Treating these as single points – the midpoints of the region, or perhaps better the single most populous point in the region – has relatively little effect on the overall distributions we find, but it does create unfortunate artefacts, tending to draw cities and other central points towards overall regional averages for a given linguistic feature. To avoid this, where texts are localised to a region, they have been localised to every specific point in that region that occurs in the database, and the weight of the text at each of these points divided by the number of points. This has the effect of spreading out the evidence offered by such ambiguous localisations across all the points which we have some independent reason to believe might be relevant.

This process is illustrated for DN IV.304 in Figure 21. The top left panel shows a localisation only to the place of issue, Stavanger: this is in line with the editorial localisation. There are, however, two other locations mentioned in the text, and we could localise it to the midpoint of all three (top right panel) or to all three (bottom left panel). If we do the latter, we weight Stavanger as 2/4 (it is both the place of issue and the professional domain of the first two signatories) and Vikedal and

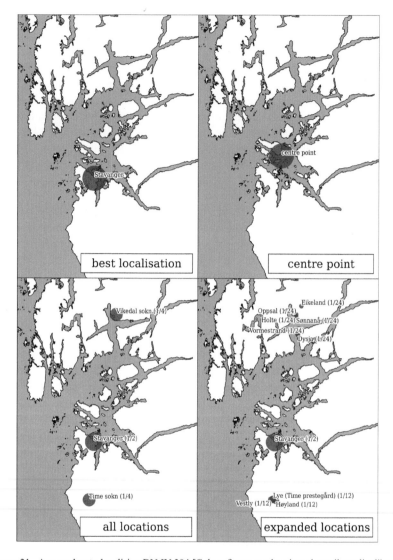

Figure 21. Approaches to localising DN IV.304 [Colour figure can be viewed at wileyonlinelibrary. com]

Time sokner each as 1/4 (each occurs just once, as the professional domain of a signatory). Finally, we can go one step further, and replace Vikedal and Time sokner with the individual points that correspond to these parishes in the database: six farms that will each be weighted 1/24 in the case of Vikedal, three weighted 1/12 in the case of Time; this is visualised in the bottom right panel.

4

V<small>ARIABLE</small> <small>DEFINITIONS AND DATASETS</small>

4.1. *Introduction*

This chapter will define a series of linguistic variables which underwent change in the Middle Norwegian period and describe the approach to data collection used for each of them. Following chapters will then explore the distributions of these variables in space and time in detail and discuss what we can take away from them, both for the history of Norwegian and for historical linguistic and sociolinguistic theory. Readers with little special interest in the history of Norwegian may be happy to accept that these datasets are good measurements of the linguistic features they purport to measure and may not wish to spend time considering the detail of how they were collected. Such readers are directed to chapters 5, 6 and 7.

The variables and changes to be examined are shown in Table 3 (note that some variables underwent more than one change over the period examined, so there are more changes than there are variables).

The questions investigated in chapters 6 and 7, those of the role of Middle Low German (MLG) contact in simplifying changes in the history of Norwegian and the types of spatial diffusion which drove change in the period examined,

Table 3. Changes studied

Domain	Variable	Change
Phonology	status of /θ/	loss of the voiced dental fricative: [ð] > /d/
Phonology	status of /θ/	loss of the voiceless dental fricative: /θ/ > /t/
Phonology	presence of svarabhakti vowels	rise of svarabhakti vowels: /Cr#/ > /CVr#/
Morphology	1sg. agreement	loss of 1sg. present verbal agreement: $-V_{1SG}$ > $-Vr_{1/3SG}$
Morphology	1pl active agreement	loss of 1pl verbal agreement: $-Vm_{1PL}$ > $-V_{PL}$
Morphology	1pl active agreement	loss of plural verbal agreement: $-V_{PL}$ > $-Vr_{PRS}/$ $-\emptyset_{PST}$
Morphology	1pl middle agreement	loss of 1pl middle verbal agreement: $-Vmz_{1PL}$ > $-Vz_{PL}$
morphophonology	1pl subject pronoun	reanalysis of 1pl pronoun: *vér* > *mér*
Morphosyntax	1pl subject pronoun	merger of 1pl pronoun into 1du. pronoun: *mér* > *mit*
Morphology	1pl subject pronoun	replacement of 1pl pronoun with loanword: *mér* > *vi*
morphophonology	1du. subject pronoun	reanalysis of 1du. pronoun: *vit* > *mit*
Morphosyntax	1du. subject pronoun	merger of 1du. pronoun into 1pl pronoun: *mit* > *mér*
Morphology	1du. subject pronoun	replacement of 1du. pronoun with loanword: *mit* > *vi*
Syntax	lexical genitives	loss of genitive objects of *millum*

require us to examine several changes. It would be difficult to draw any conclusions in these areas from the story of a single variable: whatever the result, we could not know whether it was representative of a common pattern or was a one-off. Thus the approach to data collection has been driven by the need to collect large, representative datasets for many different variables over the course of one project. A traditional, philological project might have focused on a single variable and spent the time exhaustively collecting every possible datum; the visualisation and statistical tools presented in this book would be entirely suitable for such an approach. Here, however, shortcuts have been used to allow the investigation of several variables more quickly.

The data-collection methods used generally rely on searching for specific lemmas. For the phonological variables, this means identifying a limited list of lemmas which have the relevant phonological context (and do not form orthographic minimal pairs with unrelated forms which would not be subject to the same change) and tracing the change only as it affected these words. The alternative, to identify every potential phonological context for the change in the documents and collect all the possible data, would involve manually reading and marking up each text. This is the approach taken by many of the previous scholars mentioned below, typically working only with small sub-corpora, but is extremely time consuming and not possible with a corpus of this size. Such an approach faces a problem of diminishing returns: when identifying every possible phonological context for a change, most of the time is spent identifying and categorising a large variety of rare forms which, in the end, make up only a very small fraction of the potential data. Restricting ourselves to the most common lemmas means we can collect the majority (or at least a large subset) of the potential data in a fraction of the time.

Similar comments apply to the morphological and syntactic variables, although the approach has not been identical. For the loss of lexical genitives, the approach was to choose one, specific context for lexical genitives which can easily be searched for: the preposition *millum*. Obviously it would be desirable to look at lexical genitives in a wider range of contexts (other prepositions and verbs which governed the genitive), both because this would give us a larger dataset and because we might find the change was differentiated by context. However, the investigation was limited to this context to make data collection tractable.

For the loss of 1sg. and 1pl verbal inflection, the approach was to search for subject pronouns (as these represent a short list of specific morphological forms which are therefore easy to identify in a corpus of this type) and then manually identify their associated verbs. This comes closer to a complete, philological method: it does involve examining every text and gathers a large proportion of the available data (excluding only verbs with null subjects, an infrequent type in Old and Middle Norwegian). For changes in the form of the 1pl and 1du. subject pronouns, every possible form could be identified directly by regular expression searching.

4.2. *Phonological variables*

4.2.1. *Rise of svarabhakti vowels*

4.2.1.1. *Background*

4.2.1.1.1. The change: phonology and orthography. As a result of syncopes in late Proto Norse, the phonotactics of Old Norse allowed a number of cross-linguistically marked clusters with /r/, including coda clusters with rising sonority. Synchronically, these occurred particularly in the context of certain morphological endings: nom.sg. *-r* and 2/3sg. *-r*. In late Old Norwegian, these were broken up by svarabhakti vowels so that earlier /Cr#/ and /CrC/ sequences became /CVr#/ and /CVrC/. This change eventually took place in all Nordic languages. Morphological changes later obscured most instances of this change in Continental Nordic: nom.sg. *-(V)r* was deleted by morphological change, obscuring earlier changes to its form; verbal *-r* was subject to analogical conflation with alternative endings in *-Vr*, making it a moot point whether *-r* had first become *-Vr* by sound change. Nevertheless, the change is clearly evidenced in Modern Norwegian in monomorphemic contexts such as *åker* < *ákr* 'field', in the plurals of consonant stems like *bøker* < *bækr* 'books', and in dialects where the quality of the svarabhakti vowel makes it easy to distinguish from vowels from other sources. In Insular Nordic, less morphological change has taken place and so the output of the change is clearly preserved (Icelandic/Faroese *akur*, Icelandic *bækur*/Faroese *bøkur*, but also Icelandic/Faroese *maður* 'man [nom.sg.]'). The svarabhakti vowel in Continental Nordic is usually schwa, but in Insular Nordic was /u/ (giving <u> /ʏ/ in Modern Icelandic and <u> /ʊ/ in Faroese); thus we can also clearly see the svarabhakti vowel in forms like Icelandic/Faroese *tekur* 'take [2./3sg.]' (as opposed to, say, *brúkar* 'use [2./3sg.]' where the vowel is etymological).

4.2.1.1.2. Earlier research. The two grand historians of the Norwegian language, Didrik Seip and Gustav Indrebø, both date the change very early. Seip (1955: 68,72) cites the spelling of the name of Olav Kyrre (whose reign began in 1066) as <(O)laver> on a coin, early examples of svarabhakti <a> in Icelandic manuscripts with suspected Norwegian exemplars, and further examples in Old Norwegian with <e>, <æ> and <a> from the eleventh and twelfth centuries onwards. These earliest examples are associated with religious language, particularly the lexical items *undrligr* > *undarligr* 'wonderful', *ítrligr* > *ítarligr* 'princely' and *Pétr* > *Pétar* 'Peter'. In terms of geographical variation, Seip (1955: 139) suggests that fewest svarabhakti vowels are found in charters from Trondheim and Trøndelag, but (as is his want) puts this down to a conservative writing tradition rather than spoken dialect differences. He interprets inconsistency in the orthography and abbreviation of svarabhakti vowels in West Norwegian charters as evidence that they were common in speech in this region. Indrebø (1951: 118) goes into more detail on early evidence, noting the same numismatic example and two or three runic examples of similar age in Austlandet, the first West Norwegian examples shortly after

1200 and examples in Trøndelag after 1250. He states that svarabhakti vowel spellings become more frequent in Norwegian texts from around 1325 so that they can be said to be the norm no earlier than 1350, but that in speech the sound change must have been 'quite usual'[8] already before 1300 (Indrebø 1951: 118).

Other scholars build on or contest this picture to different degrees. Schulte (2005: 1084–5) states that orthographic '[e]penthetic vowels are regularly inserted from the 13th and 14th c. onward, although some earlier attestations are found in Norwegian coin inscriptions from the 1060s' and that phonetically 'the regular intrusion of svarabhakti vowels in Norwegian starts in the 13th c., to be completed not before 1400 in early Middle Norwegian'. Klevmark's (1983) study of vocalism in charters from Hallingdal, studying twenty five charters from 1310–1463, finds extensive evidence of svarabhakti vowels from earliest documents. Farstad (1991: 56), studying vocalism in charters from Hedmark from 1356–1420, criticises Seip and Indrebø's claim that the svarabhakti vowel developed in speech centuries before it became common in writing, arguing that 'our early scribes could hardly have viewed the svarabhakti vowel as something untraditional already before a literary tradition had established itself',[9] suggesting instead that the rise in written sources is reasonable evidence for the rise in speech. Farstad discovers that only a few of the charters studied lack the svarabhakti vowel, although it is usually represented with an abbreviation mark; the proportion of fully written-out svarabhakti vowels increased over time (Farstad 1991: 60–1). Adams (2015: 234–6), studying E 8902, a late-fourteenth century Norwegian manuscript of the Swedish Birgittine revelations, notes that only sixteen tokens of over 1,100 surveyed have no svarabhakti vowel.

Thus in terms of dating the change in Norwegian sources there is agreement on the earliest evidence (the numismatic example from the 1060s) but on little else. There is a century difference in Seip and Schulte's estimations of the date the change was completed in speech. These differences are summarised in Table 4.

Turning to East Nordic, Skautrup (1968: 250) suggests that the change was common in Danish from around 1200 and in Swedish from the mid-thirteenthth century. Wessén (1968: 59–60) suggests that there are sporadic examples of svarabhakti vowels in runic Swedish and that in the earliest alphabetic Old Swedish svarabhakti vowels are already the norm, although he notes that they are lacking in the oldest attestations of the Äldre Västgötalagen, Gutalagen and Upplandslagen. This might imply a marginally later date than Skautrup. Figure 22 shows the rates of different orthographies for svarabhakti vowels in 1545 original Swedish charters dating between 1333 to 1379 and between 1401 and 1425. This seems basically in line with the more impressionistic descriptions of Skautrup and Wessén: at the beginning of the fourteenth century the conservative zero variant was already a small minority in Swedish texts.

Table 4. Previous suggested datings for the rise of svarabhakti vowels

	Indrebø	Seip	Schulte
First traces	1060s	1060s	1060s
Increasing in writing	1325	11th and 12th cc.	
Complete in writing	after 1350		
Increasing in speech			13th century
Complete in speech	before 1300		after 1400

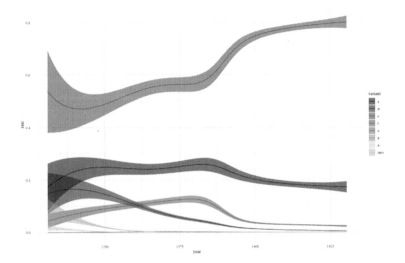

Figure 22. Kernel smoothed estimates of svarabhakti vowel orthographies in Swedish charters
[Colour figure can be viewed at wileyonlinelibrary.com]

Many scholars comment on the varying quality of the svarabhakti vowel in medieval Norwegian sources as well as its presence/absence; as this is beyond the scope of my investigation here, I will mention some of this research only very briefly. There is some agreement on the geography of this quality variation, with an association of rounded vowels with sources from Vestlandet (Adams 2015: 234–6), <a> with Østlandet (Grøtvedt 1939: 97; Adams 2015: 234–6) or specifically inner Østlandet (Klevmark 1983: 95), <æ> also with inner Østlandet (Farstad 1991: 60), and <i> with Swedish (Klevmark 1983: 96; Adams 2015: 234–6). These patterns seem to agree with modern dialect evidence on svarabhakti vowel qualities relatively well (Grøtvedt 1939: 97; Klevmark 1983: 97). Later in the period, variation decreases and <e> becomes more prevalent everywhere (Klevmark 1983: 96; Farstad 1991: 60).

4.2.1.2. Data collection
In principle, there are two types of evidence for this change. Hypercorrections, where etymological /CVr/ is spelled <Cr>, are most likely to result from a

situation in which the writing standard prescribes <Cr> spellings for etymo-logical /Cr/ sequences but these are no longer phonetically distinguishable from /CVr/ sequences for the writer in question. On the other hand, direct representations of svarabhakti vowels in the form of <CVr> spellings for etymological /Cr/ can reflect a situation in which these are now produced /CVr/ and/or a situation in which the writing standard now prescribes <CVr>. The data for hypercorrections are limited and the evidence they offer equivocal, as discussed in Blaxter (2017b: 169–76). I will not repeat the investigation of hypercorrections here but rely on my conclusion there that, as far as it is possible to square the two types of evidence, they support each other, and so we should assume that the orthographic change coincides relatively well with the sound change in the spoken language. Were it the case that the sound change postdated the orthographic change by a substantial margin, we would expect to see a long interval when direct representations of svarabhakti vowels occurred but hypercorrections did not. On the other hand, if, as suggested by Seip and Indrebø, the sound change predated the orthographic change (i.e. conservative orthographic norms were strong enough to prevent any direct representation of the sound change for some time), we would expect the opposite finding, a period with only hypercorrections and little direct evidence for the change. Neither of these situations hold. Thus here I concentrate only on direct representations of svarabhakti vowels, as the much larger source of evidence.

To estimate the rates of occurrence of svarabhakti vowels in different groups of texts we must identify a list of words to investigate that allow us to count non-occurrences as well as occurrences of the relevant spellings. This is not entirely straightforward, since most svarabhakti vowels occur in morphologically complex forms and so identifying good candidates is complicated by unrelated analogical change. Strong verbs and class one weak verbs with 2./3sg. -r could be subject to analogy from other verb classes with endings in -ir and -ar. As a result, it is impossible to tell whether a form like <binder> for Old Norwegian (strong III) bindr 'bind' in DN VII.280 reflects sound change or analogy with forms like (weak 1) bendir 'bend'. Similarly, nominals with nom.sg. in -r could be subject to analogy from the ija-stem declension with nom.sg. in -ir and from nom.pl forms in -ir and -ar, and so present the same problems of interpretation.

However, the potential for analogical interference in nominals seems much lower than in verbs. In the case of nominal forms, nom.sg. nouns in -ir represent a minor class with no highly frequent members: it seems unlikely that analogical transfer into this class was ever a productive process. As the singular-plural distinction in nouns has been maintained extremely well for the entirety of the history of Norwegian, analogical transfer between nom.sg. and nom.pl endings also seems unlikely. By contrast, in the verbal case the analogical transfer concerned would be from the largest, most productive verb classes (all weak verbs excepting light stemmed class one weak verbs) to smaller classes. It seems very probable that such analogy took place. Accordingly, no verb forms were used in this study.

All tokens of the adverbs *aptr* 'back', *áðr* 'earlier' (also in the compound *áðrnefndr* 'aforementioned') and *niðr* 'down', the preposition *meðr* 'with', the conjunction *eðr* 'or' and the nom.sg. of the common nouns *konungr* 'king' and *maðr* 'man, person' (including compounds in *-maðr*) and the personal names *Arnfinnr, Aslákr, Ásmundr, Barðr, Eiríkr, Erlingr, Guðbrandr, Guðleikr, Hallvarðr, Haraldr, Ingimundr, Ingivaldr, Knútr, Oddr, Ólafr, Ormr, Pétr, Ulfr* and *Þórðr* were identified in original texts. This comprised a total of 25,076 tokens. The nominals were checked to ensure that they were not (analogical) *-ar* genitives or *-Vr* plurals and all such instances excluded. The frequencies of different orthographic variants for these lemmas in original texts in the dataset are given in Table 5.

4.2.1.2.1. Editorial intervention. Seip notes that 'in manuscripts and charters the svarabhakti vowel is often written with an abbreviation mark, so it is impossible to determine its quality'.[10] We must be wary of the evidence here: svarabhakti vowel quality and perhaps presence may be obscured by abbreviation.

In order to assess the scale of this problem, 237 tokens in sixty six charters which were independently transcribed in Hødnebø (1960) were examined in detail. In sixty two (26.16 per cent) the svarabhakti vowel and/or the /r/ were abbreviated in one of two ways. Firstly, there are cases where an entire word was abbreviated, leaving just the first letter and abbreviation mark. In the sample, there were seventeen such abbreviations (7.17 per cent) (mostly the noun *konungr* and preposition *með(r)*). Clearly, it would be desirable to exclude this type as it offers no actual evidence about the form of the word. The second type uses a hook, to abbreviate a /Vr/ sequence or conceivably a /r/ alone: these abbreviations should be expanded according to unabbreviated examples in the same document. We would not expect to find disagreement between the DN and Hødnebø if both followed this practice, yet disagreements are found.

DN IV.6 (1293) is an instructive example. Here, ten tokens were collected for this study: five of *maðr*, one of *lǫgmaðr*, and one each of *Pétr, Áslákr, Eiríkr* and *Ormr*. In the DN, just one of these tokens has a svarabhakti vowel: <Ormær>. By contrast, Hødnebø also transcribes svarabhakti vowels in <Petær>, <Eírikær> and <Aflakær>, reflecting different decisions about how to expand the hook abbreviation. Both Hødnebø's and the DN's transcriptions are defensible. There are unabbreviated svarabhakti vowels in the text, but they are outnumbered by many examples with no svarabhakti vowel (and no abbreviation mark). We could take these clear svarabhakti vowels as slips of the pen that reveal the 'real' language of the scribe, contrasting with forms without svarabhakti vowels as uninformative normative forms: this, it seems, was Hødnebø's interpretation (although not for all tokens, as he expands some abbreviation marks simply as <ꝛ>). Alternatively, we could expand

---

[10] '[i] hss. og diplomer er svarabhaktivokalen ofte skrevet med et forkortningstegn, så det er umulig å avgjøre kvaliteten' (Seip 1955: 138).

Table 5. Number of tokens in the svarabhakti vowel dataset by lemma and variant

Lemma	Svarabhakti vowel orthography							
	Ø (<Cr>)	a	æ	e	i	o	ø	u
áðr	268	41	32	308	6	2	0	9
áðrnefndr	225	64	16	1443	28	2	1	0
aptr	159	36	29	343	8	2	0	8
Arnfinnr	46	7	8	47	4	2	0	3
Aslákr	62	37	36	128	6	2	0	0
Ásmundr	20	16	8	71	0	0	0	0
Barðr	122	12	15	159	2	6	0	1
eðr	868	244	262	7912	59	6	0	12
Eiríkr	122	63	63	411	7	0	0	2
Erlingr	79	21	27	140	4	0	0	2
Guðbrandr	101	15	11	166	4	0	0	3
Guðleikr	25	7	4	47	1	2	0	0
Hallvarðr	160	53	48	596	14	0	0	0
Haraldr	31	11	25	161	0	0	0	0
Ingimundr	24	0	1	15	0	0	0	0
Ingivaldr	1	0	0	0	0	0	0	0
Knútr	5	0	0	7	0	0	0	0
konungr	240	9	10	142	2	0	0	0
maðr	456	38	47	394	0	0	0	2
meðr	880	128	142	1862	8	0	0	3
niðr	32	9	10	398	1	0	0	0
Oddr	57	12	8	106	1	3	0	0
Ólafr	64	68	61	698	7	0	0	2
Ormr	57	24	34	212	3	1	0	3
Pétr	97	55	33	2257	7	1	0	7
Ulfr	10	6	0	158	6	2	0	3
Þórðr	117	50	30	306	4	0	0	1

abbreviations according to the majority pattern, as the DN does. From a purely statistical standpoint the DN practice is reassuring here, since expanding ambiguous examples according to the majority pattern for the charter should not change the average across many charters (although it would change the variance).

In total, of the 220 examples where there was a partial word with an abbreviation mark rather than a fully abbreviated word, for just eight (3.64 per cent) was there disagreement between Hødnebø and the DN. This low rate offers some reassurance about the scale of the problem. Regardless, there is no option but to take the judgement of the DN: the work involved in retranscribing all relevant texts to identify the unambiguous data would be enormous and facsimiles are available only for a small subset of texts. Thus this source of uncertainty must be borne in mind.

However, as already discussed more generally in section 3.3.1.1, there is reason for optimism: it is not clear how editorial intervention could introduce any specific biases. There is no clear or consistent view in the scholarly literature even now on the geographical distribution of svarabhakti vowels in early sources and minimal opinion on their pathway of diffusion; when most DN texts were transcribed there was no scholarship on this topic at all. Accordingly, there could be no prior expectation to bias transcribers to interpret abbreviations as representing svarabhakti vowels in some regions but not others. There is scholarly opinion on the geographical distribution of svarabhakti vowel qualities and, anyway, only a short logical leap is needed to expect <u> to be more common on the west coast (the region in closest contact with Iceland and the Faroes and from which they were settled). Accordingly, a study of svarabhakti vowel qualities in the DN might face a more serious problem. But for our purposes, focusing only on the presence or absence of svarabhakti vowels, we can assume that transcription practices have introduced noise into the dataset but are unlikely to have introduced spurious patterns.

4.2.2. Loss of voiceless dental fricatives

4.2.2.1. Background
Several changes affected the dental fricative /θ/ in Middle Norwegian, resulting in its disappearing in all of Continental Nordic.

4.2.2.1.1. Phonology and orthography before the change. Two orthemes are used for dental fricatives in normalised Old Norse orthography: <þ> in word-initial position (or morpheme-initial position in the second element of a compound) and <ð> elsewhere. This broadly reflects Old Norwegian manuscript orthographies. The voiced and voiceless fricatives were predictable allophones of the same phoneme, with [θ] appearing in stressed onset (including the initial syllable of the second element of a compound) and [ð] elsewhere. As a result, in all instances but the onset of the stressed syllable in function words, <þ> represented [θ] and <ð> [ð]; function words were chronically under-stressed, and so in these cases <þ> could represent [ð]. Different changes took place in these three contexts (stressed onset in content words, stressed onset in function words, elsewhere), with different outcomes in the different modern languages. As we shall see, there is also orthographic evidence that the timing of these changes differed in the different contexts, with changes affecting <þ> [ð] in function words taking place later than changes affecting /θ/ in other contexts. This raises the question of how many changes we are talking about; this is dealt with in more detail in chapter 5. Either way, because different lexical items are involved and the orthographies are different, we must gather data for voiced and voiceless contexts separately. We begin with the changes affecting the voiceless dental fricative in stressed onset. Changes affecting the voiced allophone in coda and in unstressed, word-internal syllable onset are dealt with in section 4.2.3.

4.2.2.1.2. The nature of the change. Two orthographic changes affected words with voiceless dental fricatives in Middle Norwegian. The thorn orthography <þ> could be replaced by the digraph <th> (the orthography used for the dental fricative in later Old Swedish) or it could be replaced by <t>. Thus a word with initial /θ/ like *þórsdagr* 'Thursday' might be spelt <þorsdagr> in early manuscripts, but later we see spellings like <thorsdager> and <torsdager>. In terms of phonology, the end result in Modern Norwegian is a voiceless stop: *torsdag* /tuṣdɑg/ (or similar).

4.2.2.1.3. Earlier research. According to Indrebø (1951: 226–30), the letter thorn fell out of use over the period 1420–1450, with initial signs as early as 1334 in Bergen. Indrebø suggests that these orthographic changes were not a direct expression of the sound change, but rather that the letter fell out of use in script before the sound change affecting /θ/ was completed. Seip (1954: 201–2) dates the orthographic change slightly earlier, between 1400 and 1450, noting the same earliest instance from 1334 and increasingly frequent examples from 1370 onwards. On the relationship between pronunciation and orthography, he takes a somewhat different position to Indrebø, stating that the change of <þ> to <th> is initially purely orthographic except in Jämtland (although <th> later came also to be used for /t/) but otherwise assuming that the earliest examples of a change from <þ> to <t> in writing reflected a change which had already taken place in speech (Seip 1955: 294). In terms of spatial distribution, he suggests the orthographic change occurred earliest in Jämtland (Seip 1955: 294). Schulte (2005: 1085) states simply that 'these transitions pertain to the 14th and 15th c.'. Mørck (2011: 531) suggests that <þ> transitioned to <th> and <t> gradually during the fifteenth century and that the sounds it represented disappeared at the same time (Mørck 2011: 537). Thus we see all possible options supported in the literature: that the orthographic change preceded the sound change, that it followed it, or that the two were concurrent.

None of these authors comments in detail on geography. Adams (2016: 64–5), studying the orthography of the late-fourteenth century Norwegian Birgittine manuscript E 8902, sees the use of <th> for /θ/ and particularly for /t/ as evidence of Swedish influence, commenting 'a Norwegian would never use <th> for <t>': he thus assumes that the change was normal in Swedish at this point but unknown in Norwegian. Certainly it seems clear the change happened earlier in East Nordic than Norwegian: Skautrup (1968: 252) dates the change in Danish to 1250–1300 at the latest and in Swedish to the 1300s. Wessén (1968: 82) states that the letter <þ> disappeared from Old Swedish texts around 1375 to be replaced by <th> in word-initial position and <dh> elsewhere, and that the sound change [θ] > /t/ happened at latest by 1400.

4.2.2.2. Data collection
4.2.2.2.1. Method of data collection. As with svarabhakti vowels we can gather data on voiceless dental fricative stopping by looking at direct representations of

the change or at hypercorrections, and as with svarabhakti vowels, I investigated the distribution of hypercorrections in Blaxter (2017b: 223–6, 230). As in the case of svarabhakti vowels, hypercorrections (i.e. instances where <th> or <þ> are written for etymological /t/) are always very low in frequency, reducing their utility as evidence for the spatial distributions of an underlying sound change. The evidence from hypercorrections is easy to integrate and in close agreement with the evidence from direct representations of the change. Hypercorrect <þ> begins to rise in frequency at the same time that <t> begins to occur for etymological /θ/, and only falls when the disappearance of <þ> is nearing completion. Thus we can consider hypercorrections useful confirmation that the orthographic change from <þ> to <t> in words with etymological /θ/ is indeed a reflection of a change happening at the same time in speech. The picture of hypercorrect <th> is rather more complex: it is slightly more common in very early texts than hypercorrect <þ>, and becomes far more common after the loss of <þ> is fully complete. It seems, then, that the ortheme <th> was later recruited for other purposes, making it rather ambiguous evidence for the phonology of etymological /θ/.

All tokens of thirteen content words with /θ/ in stressed onset were identified: these were common nouns *samþykkt* 'agreement', *þjónusta* 'service', *þórsdagr* 'Thursday', *þriði* 'third' and *þrír* 'three' and personal names/patronymics *Þórbjǫrn, Þórbjǫrnsson, Þórgeir, Þórgeirsson, Þórir, Þórisson, Þórsteinn* and *Þórsteinsson*; these totalled 10,892 tokens. The different orthographies of the dental consonant in these words were tallied.

4.2.2.2.2. Categorisation of orthemes. The relevant orthographies are summarised in Table 6. In practice, because <th> forms are ambiguous between Swedish-influenced spellings for [θ], Latin-influenced spellings for [θ], and later spellings for [t], these are excluded in the work here. <d>-spellings are assumed to represent loanwords from MLG rather than internal sound change, and so are also excluded. <tt> will be treated together with <t>. The frequencies of the different variants in the final dataset by lemma are given in Table 7.

Table 6. Variants and example forms in the voiceless dental fricatives dataset

Variant	Notes	Example forms
þ	earliest ortheme in West Norse for etymological /θ/	<þorbiørnson> Þórbjǫrnsson, <þushundrat> þúshundrað, <þorssz dagh> þórsdagr
th	typical ortheme in later Old East Norse for etymological /θ/	<thionæsth> þjónusta, <samthøkt> samþykkt, <thorerson> Þórisson
t	typical ortheme for /t/	<tosteyn> Þórsteinn, <twri> Þórir, <tørgerszøn> Þórgeirsson
tt	a common ortheme for /t/ in texts which do not mark length, especially in texts showing MLG influence on orthography	<ttorsdagen> þórsdagin, <ttoresson> Þórisson, <ttorbyørn> Þórbjǫrn
d	probably borrowed MLG form; excluded	<Deneste> þjónusta

Table 7. Number of tokens in the voiceless dental fricatives dataset by lemma and variant

| Lemma | Dental Consonant Orthography | | | |
	t	th	tt	þ
samþykkt	363	60	0	412
þjónusta	703	514	0	101
Þórbjǫrn	295	20	0	267
Þórbjǫrnsson	126	31	0	92
Þórgeir	413	77	0	491
Þórgeirsson	223	57	0	216
Þórir	601	458	0	931
Þórisson	253	181	0	277
þórsdagr	307	50	0	348
Þórsteinn	430	135	3	694
Þórsteinsson	248	56	0	216
þriði	360	22	0	330
þrír	439	127	0	526

In practice, because <th> forms are ambiguous between Swedish-influenced spellings for [θ], Latin-influenced spellings for [θ], and later spellings for [t], these are excluded in the work here. <d>-spellings are assumed to represent loanwords from MLG rather than internal sound change, and so are also excluded. <tt> will be treated together with <t>. The frequencies of the different variants in the final dataset by lemma are given in Table 7.

4.2.2.2.3. Formulae and editorial intervention. As many of the words are proper nouns, formulae are not a major issue: even where proper nouns occur in formulae, they are unlikely to have been copied directly from an exemplar in a kopibok or earlier charter as such exemplars would have referred to different people. Similarly the main source of editorial intervention, the silent expansion of abbreviations, does not present a problem: in all but one of the words the relevant consonant is word-initial and thus is never abbreviated.

4.2.3. Loss of voiced dental fricatives

4.2.3.1. Background
4.2.3.1.1. The nature of the change. The voiced allophone of /θ/ went through related changes, with the result that [ð] become a voiced stop [d] in onset (as in Modern Norwegian *da* /dɑː/ < ON *þá* /θɑː/ [ðɑː] 'then, when') and elsewhere zero (as in Modern Norwegian *med* /meː/ < ON *með* /meθ/ [með] 'with') or a voiced stop (as in Modern Norwegian *tidig* /tiːdi/ < ON *tíðigr* 'early') (cf. Seip 1934: 72–105). In medieval texts we see a change from Old Norwegian <ð> to later <d> and <dh>, which I will argue reflects an underlying sound change. We

also see a rise in <th> spellings; these are very common in East Nordic texts, but in West Nordic texts are largely restricted to function words. The change we focus on here is the loss of <ð>, the distinctive ortheme for [ð], regardless of what came to replace it; this is taken to represent a structural change by which the phoneme /θ/ merged with /d/ in certain positions, and probably a phonetic change by which [ð] became [d].

4.2.3.1.2. Earlier research. Seip (1954: 203–5) suggests that [ð] had been lost entirely in most positions in speech by 1200, but that due to <ð> and later <d> being preserved in writing, a 'reading style' evolved which retained some kind of dental consonant here. This is based on the minority of tokens where <t> appears in the orthography for historical [ð] (such as <vmbodt> for *umboð*), where svarabhakti vowels appear following historical [ð] (such as <Ghwderid> for *Guðríðr*), and other orthographic irregularities which are hard to interpret without the presence of some consonant. Indrebø (Seip 1954: 226–9) notes that there is occasional evidence for the loss of [ð] after vowels from 1200 onwards, and similarly suggests that the writing system which retained <d> or <dh> in these positions throughout the Middle Norwegian period was archaising (although he also summarises a wide range of exceptional cases in which historical [ð] is retained as /d/ in Modern dialects). He suggests that [ð] was preserved longer in these positions in Danish than in Norwegian or Swedish varieties. The development of [ð] into /d/ in post-consonantal position he dates to early in the Middle Norwegian period (he also discusses morphologically motivated complications in some detail). Turning to Old Swedish, Wessén (1968: 82) states that [ð] remained in the language throughout the period and that <dh> remained as a way of writing it until the eighteenth century. [ð] was deleted in a larger or smaller range of contexts in different dialects at different times during the Younger Old Swedish period, with the remaining instances becoming [d] probably during the seventeenth century (Wessén 1968: 162–3).

Both Seip and Indrebø work from the a priori assumption that orthography is likely to be conservative as well as the assumption that change should be entirely regular. In this framework, if we find inconsistent written evidence for a sound change from a very early point, we arrive at the conclusion that the sound change must have been regularly carried out in speech and that where the orthography does not agree, this must be because it is archaising. However, this means that they are prioritising accounting for a small minority of the evidence (occasional early instances of <ð> being deleted) at the expense of a straightforward reading of the vast bulk of the evidence (in most instances, <ð> remained) and then still need to posit relatively elaborate scenarios to account for further details (Seip's 'reading style' [ð]). I take the position that we should instead describe the bulk of the evidence – the changing orthographies for historical [ð] – working on the assumption that it reflects spoken reality, and only move to a more involved explanation if it is impossible to arrive at a coherent account this way. In this account, then, the loss of the ortheme <ð>

and its replacement by <d> reflects a sound change affecting [ð] /θ/ which had been preserved until this point, and sporadic instances of <ð> missing in earlier written sources reflect errors or the representation of fast speech processes. Whatever position is taken, it does appear that changes affecting [ð] were earlier in West than in East Nordic.

4.2.3.2. Data collection

Hypercorrections were not investigated for this change and so only words with an etymological /θ/ in coda or unstressed onset were investigated. All relevant tokens of 40 lexical items were identified. The lexical items were the adverbs *áðr* 'before, already' and *síðan* 'after, later', the personal names *Barðr, Sigurðr* and *Þórðr*, the conjunctions *eða* 'or' and *eðr* 'or', the weak past of verbs *biðja, hafa, heyra, líða, rita, segja* and *virða*, the prepositions *með/meðr* 'with' and *við/viðr* 'with, against', the pronoun *yðr* 'you (pl.)', the adjective *góðr* 'good', and the common nouns *bróðir* 'brother', *burð* 'birth', *faðir* 'father', *garðr* 'estate', *guð* 'god', *jǫrð* 'land', *kórsbróðir* 'chorister', *lǫgmaðr* 'lawyer', *maðr* 'man', *mánaðr* 'month', *móðir* 'mother', *náð* 'grace, peace', *orð* 'word', *skilorð* 'agreement', *staðr* 'place' *tíð* 'time', *umboð* 'errand' and *vitnisburðr* 'testimony'. This was a total of 101,160 tokens in original texts in the corpus. The relevant orthographies are summarised in Table 8 and the variant counts by lemma are given in Table 9.

Table 8. Variants and example forms in the voiced dental fricatives dataset

Variant	Notes	Example forms
<ð>	typical ortheme in Old West Norse for /θ/ in positions other than stressed onset	<Sigvrðr> Sigurðr, <siðæn> síðan, <Guðs> Guðs
<þ>	typical ortheme in Old East Norse for /θ/ in all positions	<siþan> síðan, <faþer> faðir, <gaarþ> garð
<th>	typical ortheme in Middle Swedish and Danish for /θ/, and in Middle Norwegian for /θ/ in in function word onset	<ethr> eðr, <fathir> faðir, <korsbrøther> kórsbrœðr
<tth>		<gwtth> guð, <matther> maðr, <noth> náð
<dh>		<syddhan> síðan, <Bardher> Bárðr, <gardhæ> garði
<ddh>		<æddher> eðr, <maddher> maðr, <orddh> orð
<d>	typical ortheme in later Norwegian	<uitnisburdr> vitnisburðr, <brœdar> brœðr, <bwrd> burð
<dd>		<addar> áðr, <gaardde> garði, <gvdds> Guðs
<ðh>	contamination of <ð> and <dh>?	<naðh> náð

Table 9. Number of tokens in the voiced dental fricatives dataset by lemma and variant

Lemma	Dental Consonant Orthography				
	ð	dh	d	t	th
áðr	118	94	453	0	127
annarr	235	205	1,183	2	128
bæði	40	198	591	2	201
Barðr	83	33	259	0	0
biðja	27	60	158	0	1
bróðir	127	816	1,281	0	12
burð	113	48	265	0	2
eða	479	36	460	0	0
eðr	359	3,553	6,696	0	8,484
faðir	25	760	0	0	46
garðr	114	628	1,398	0	7
góðr	46	343	457	0	1
guð	607	1,368	8,630	1	74
hafa	272	716	6,775	0	16
heyra	46	402	2,340	0	0
jǫrð	260	1,268	2,734	1	8
kórsbróðir	264	126	731	0	3
líða	58	53	261	23	19
lǫgmaðr	90	0	101	0	0
maðr	109	26	162	0	2
mánaðr	146	46	254	0	14
með	518	2,354	14,614	0	1,665
meðr	377	383	2,262	0	2
móðir	35	361	600	8	8
náð	71	1,050	1,487	0	79
orð	56	425	744	0	6
rita	33	0	34	0	0
segja	43	183	1,307	0	0
síðan	80	525	1,284	0	23
Sigurðr	185	78	911	0	0
skilorð	46	180	722	0	0
staðr	83	393	499	0	0
tíð	28	521	1453	111	62
umboð	64	9	167	10	0
við	94	300	676	0	77
viðr	197	338	1,454	0	41
virða	25	13	21	0	0
vitnisburðr	179	4	369	0	0
yðr	338	331	1,676	0	13
Þórðr	2	41	72	0	0

4.2.3.2.1. Formulae and lexical effects. Many of these lexical items are predominantly found in particular formulae; examples of some of the more common formulae found in the dataset are given in Table 10. Generally, the fact

Table 10. Most significant formulae appearing in the voiced dental fricatives dataset

Lexical item	Examples	
guð 'god'	sender Nikulas biscup 7 korsbrœðr í Oslo queðiu **guðs** 7 sína	DN I.7, 1225
	'bishop Nikulas and choristers in Oslo send **god's** greetings and their own'	
	Ollum **guðs** vinum oc sinum	DN V.16, 1286
	'to all **god's** friends and his own'	
	firir **guðs** saker	DN I.82, 1294
	'for **god's** sake'	
	vid **gud**, hellga kirkiu, ok oss	DN IV.70, 1307
	'before **god**, [the] holy church, and ourselves'	
	sextande are rikis wars wirdolegs herra Hakonar mæðr **guds** nad Noregx konongs	DN IV.110, 1315
	'in [the] sixteenth year of [the] reign of our worthy lord Hákon with **god's** grace king of Norway'	
	J namfne **guðs** amen	DN II.89, 1307
	'In **god's** name amen'	
	Erikr með **guðs** miskunn Noregs konongr	DN II.20, 1283
	Erikr with **god's** grace king of Norway	
burð 'birth'	þa er liðnir varo j fra **burðar** tið vars herra Jesu Christi	DN I.80, 1292
	'when there had passed since [the] time of **birth** of our lord Jesus Christ..'.	
faðir 'father'	skylgeten bæde till **fadur** ok modor	DN III.319, 1361
	'legitimately begotten both to **father** and mother'	
vitnisburðr, 'testimony'	til sanz **vitnisburðr**, sættom ver wor jnsigli firir þætta bref	DN II.130, 1317
	'in true **testimony**, we set our seals on this charter'	
náð 'grace'	herra Magnus med gvs **nad** Norges konvngh	DN VII.136, 1332
	'lord Magnus with god's **grace** king of Norway'	
orð 'word'	so vattar **ord** efttir **ordde** sem her segir.	DN I.121, 1309
	'thus [it] attests, **word** after **word** as [it] says here'	
	vattande **ord** j fra **orde** sem her sæigir.	DN V.167, 1343
	'attesting **word** from **word** as [it] says here'	
	saam ok herdwm a **ord** þeira ok handeband	DN IV.520, 1380
	'we saw and heard their **words** and hand-shake'	
	þær saghom handarband ok høyrdum ord þæiræ	DN V.303, 1378
	'there we saw [their] hand-shake and heard their words'	

that a word occurs in a particular formula has no effect on its orthography and so will not influence the distribution of the variants we are interested in. However, some of the formulae in question are particularly associated with certain document types and social groups, and these may affect the distribution of orthemes. For example, the formula *með guðs náð* 'with god's grace' is more typical of later charters with signatories from the higher social classes, and so *náð* shows a higher rate of East-Nordic-influenced <th> in the fifteenth and sixteenth centuries than the other lexical items do. However, there are no obvious such effects in the early period covered by the dataset, the late thirteenth and first half of the fourteenth centuries, and this is the period relevant to the change we are interested in here.

4.2.3.2.2. Editorial intervention. Transcription practices and intentional editorial intervention could plausibly have a substantial effect on these data. Edh <ð> and insular *d* <ð> can be hard to distinguish in medieval hands, resulting in different decisions by different transcribers. Similarly, different decisions can justifiably be made when expanding abbreviations. The 1,149 tokens from the dataset which occur in documents published in Hødnebø (1960) were checked against Hødnebø's transcriptions; the results are summarised in Table 11. Note that this includes documents which are copies and so will not be included in other analyses of these data. The overall agreement rate is 92.66 per cent[11].

Of the 108 non-agreeing tokens, twenty seven represent a case where Hødnebo and the DN have different manuscript sources: Hødnebø's text seventy four is apparently based on Ch 26049 at the British Library (although if this class mark did indeed refer to this charter at the time that Hødnebø was writing, it must since have been reassigned) and always has <ð>, whereas DN I.92 is based on Arne Magnussen's transcription which consistently has <d>. Such a discrepancy could only happen with a copied document and so is not representative of the final dataset we are using here. If we restrict ourselves to original documents, we find the patterns in Table 12; the overall rate of agreement is 95.40 per cent.

Of the fifth eight non-agreeing tokens in this more representative dataset, eight reflect different decisions about the expansion of abbreviations, often where both decisions are justifiable. The others are hard to explain. There are no obvious patterns here: the DN's apparent slight preference for <d> readings compared with Hødnebø is non-significant. Assuming this is a good reflection of tendencies throughout the entire dataset, this suggests that transcription errors and ambiguous readings will not create any specific effect when working with the DN. However, it is a substantial additional source of noise that should be borne in mind.

---

[11] The digital copies of the DN were not checked against the published volumes, so it is possible that these differences reflect errors in the digitisation process rather than differences of opinion in transcription of the original documents. However, since we cannot go back to the paper copies of the DN for a dataset of this size any more than we can go back to the medieval manuscripts, it makes no practical difference at what stage the differences were introduced.

Table 11. Comparison of transcriptions of voiced dental fricatives in the DN and Hødnebø (1960)

		DN transcription				
		d	ð	þ	dd	ðð
Transcription in Hødnebø (1960)	d	410	33	0	0	0
	ð	73	933	0	0	0
	þ	0	0	16	0	0
	dd	0	0	0	1	0
	ðð	0	1	0	0	4
	g	1	0	0	0	0
Agreement		84.71 per cent	96.48 per cent	100 per cent	100 per cent	100 per cent

Table 12. Comparison of transcriptions of voiced dental fricatives in original charters in the DN and Hødnebø (1960)

		DN transcription				
		d	ð	þ	dd	ðð
Transcription in Hødnebø (1960)	d	379	32	0	0	0
	ð	25	819	0	0	0
	þ	0	0	0	0	0
	dd	0	0	0	1	0
	ðð	0	1	0	0	4
	g	0	0	0	0	0
Agreement		93.81 per cent	96.13 per cent	n/a	100 per cent	100 per cent

4.3. Morphological variables

4.3.1. Changes in agreement of verbs with 1sg. subjects

4.3.1.1. Background

4.3.1.1.1. Verbal conjugation before the change. Present tense verbs in pre-alphabetic Old Norse had subject-verb agreement for three persons in both numbers (separate agreement patterns for the dual disappeared before the earliest records of North Germanic). By regular sound change this agreement would be expected to survive into alphabetic Old Norse, but in reality early Old Norwegian and Old Icelandic verb conjugation already shows some analogical levelling. This removed vowel alternations within verb conjugations caused by breaking, u-umlaut and i-umlaut and merged the 2sg. and 3sg. endings for many verbs as *-(V)r* (Indrebø 1951: 123–4). The conjugations for present tense singular active verbs for Old West Norse are given in Tables 13 to 15, reproduced from Noreen (1903: 353, 355) and Gordon & Taylor (1956).

As can be seen, at the beginning of the period we expect the 1sg. to be distinct from the 3sg. for regular verbs, *vilja* and *vera*, but not for the preterite-presents. We can thus exclude the preterite-presents from consideration here. For two classes of verbs (*vilja* and heavy stem strong verbs in -*s*, -*l* or -*n*), the only difference between the 1sg. and 3sg. was the length of the final consonant; as consonant length is not consistently represented in Old Norwegian orthography, we must also exclude these. Noreen (1903: 358) suggests this pattern sometimes extends to weak verbs.

4.3.1.1.2. The nature of the change. The distinction between the 1sg. and 3sg. was lost, with 3sg. endings in -*(V)r* spreading to 1sg. contexts. This was part of the larger loss of subject-verb agreement: the ending -*er* eventually came to be used in all persons and numbers as a marker of present tense. We can think of this change as the spread of 1/3sg. syncretism from other parts of the paradigm to the present indicative or as the removal of a person constraint on the 2/3sg. ending so that it could be used in the 1sg. Note that parallel changes took place in the subjunctive and in the past tense of weak verbs, in which 3sg. endings replaced 1sg. endings; as the data in this corpus is less good for these changes, they are not dealt with further here.

A parallel change also affected the middle voice, with the 1sg. ending -*umk* being replaced by the 3sg. ending -*iz*. There is insufficient evidence in this corpus to investigate this: the ending -*umk* occurs only once in an original document in the DN, as shown in Extract (1):

---

(1) Archaic 1sg present middle ending
DN I.51, undated between 1226 and 1254
Til vinatto þyckiumc ek oc gortt hava við   I think that I also have dealt
þa er firir staðenum raða.   in friendship with those who
oc raðande verða   rule the place and come to rule

It is striking that this is the earliest example of a 1sg. present middle verb in the corpus: the next oldest such verb (Extract (2)) and all later examples have the

Table 13. Old West Norse regular present singular active verb conjugations

		Strong	Strong (heavy s-, l- and n-stems)	Weak 1 (light stems)	Weak 1 (heavy stems)	Weak 2 and 3
indicative	1st	-Ø	-Ø	-Ø	-i	-a
	2nd	-r	-ː	-r	-ir	-ar
	3rd	-r	-ː	-r	-ir	-ar
subjunctive	1st	-a	-a	-ja	-a	-a
	2nd	-ir	-ir	-ir	-ir	-ir
	3rd	-i	-i	-i	-i	-i

Table 14. Old West Norse preterite-present present singular active verb conjugations

		vita 'know'	eiga 'own'	kunna 'be able'	unna 'love'	þurfa 'need'	muna 'remember'	munu 'will'	skulu 'shall'	mega 'be able'	knáttu 'be able'
indicative	1st	veit	Á	kann	ann	þarf	man	mun	skal	má know'	kná
	2nd	veizt	átt	kannt	annt	þarft	mant	munt	skalt	mátt	knátt
	3rd	veit	Á	kann	ann	þarf	man	mun	skalt	má	kná
subjunctive	1st	vita	eiga	kunna	unna	þurfa	muna	myna	skyla	mega	knega
	2nd	vitir	eigir	kunnir	unnir	þurfir	munir	mynir	skylir	megir	knegir
	3rd	viti	eigi	kunni	unni	þurfi	muni	myni	skyli	megi	knegi

Table 15. Old West Norse irregular present singular active verb conjugations

		vera	vilja
indicative	1st	em	vil
	2nd	ert	vill(t)
	3rd	er	vill
subjunctive	1st	sé	vilja
	2nd	sér	vilir
	3rd	sé	vili

levelled 3sg. ending. This suggests this change took place in middle verbs at the same time as or perhaps slightly earlier than in active verbs. We can, however, say little more on the basis of such limited data;

(2) Levelled 1sg present middle ending
DN II.29, 16th of March 1291

| ok ek <u>kennez</u> þar viðr at minn | and I acknowledge in that regard that |
| herra Andres biscup j Aslo | my lord Andræs of Oslo... |

4.3.1.1.3. Earlier research. Several histories of Norwegian deal with this change. Seip (1955: 199) suggests that 2/3sg. *-(V)r* sometimes spread to the 1sg. in strong verbs already in 1150–1300; he also points out the parallel change in *vera* 'to be', with 3sg. *er* sometimes occurring for expected *em* in this period. Seip also notes the reverse change, with 3sg. verbs sometimes occurring without a final *-r*. Seip's description suggests this was a phonological change – an early instance of the *-r* dropping that became general in certain dialects later – but it is better seen as morphological, as final *-(V)r* remains well-preserved in later centuries, playing a major role in the phonology (being a conditioning environment for svarabhakti vowel insertion) and the morphology (eventually spreading to be a marker of all present-tense verbs). Thus, in these early data, we see a tendency towards the analogical elimination of singular person distinctions in present tense verbs that could be carried out in either direction. Seip (1955: 321) goes on to suggest that the loss of all person distinctions on the verb was probably complete in speech by 1300 but that they were maintained rather longer in the plural in writing.

Indrebø (1951: 124), discussing the wider process of conjugation simplification from the syncope period onwards, notes that 3sg. endings are found in the 1sg. present tense of weak and strong verbs from around 1250 and in *vera* 'to be' from 1280. Mørck (2005: 1142; 2011: 554), describing the transition from Old to Middle Norwegian, suggests the 1sg. present merged with the 2/3sg. in late Old Norwegian and gives a paradigm with no person distinction in the present indicative singular for Swedish and Norwegian in the early fourteenth century. Tønnessen (1995: 29–30,46–8), examining verbal inflection in Oslo charters in the latter half of the fifteenth century, confirms that no distinction between 1sg. and 3sg. remains in this period.

There is one detailed study of the change, Ottosson (2003: 120–9), based on samples from the early major Norwegian manuscripts and a selection of charters dating before 1370 (including all charters before 1300). Ottosson examines present indicative, present subjunctive, weak past indicative and weak past subjunctive verbs separately; the results of his study for indicative verbs are given in Figure 23 (some numbers are estimates). As can be seen, Ottosson finds that the change was ongoing during the thirteenth century, that it probably happened earlier in the past tense than the present, and that it moved towards completion in the early-fourteenth century.

Thus we expect to find the merger of the 1sg. and 3sg. in the present indicative well under way in the earliest period covered by the corpus and going to completion in the first half of the fourteenth century. From Seip's comments, we might expect to find it affected strong verbs before weak verbs. No scholar makes any suggestion about how it diffused through the speech community or the country.

It seems likely that this change happened earlier in Swedish and Danish than Norwegian. In the earliest Swedish sources, the -(V)r and zero endings are found for both 1sg. and 3sg.: there is no categorical distribution as in the earliest Old Icelandic and Old Norwegian (Jansson 1934: 233; Delsing 2002: 935, 936; Mørck 2005: 1142). In Danish the change seems to have been even earlier: already in the earliest sources distinctive 1sg. forms are restricted to occasional formulae (Skautrup 1968: 273).

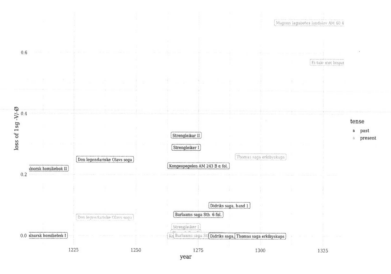

Figure 23. Rates of the loss of the 1sg. ending in Old Norse manuscripts from Ottosson (2003), ranging from 0 (complete retention of the conservative form) to 1 (complete loss) [Colour figure can be viewed at wileyonlinelibrary.com]

4.3.1.2. Data collection

4.3.1.2.1. Method of data collection. To collect all examples of 1sg. present-tense verbs, forms of the 1sg. nominative pronoun were identified and corresponding finite verb(s) recorded for each. This included both (or all) verbs in co-ordinated phrases even if the subject pronoun is not repeated with each verb, as shown in Extract (3); 1sg. verbs with null subjects were not investigated.

---

(3) Co-ordinated verbs
    DN IV.412, 22nd of November 1360

ek <u>lukr</u> ok <u>afhender</u> meder þesso	I pay and transfer with this my open
minu opno brefue sambrœðrum	charter to my fellow brothers and
minum ok korsbrœdrum aat	choristers at [the] aforementioned
fyrnæmfdre Marikirkiu	Church of [St.] Mary...

Subjunctive verbs, as in the example in Extract (4), were also excluded:

---

(4) Subjunctive verb
    DN IV.469, 13th of January 1368

stændr iorden j byghslu vttan ek	[if] the land comes to be rented out but
sialfr a <u>siti</u>, þa skal hon æigha	I myself am not occupying [it], then
landskyld	she will have a right to [the] rent...

Verb conjugations were identified from dictionaries (Cleasby et al. 1894; Zoëga 2004; Hægstad & Torp 2015) and verbs like *velja* 'choose' which would not be expected to have a distinct 1sg. form were excluded. Data was gathered from original texts until 1375, at which point the change had clearly gone to completion.

4.3.1.2.2. Categorisation of endings. The relevant change for all verbs except *vera* 'to be' is the spread of *-(V)r* to the 1sg. The endings identified are summarised in Tables 16 and 17.

All of these were included with the exception of instances of *-Ø* which plausibly represented *-ir* with haplology (i.e. where *-ir* would be the expected 2/3sg. form and the stem ended in *-Vr-*); this comprised a total of 688 tokens. The counts of tokens of different forms included in the dataset are given in Table 18.

4.3.1.2.3. Formulae. Due to the restricted range of text types among these early documents, the vast majority of tokens were in formulae. The main text types represented are wills, property charters and charters reporting legal hearings. In property charters and those reporting legal hearings, the main body of text is usually in the preterite (reporting what took place in a transaction or what was said at a hearing, the content of which is itself past-tense narrative); the only

Table 16. 1sg. forms not showing the change

Form	Notes	Example
-Ø		\<gæf\> 'give', DN II.77 (1304)
-Ø	*-Vr-Vr* with haplology	\<gør\> 'make', DN VII.280 (1370)
-i		\<hefi\> 'have', DN I.63 (1269-1271)
-e		\<hafe\> 'have', DN II.67 (1303)
em	1.sg. of *vera* 'to be'	\<em\>, DN I.51 (1226-1254)

Table 17. 1sg. forms showing the change

Form	Notes	Example
-ær	*-r* with svarabhakti vowel	\<bindær\> 'bind', DN VII.290 (1372)
-ær		\<pant sætær\> 'give as security', DN XVIII.29 (1374)
-ar		\<æthlar\> 'suppose', DN IV.282 (1343)
-ar	*-r* with svarabhakti vowel	\<gefuar\> 'give', DN II.334 (1356)
-r		\<biðr\> 'ask', DN II.305 (1349)
-r	*-er/-ir* with hypercorrection	\<afhenðr\> 'transfer', DN X.48 (1341)
-er		\<afhænder\> 'transfer', DN IV.162 (1323)
-er	*-r* with svarabhakti vowel	\<gengher\> 'walk', DN VI.67 (1299-1305)
-ir		\<gerir\> 'make', DN IV.85 (1310)
-ir	*-r* with svarabhakti vowel	\<giuir\> 'give', DN III.342 (1364)
-yr		\<aafhendyr\> 'transfer', DN III.332 (1363)
er	2./3sg. of *vera* 'to be'	\<er\>, DN I.326 (1351)

Table 18. Number of tokens in the 1sg. agreement dataset by form

Form	Count
-Ø	33
-a	2
-e	21
-i	9
-r	60
-ær	21
-ar	31
-er, er	291
-ir, -yr	212
-ur	8

present verbs in these texts are usually in introductory and closing formulae. Extract (5) gives introductory formulae and the beginning of the body from a charter reporting a legal hearing. Extract (6) gives the beginning of the body from a charter recording a property transaction.

(5) Example verbs in a murder charter
DN XIII.23, 1360

Sinum hæiderlegom herra herra Magnus med gudsnaad (Suia) ok Noregs kononge sender Þrond Reidarsson i umbode Kæitiuls Viglæiksonar æuerdelega hæilsu med varom herra ok sinæ uiliulega Þionosto yddr min herre **gerer ek** kunnikt at a æinu are ok fiortukta rikis ydars uar ek a Igufstvæit a Þinginu er ligger a Þilamorkene tisdagen æiptir Midfaustu tok ek prof Þæira Solua Olafs sonar [...] ok Þoorder Glødes sonar ...	To his worthy lord lord Magnús with god's grace king of Swedes and Norway[,] Þróndr Hreiðarsson as representative of Ketill Vígleikssonr sends eternal greeting with our lord and his own willing service to you my lord [.] I make known that in the forty-first year of your reign I was at Igufsþveit at the Thing which is located in Telemark on [the] Tuesday after Mid-Lent I took evidence from Sǫlvér Ólafssonr and Þórðr Glǫðissonr ...

(6) Example verbs in a property charter
DN XIII.18, 1343

ek gerer yder kunnikt at **ek hefuer** gefuet ok afhænt Birnj synj minum ser till kuænfangs tolf marka booll j þæima anemfdum jordum ...	**I make** known to you that **I have** given and transferred to my son Bjǫrn for bride-price twelve merkisból in the aforementioned farm ...

As can be seen, typically only verbs in the introductory formulae are in the present tense; when present verbs are found in the body, as in DN XIII.18, these are usually in formulae characterising the type of charter in question. Wills are often entirely in present tense, but are still typically made up of formulaic phrases. Extract (7) shows an extract from a will.

(7) Example verbs in a will
DN II.78, 1304

Jn nomine domini amen. **Ek** Ingimundr korsbroðr j Stawangre hafande alla mina skynsæmd ok samuizko þa sæm gud hefer gefet mer sua sæm þa er æk være heil ok vsiuker **gerer** mit testamentum guði til lofs ok dyrðar ok mer til synda aflausna ok salohialpar. fyrst at **æk gæf** guði sal mina ok kys æk mer lægstað þar sæm herra biskup ok brœðr gera rað fyrer. **gæf æk** til staðarens j Stawangre ...	In nomine domini amen. **I**[,] Ingimundr [,] chorister in Stavanger[,] having all my senses and wits which god has given me just as when I was healthy and unsick[,] **make** my testament for praise and glory to god and my forgiveness of sins and salvation. First that **I give** to god my soul and I choose [a] resting-place for myself where [the] lord bishop and brethren advise. **I give** to the place in Stavanger ...

As can be seen, most present tense verbs in this type of charter are in the formulae *ek gef* 'I give' and *ek kýs* 'I choose'.

As almost all data are in formulae it would be fruitless to try to exclude or separate out formulaic uses. However, we should remain mindful that these formulaic data may be particularly conservative relative even to other written data.

4.3.1.2.4. Editorial intervention. In one example in DN IV.359 (1352) the editor has 'corrected' a conservative 1sg. verb form to an innovative form with an -*r*: the printed edition reads <offra[r]>. This editorial intervention has been discounted and this form counted as an example without the change.

Eighteen texts in the dataset have been printed elsewhere: DN I.51, I.63, I.70, II.19, II.24, II.29, II.39, II.45, II.58, II.61, III.30, III.45, IV.18, V.16 and V.41 were printed in Hødnebø (1960) and DN I.343, I.409, III.332 and III.328 in Hødnebø (1966). The fifty seven tokens in these texts were checked against Hødnebø's transcriptions. For none was there disagreement regarding the suffix: Hødnebø distinguishes between orthemes which the DN merges, such as <f ꝼ>, <r ꝛ> and <i í>, and notes where abbreviations have been expanded, but such abbreviations do not render this variable ambiguous and there were no other differences between the two sets of transcriptions. This is encouraging evidence that transcription practices have not interfered with this dataset.

4.3.2. Changes in the form of 1pl and 1du. subject pronouns

4.3.2.1. Background

4.3.2.1.1. Introduction. Multiple changes affected 1pl and 1du. pronouns over the Old and Middle Norwegian periods: a reanalysis of the word boundary between verb and subject pronoun took place in certain contexts, resulting in new forms of the pronouns without any change in their meaning; the distinction between dual and plural pronouns was lost; and a new form, *vi*, which I argue was borrowed from East Nordic, replaced the older forms. These changes applied unevenly across localities, leaving dialectal variation in the form of the 1pl pronoun in Modern Norwegian. Related changes affected the object forms of the pronouns, but here I concentrate only on the subject pronouns.

4.3.2.1.2. Morphology before the changes. Old Norse inherited two variants of the Proto Germanic 1pl.nom. pronoun **wīz*, reflecting variable stress: *vér* in West Nordic and *vi(r)* in East Nordic. In the case of the 1du.nom. pronoun, **wet*, only the unstressed variant survives, giving *vit* in both West and East Nordic. Thus at the beginning of the time covered by the corpus, the Old Norwegian period, we find 1pl *vér* and 1du. *vit* in Norwegian texts.

4.3.2.1.3. The nature of the changes. I will treat the several changes affecting these pronouns over the period covered separately. First, the initial consonant of the two pronouns changes from *v-* to *m-*: *vér* > *mér*, *vit* > *mit*. Secondly, the distribution of these pronouns changes, resulting in the loss of the dual-plural distinction. If we examine their reflexes in Modern Norwegian we find that there is no dual-plural distinction anywhere, but that some traditional dialects have a 1pl subject pronoun which is a reflex of *mér* (*me, mø*, etc.) while others have a 1pl subject pronoun which is a reflex of *mit* (*mi, mid*) (this position conflicts with that taken by some earlier scholars: see further 4.3.2.1.4 below). Thus we can assume that the loss of the dual-plural distinction reflects at least two more-or-less separate changes, one in which *mér* spread to dual subjects and one in which *mit* spread to plural subjects, which might have taken place in different dialects and/or at different times. Thirdly, the East Nordic pronoun *vi*, which had already expanded to be used for dual subjects, was borrowed from Swedish and/or Danish into Norwegian (again, this interpretation conflicts with that of some previous scholars).

4.3.2.1.4. Earlier research. Indrebø (1951: 122–3) notes that *m-* forms first appear in Norwegian sources around 1200. Seip (1954: 229–30) notes that *m-* forms are the norm in Old and Middle Norwegian sources from regions in Østlandet that do not have *m-* forms today, and that a division seems to exist in Middle Norwegian where *vér* is used for the *pluralis majestatis* and *m*-forms elsewhere. He argues for the following account: written norms with *v*-forms developed at a point before the *m-* forms developed in speech; *m*-forms developed in speech; later these spoken *m*-forms found their way into writing and became the written norm even in regions where they were never used in speech; but that *vér* was retained in the written standard for the *pluralis majestatis*. This line of thinking reflects an assumption that modern *vi* and dialectal *ve* (which I see as phonological variants of East Nordic loanword *vi*) are closely connected to the Old Norwegian *v*-forms *vér* and *vit*. Tylden (1944: 62) too notes that *m*-forms are found across a much larger area in the Old and Middle Norwegian periods than they are today, and suggests that they were innovated and first spread across a huge area of inland Norway: Østerdalen, Gudbrands-dalen, Valdres, Hallingdal, Numedal, Telemark and the inland parts of Hardanger and Sogn. Unlike Seip, he concludes (seemingly reluctantly) that the *m*-forms were a part of the spoken language even in regions they do not occur in Modern Norwegian dialects, but he argues that the older *v*-forms must have remained as variants in speech to explain *vi* in Modern dialects. Few scholars have written about the loss of the dual-plural distinction in the abstract, but Indrebø (1951: 255) identifies the earliest evidence in 1364 and 1370, suggesting that the distinction must not have been lost fully until the early Modern period.

We can get an idea of Old and Middle Norwegian usage in Vestlandet specifically from the works of Marius Hægstad and Egil Pettersen. Hægstad (1915: 82) states that *mid* and *mer* must have alternated with *v-* forms in speech in Ryfylke in the Old Norwegian period but replaced them in the Middle

Norwegian period. Hægstad (1916: 186) notes that *v*- forms seem to have lasted much longer in Bergen than anywhere else in Vestlandet. With this caveat, he states that the *m*- forms are generally in the majority in charters from Vestlandet until the end of the fifteenth century when *vi* becomes the written norm. Pettersen (1991: 309) suggests that *vér* is very rare throughout Vestlandet by 1450 and absent from 1500, and that *vi* is the only form found from Nordvestlandet and Bergen throughout this period. However, he also suggests that *mer*, *ver* and *mit* all represent spoken forms which appear in texts 'through carelessness' in contrast to *vi* which should be seen as a written feature, and that these spoken forms are maintained much better in Agder and Rogaland than further north (Pettersen 1991: 309–11). On the loss of the dual-plural distinction, Hægstad notes that the merger begins very early in the southern part of Vestlandet, with examples from 1380, and that plural *mer* and related forms disappear altogether in this area after 1462 (Hægstad 1915: 82). Further north (Sunnmøre, Nordfjord og Sunnfjord) the dual and plural seem to have remained distinct somewhat longer, with the earliest example of dual forms for plural meaning in 1394 (Hægstad 1907: 26). Pettersen (1991: 308) argues that there is no trace of the dual-plural distinction left anywhere in Vestlandet in the period he studies (1450 onwards), with *mer*, *ver*, *mit* and *vi* all alternating as variants of the plural. He finds that *mit* is used much more than *mer*, especially in Agder (Pettersen 1991: 310).

On the relationship between medieval and modern forms, Indrebø (1951: 122, 256) suggests that both *me* and *mi* are (primarily) reflexes of Old Norwegian dual *mit* rather than plural *mér*. Hægstad (1915: 82) too, although he expresses some doubt, concludes that the historical dual forms probably won out over the plural forms in speech in all but religious contexts, and thus that *mit* and related forms are the ancestors of the modern dialect forms. However, on the basis of the clear similarity between the *mi-me* isogloss in Modern Norwegian dialects and the isogloss dividing majority *mit* from majority *mér* areas in Middle Norwegian, and the fact that the object forms in different Modern Norwegian dialects clearly descend from dual and plural forms with the same spatial pattern, I have argued elsewhere that we should assume *mi* is a reflex of *mit* and *me* of *mér* (Blaxter 2019: 30–1). I will assume this here.

There were never *m*- forms in East Nordic and so many of these changes need not be explored there, but the dual-plural distinction did exist and was lost. Wessén (1968: 116) notes that dual forms are already rare in the oldest manuscripts of the earliest Old Swedish sources and disappear immediately after this: we can assume the change happened there much earlier in than in Norwegian.

4.3.2.2. Data collection
4.3.2.2.1. Method of data collection. All 1pl.nom. and 1du.nom. pronouns in original texts dated 1375 or later were identified. This involved identifying all potential forms, excluding those which raised philological problems, and disambiguating homographs: the forms *me*, *mi*, *mid* and *mit* were disambiguated from forms of the preposition *með* 'with'; the form *vid* was disambiguated from

the preposition *við(r)* 'against, with'; the forms *vir* and *vér* were disambiguated from forms of *vera* 'to be', *verja* 'to defend', *verr* 'worse' and *værr* 'comfortable'; the forms *mér* and *mir* were disambiguated from the 1sg.dat. pronoun *mér* and from *meir* 'more'; the form *mit* was disambiguated from the nt.nom-acc.sg. of the first person possessive adjective; and the form *vi* was disambiguated from the Roman numerals *VI*, *VII*, *VIII* and *VIIII*. Only one known form was not investigated: *med* occurs extremely rarely as a form of the 1pl pronoun, but is a homograph of the preposition *með* 'with'; with nearly 40,000 occurrences in the corpus, the work of disambiguating these was not deemed worth the tiny number of additional tokens it would produce. The forms included, a total of 18,950 tokens of 84 types, are summarised in Table 19.

4.3.2.2.2. Formulae. Much of the data in this investigation come from formulae. These formulae always include active verbs as well as a pronoun and are more relevant to the exploration of changes affecting 1du./pl verbal agreement than the pronouns themselves; for that reason, the major formulae are listed in Tables 26 to 28, in the discussion of changes in verbal agreement. Pettersen (1991: 312) suggests that different formulae favour the use of different variants, but it seems clear that, if such patterns are present, they must be specific to particular times and a places.

4.3.2.2.3. Editorial intervention. The nature of the forms in question makes it relatively unlikely editorial intervention or transcription practices would pose a problem: there are no obvious abbreviations that could render the distinctions between the variants defined here ambiguous. To confirm this, the 271 tokens in this dataset which occur in texts transcribed in Hødnebø (1960) were identified and Hødnebø's transcription compared with the DN; all distinct pairs identified in this way are given in Table 20. As can be seen, there are a range of differences. The relevant volumes of the DN silently expand abbreviations, do not distinguish between certain letter forms (<ʀ> and <r>, <ɣ> and <v>), usually ignore diacritics, and introduce their own capitalisation scheme; as a result, there are often many possible transcriptions in Hødnebø corresponding to a single transcription in the DN. Nevertheless, none of these would affect the assignment of variants and so there is no reason to think that transcription practices would influence their distributions.

4.3.3. Changes in agreement of verbs with 1pl and 1du. subjects

4.3.3.1. Background
4.3.3.1.1. Introduction. This section will examine two changes: the loss of 1pl subject agreement with active verbs, and the loss of 1pl subject agreement with middle verbs.

4.3.3.1.2. Verbal conjugation before the change. Verbs in early Old Norwegian and Old Icelandic agreed with subjects for person and number, distinguishing all

Table 19. Forms, orthographies and token counts of 1pl.nom. and 1du.nom. pronouns

Form	Orthographies	Count
me	<me>, <mee>	9
mér	<mæær>, <mæer>, <mæir>, <mær>, <meær>, <meer>, <meerr>, <meir>, <mer>, <merh>, <merr>, <meyr>, <mœr>	2403
mi	<mi>, <mi(t)h>, <my>	5
mid	<mid>, <midh>, <miid>, <mjd>, <myd>, <mydh>, <mydt>	252
mir[12]	<mir>	3
mit	<miit>, <miith>, <mijth>, <mit>, <mith>, <mitt>, <mitth>, <mjjt>, <mjt>, <myt>, <myth>, <mytt>, <mytth>	2468
miz	<midz>, <mitz>	23
ve	<væ>, <ve>, <wæ>, <we>, <wee>	9
vér	<uær>, <uer>, <vær>, <veer>, <ver>, <wær>, <weer>, <weir>, <wer>, <wuer>	1324
vi	<ui>, <uii>, <uij>, <uy>, <vi>, <vii>, <viii>, <viiij>, <viij>, <vij>, <vj>, <vy>, <whij>, <wi>, <wii>, <wij>, <wj>, <wjj>, <wy>	12423
vid	<vid>, <við>, <vidh>	12
vir	<vier>, <vijr>, <vir>	6
vit	<uit>, <vit>, <wit>	13

three persons in the plural. Conjugations for Old West Norse plural verbs are given in Table 21 and 22, reproduced from Noreen (1970: 355, 361, 363, 369) and Gordon & Taylor (1956). As can be seen, at the beginning of the period 1pl is always distinct from 2pl and 3pl.

4.3.3.1.3. The nature of the change. Modern Norwegian has lost nearly all verbal person/number marking (there are relics of number agreement in some dialects); finite verb forms descend from earlier 3sg. forms. However, existing literature, comparison with Early Modern Swedish, and the vestiges in some dialects all suggest that Norwegian went through an intermediate stage in which number was distinguished but person was not: singular was marked with the reflex of the 3sg. for all persons, and the plural was marked with the reflex of the 3pl. This implies two changes in 1pl verbs: one in which the 1pl ending was levelled to the historical 3pl ending, and a later change in which it was levelled further to the 3sg. ending. Due to the timing of these changes, I concentrate here primarily on the earlier change (*-um* > *-u/-a*) in the active, with the latter change

---

[12]These occur in a single, extremely late charter from Telemark, DN XI.715, and are difficult to interpret. The <r> could represent a way of writing some lenited reflex of /t/, making these a reflex of mit (cf. Hægstad's (1907: 26) comment on the form mir in modern Sunnmøre dialect). But the text also contains the form <Tyllemarken> in which we see close <y> written where other texts of the period would write <e>, implying that perhaps we should see these as forms of mér. There are a further fourteen examples of <mir>-type forms in ten copied documents, but these could easily represent misinterpretations of older mit or mér manuscript forms by later copyists unfamiliar with them.

Table 20. Transcriptions of 1pl and 1du. nom. pronouns in the DN and in Hødnebø (1960)

Variant	DN transcription	Hødnebø transcription
mér	Mer	Mer
	Mer	Mer
mit	Mitt	mitt
		mítt
vér	Uær	Uer
	Ver	V*er*
		Ver
		Ve<small>R</small>
		v*er*
		ver
	Uer	u*er*
		uer
	Vær	vær
	Veer	veer
	Ver	'v*er*'
		Uer
		V*er*
		v*er*
		v*er*
		ver
		er
		er
		e<small>R</small>
	Wer	Wer
vet	Vet	Vet
	Vet	vet
vit	Vit	vit
		vít
	Vitt	vítt

Table 21. Old West Norse regular plural active verb conjugations

		Present strong, weak 1 and 3	weak 2	Preterite
Indicative	1st	-um	-jum	-um
	2nd	-ið, -it, -ir	-ið, -it, -ir	-uð, -ut, -ur
	3rd	-a	-ja	-u
Subjunctive	1st	-im		
	2nd	-ið, -it, -ir		
	3rd	-i		

Table 22. Old West Norse regular plural middle verb conjugations

		Present		Preterite
		strong, weak 1 and 3	weak 2	
Indicative	1st	-ums(k), -umk, -umz	-jums(k), -jumk, -jumz	-ums(k), -umk, -umz
	2nd	-is(k), -iz(k)	-uz(k)	
	3rd	-as(k), -az	-jas(k), -jaz	-us(k), -uz
Subjunctive	1st	-ims(k), -imk, imz		
	2nd	-iz(k)		
	3rd	-is(k), -az		

(-u/-a > -er) receiving less attention. In the middle voice it is hard to make these distinctions cleanly, and so I will treat this as a single change: -umz > -iz.

4.3.3.1.4. Earlier research. The loss of the middle 1pl ending -umz has received little attention in previous scholarship: Noreen (1970: 370) simply notes that middle 1pl endings were replaced by 3pl endings in Middle Norwegian. The most detailed study is Ottosson (2003: 165–6), which suggests that the old 1pl ending is first replaced by 3pl forms before later being replaced by 3sg. forms. Ottosson suggests this happened earlier than the corresponding change in active verbs, although this might be because a large proportion of middle voice examples are with the verb *kennast* 'acknowledge' in a formula that is originally Danish (Ottosson 2003: 169–70). Pettersen (1991: 276), studying charters from West Norway, claims that singular forms are used consistently for the 1pl middle over 1450–1500, suggesting both changes were complete by this period, although Ottosson (2003: 170) cites counterexamples.

More has been written on the loss of active 1pl -um: it is dealt with in histories of Norwegian and in studies of the language of charters from particular regions; the allomorphic variation which preceded it and new pronouns which emerged as part of the change are discussed even more widely. One extensive study, Ottosson (2003), has been undertaken. We will first discuss the sound change and reanalysis which innovated the possibility of using 3pl endings with 1pl verbs; we will then discuss the literature on the loss of 1pl inflection; finally, Ottosson's findings will be reported in detail.

There is consensus that 3pl forms with 1pl subjects first arose through a reanalysis which also created the Norwegian 1pl.nom. pronouns in *m-*. When the verb preceded the subject pronoun, the sequences -um vér (plural) and -um vit (dual) underwent sound changes which deleted the initial consonant of the pronoun: either progressive assimilation and degemination (Hægstad 1917: 46; Indrebø 1951: 122; Christiansen 1956: 176) or simply deletion (Seip 1955: 76, 164). In either case, this must be an irregular sound change, since we do final -mv- sequences elsewhere in Old Norse (e.g. samvit, Modern Norwegian samvett 'conscience'). The final -m was reanalysed as part of the pronoun, giving pronouns mér and mit and 1pl ending -u; the new pronouns are found in sources a little after 1200 and spread rapidly after 1325 (Seip 1955: 194–5, 317; Haugen 1976: 302–3).

We also find 1pl -*u* in the sequence verb + pronoun in Old Icelandic where pronouns in *m*- never arose (Noreen 1970: 358; Faarlund 2004: 50–3), so we must assume an alternative development deleted the final consonant of the verb but left the initial consonant of the pronoun intact. In this form, this change is present inconsistently from late-twelfth century sources onwards in both Old Icelandic and Old Norwegian (Seip 1954: 229; Noreen 1970: 358).

A united account of the development might go as follows. Firstly, the final consonant of the verb was variably deleted when it directly preceded the pronoun. Assuming this took place before /w/ became [v], this left a sequence [-uweːr] (dual [-uwit]) which was ambiguous between /uweːr/ (dual /uwit/) and /ueːr/ (/uit/), varying with a conservative form retaining the /m/. This is the situation in Old Icelandic and the earliest Old Norwegian. Then, in Old Norwegian alone, the optional /m/ in this sequence was reanalysed as belonging to the pronoun.

In the past tense these changes created an ending that was identical to the 3pl ending, but in the present the two remained distinct: 3pl -*a* and 1pl -*u*. The eventual appearance of 3pl endings in 1pl contexts in the past tense thus involves this sound change and reanalysis alone, whereas in the present there must have been additional analogical change (Hægstad 1916: 158; Indrebø 1993: 140, 143–4) or sound change (Grøtvedt 1970: 240) merging 1pl -*u* and -*a*. Conservative -*um* and innovative -*u* and -*a* then competed, with the eventual result that the conservative form disappeared and person marking was lost in the plural.

A range of chronologies have been suggested: Seip (1955: 199, 321) suggests the new forms arose in Old Norwegian and that all person distinctions were lost on the verb in speech by 1300, although they were preserved in writing until around 1370; Skard's account (1973: 97, 146) is similar. Trosterud (2001: 166–9) suggests that 3pl endings only begin to appear on 1pl verbs in the fifteenth century, while Indrebø (1951: 215) suggests that new and old forms competed in the fifteenth century but that -*um* survived into early Modern Norwegian. Other authors converge on a similar chronology: 3pl endings begin to appear on 1pl verbs outside the sequence verb+subject pronoun in the late-fourteenth or early-fifteenth century; these increase in frequency gradually in the first half of the fifteenth century and more rapidly after 1450; -*um* largely disappeared shortly after 1500, although isolated examples occur later (Hægstad 1902: 201; Hægstad 1916: 158, 202; Tylden 1944: 126–7; Pettersen 1991: 659–60).

In terms of internal linguistic factors, most authors comment that the sequence verb+pronoun was a leading environment; this is expected since this was the context the change was innovated in. Grøtvedt (1970: 240) also suggests that the weak past was a leading context. Indrebø (1993: 139–40) observes that the verb *setja* 'set' leads the change, but suggests this is probably an artefact of formula-usage. Kinn (2010: 93–107; 2011) investigates the distribution of overt non-referential subjects in late Middle Norwegian charters with and without merger of 1pl and 3pl, finding no clear association between these two changes, contrary to previous predictions.

There are also comments on external factors. Tylden (1944: 126–7,135–7) suggests that changed forms are associated with the incoming 1pl.nom. pronoun *vi*: as this pronoun was borrowed from East Nordic, this might indicate that the loss of 1pl endings is associated with Swedish/Danish influence. Tylden also finds that changed forms are associated with the sequence *henge vi* 'we hang' in an eschatocol formula borrowed from Danish. This observation is also made by Tønnessen (1995: 31,48–50). Pettersen (1991: 659–60) suggests that, within West Norway, the change is earliest and strongest in Bergen and weakest in Agder. This agrees with Hægstad's (1916: 158, 201) suggestion that within West Norwegian the change is first found in the upper classes in Bergen and only reaches rural areas when Danish influence becomes more general.

Looking outside Norwegian, already in the earliest Old Danish manuscripts we find 1pl *-um* only infrequently and only in formulaic contexts; by the early-sixteenth century *-um* disappears altogether (Skautrup 1968: 273; Trosterud 2001: 169–71). It is worth noting that this highlights the complex nature of the relationship between the changes affecting the inflectional ending and the changes affecting the pronouns: it seems clear that the two must be related, but clearly the change affecting the inflectional ending can happen independently of the changes affecting the pronouns since the *m-* pronouns do not occur in Danish.

Finally, we come to Ottosson's (2003) study, a work based on examples from earlier studies (particularly Tylden 1944) and examination of a selection of charters from specific regions. Ottosson outlines the change as follows: the final *-m* of the suffix is dropped by sound change when the pronoun directly follows, causing a merger with the 3pl ending in the past but a distinctive ending the present; unstressed vowels merge by sound change in some dialects, creating a merger with the 3sg. ending in the weak past and with the 3pl ending elsewhere; the 3pl ending spreads to 1pl contexts by morphological change; and finally the 3sg. ending spreads to 1pl contexts by morphological change (Ottosson 2003: 158). A key part of Ottosson's argument is that, in spite of some phonological steps, the changes are primarily morphological (Ottosson 2003: 163–4). He also argues the importance of distinguishing tenses and verb classes, as the sound changes which took place have different morphological implications in different paradigms (Ottosson 2003: 161–2).

For the change from *-um* to *-u* in the past (merging 1pl and 3pl), Ottosson suggests there are sporadic examples before 1450 (particularly in weak verbs) after which the change progresses more quickly (Ottosson 2003: 163). This slightly predates the change from *-um* to *-a* in the present (Ottosson 2003: 163): innovative present tense forms are found sporadically in the first half of the 1400s, becoming common by the middle of the century (Ottosson 2003: 164). The change from *-a/-u* to *-e/-æ* is found sporadically in the early 1400s but becomes more common after 1450 (Ottosson 2003: 166). The early examples of this unstressed vowel weakening are in charters from the higher levels of ecclesiastical and secular administration and are associated with signs of Danish influence, but, due to good evidence of dialectal use in regions like Romerike, the change cannot be written off as a Danish feature (Ottosson 2003: 166). This change, too, appears later in the present than the past, implying that it is at least partly morphological rather than phonological (Ottosson 2003: 166). In terms of geography, Ottosson notes that material from Toten, West Telemark and Voss is more conservative than that from Vestfold, with little change in the former regions before 1470 (Ottosson 2003: 168).

Overall we have a consistent picture in some respects: the initial context of the change is agreed to be the sequence of verb+pronoun; the reanalysis of this sequence also produced the Norwegian *m-* pronouns. Analogical change spread 3pl endings to 1pl verbs in other contexts, with the past leading. There is substantial variation in the dating of the change, ranging from Seip's suggestion that person distinctions had been completely lost on the verb in speech by 1300 to Trosterud's claim that 3pl forms do not *begin* to appear in 1pl contexts until the fifteenth century (although it is not clear whether this applies to speech in addition to text). A change progressing rapidly in the mid-fifteenth century with sporadic examples earlier seems most likely. Between Ottosson and Pettersen's comments we might expect to find the change spreading from east to west and earlier in Bergen than the rural west.

It is also worth noting that a similar phenomenon is found elsewhere in Germanic. Old Frisian shows reduction of pl *-ath* to *-a* when the verb directly precedes a 1pl or 2pl subject pronoun (Bremmer 2009: 86). MLG itself has reduction of pl *-en/-et* to *-e* when the verb directly precedes a 1pl or 2pl subject pronoun; this is nearly categorical, with no discernible differentiation by tense, mood or person. An obvious difference from the Middle Nordic case is that MLG had lost person distinctions in the plural already at this point (Lasch 1974: 224–227). This pattern is not found in Old Saxon. Old English, which likewise lacked person distinctions in the plural, sometimes has pl *-e* instead of *-að* when the verb directly precedes the 1pl or 2pl subject pronoun (Davis 1953: §56); this is often ascribed only to southern Old English or only to West Saxon and referred to as 'West Saxon concord'. Benskin (2011) gives a thorough account of this form in Ingvaeonic, relating West Saxon concord to the later 'northern subject rule', a pattern in which a plural (including 3pl) verb takes *-e* or zero suffix if the subject pronoun is adjacent but *-(V)s* otherwise. Benskin (2011: 159–65) reports various suggested origins for West Saxon concord, including survival of dual verb agreement, phonological reduction of the consonant cluster after encliticisation of the pronoun, and spread of subjunctive forms with loss of final *-n* either in early Northumbrian or Late West Saxon.[13] The account involving phonological reduction after encliticisation (originally Luick 1922;

---

[13] Benskin's main line of argument has to do with the possibility of a role for Celtic influence in the development of West Saxon concord into the northern subject rule, and so is not relevant here.

1924) is a particularly relevant comparison. In broad terms, the proposal is that /θw/ and /θj/ do not occur in unstressed onset and so when these sequences were created by encliticisation of 1pl *wē* or 2pl *ġē* after pl *-að* they were reduced.

If we were to assume that the pattern of a reduced ending in the sequence VERB-SUBJECT PRONOUN was not an independent innovation in each branch, this either pushes its innovation back to a very early point or implies that the change diffused among Germanic dialects in contact. In this case, the relationship between the reanalysed 1pl and 1du. subject pronouns and the reduced ending could not be direct, since these reanalysed pronouns do not occur more widely in Germanic. Alternatively, we might take this as implying that this is (for some reason) a very natural change which has recurred multiple times in Germanic. In this case, we might even imagine that it recurred in different branches of *North* Germanic, and that the creation of the *m-* pronouns was a unique feature of the Norwegian iteration. Either way, since the reduced ending was near-categorical in VERB-SUBJECT position in MLG, it is possible that contact with MLG played a direct role in pushing forward the change in Nordic.

4.3.3.2. Data collection
4.3.3.2.1. Method of data collection. The dataset gathered to explore the forms of 1pl and 1du. pronouns was taken as a starting point. For every pronoun, each associated verb was identified, including verbs in co-ordinated clauses; after philological exclusions, this totalled 23,870 verbs.

Two other approaches could have been taken. A traditional method would have been to read the texts and identify 1pl verbs manually. However, this was infeasible with a dataset of this size. Alternatively, it might seem more intuitive to search the corpus for 1pl verbs themselves. However, various homographic morphological endings would have caused practical difficulties: for example, the original 1pl ending *-um* is the same as various dative endings, meaning that it would have been necessary to disambiguate between verbs and an enormous number of dative nominals. Putting aside issues of practicality, to search directly for 1pl verbs it would have been necessary to predetermine the range of possible endings; by searching for subjects and then identifying their associated verbs, no prior assumptions about the range of possible endings were needed.

The disadvantage of the methodology used is that verbs with null subjects were not included (although verbs whose subject was omitted under co-ordination were). This does not represent a large proportion of verbs: Kinn (2016: 224) estimates the rate of 1pl null subjects in Middle Norwegian at 11.9 per cent. Kinn's estimation treats the verbs *sjá* 'see' and *heyra* 'hear' in the protocol formula exemplified in Extract 8 as having null subjects whereas in this study these were treated as having had their subject omitted under co-ordination and thus were included. Omitting this formula, Kinn's figure for 1pl null subjects is as low as 3.6 per cent (Kinn 2016: 225). The exclusion of these verbs is unlikely to have materially affected results.

(8) Protocol formula with sjá and heyra in DN VII.488	
DN VII.488, 4th of February 1481	
myt varom a Byrttom Agatæmessa	we were in Byrtum on [the] eve of
æftæn anno dominj mcdlxj saghom	[St.] Agatha's mass AD 1481[,] saw
ok hørdhom a thera samptaal	and heard their interview

4.3.3.2.2. Categorisation of verbs. All verbs were identified and categorised into conjugation, tense and their position relative to the subject pronoun. The token counts are given in Table 23.

4.3.3.2.3. Categorisation of endings. All endings identified are given and classified in Tables 24 and 25. Although the original classification distinguished different vowels (distinguishing *-u* from *-a*, *-ir* from *-ar*, etc.), it became clear that changes in unstressed vowel orthographies rendered these distinctions meaningless without considerable further work. <e> and <æ> in unstressed positions indicated a front vowel in the early part of the corpus but later became spellings for schwa; unstressed <i> earlier indicated a front vowel but later could be used to indicate palatalisation of the preceding consonant or as a hypercorrect spelling for schwa. Furthermore, contrary to the suggestions of previous scholars, the replacement of 1pl endings by 3pl endings and the merger of unstressed vowels do not represent clearly distinguishable changes in Middle Norwegian: there is no period in which typical Old Norwegian 3pl endings (<-u/-o> and <-a>, <-az> and <-uz/-oz>) become common on 1pl verbs; rather, the weakened endings <-e> and <-iz> replace earlier endings directly (cf. Figures 24–27).

Accordingly, in this investigation, no distinctions are made between endings with different vowels. This leaves four active verb endings (*-Vm, -V, -Vr, -Ø*) and two middle verb endings (*-Vmz, -(V)z*).

Table 23. Number of verbs by conjugation, tense and position relative to subject pronoun

Tense	Position	Major class			
		anomalous	*weak*	*strong*	*preterite-present*
present	V... S	4	60	4	4
	VS	532	4003	1302	243
	SV	702	1083	202	323
	S... V	210	1629	258	211
past	V... S	3	26	12	2
	VS	763	2598	771	216
	SV	2508	353	332	316
	S... V	210	2619	2140	190

Table 24. 1pl active endings

Ending	Variants	Examples
-um	<-m>, <-æm>, <-am>, <-åm>, <-em>, <-im>, <-om>, <-öm>, <-øm>, <-um>, <-unm>, <-vm>, <-wm>, <-ym>	<dømdøm> 'judged' (DN V.570, 1424) <settum> 'set' (DN IX.350, 1464)
-a	<-a>	<heingia> 'hang' (DN III.869, 1464) <hafwa> 'have' (DN VIII.412, 1484)
-i	<-e>, <-i>, <-j>	<fwnne> 'found' (DN VIII.413, 1484) <sæti> 'set' (DN IV.737, 1403)
-i/-a	<-æ>	<hængiæ> 'hang' (DN V.458, 1408) <kungøræ> 'make known' (DN VI.429, 1427)
-u	<-o>, <-ø>, <-u>, <-v>, <-w>	<setto> 'set' (DN II.698, 1428) <settu> 'set' (DN VII.358, 1412)
-ar	<-ar>	<wndrar> 'wonder' (DN XI.216, 1464) <helsar> 'greet' (DN IX.234, 1423)
-ir	<-er>, <-ir>, <-yr>	<hafuer> 'have' (DN I.696, 1424) <haffuir> 'have' (DN XI.396, 1523)
-ir/-ar	<-ær>	<trøcheær> 'print' (DN VIII.574, 1527) <havær> 'havve' (DN IX.696, 1531)
-Ø	-Ø	<kand> 'can' (DN IX.696, 1531) <ransaghet> 'investigated' (DN XIV.728, 1533)

4.3.3.2.4. Formulae. As mentioned above in the discussion of 1du. and 1pl pronouns, a large majority of the data for these variables come from formulaic contexts (Tables 26–28). If formulae exert a conservative effect on this variable, this effect should apply across all of the data and so should not interfere with the patterns we are interested in. One downside of this property of the data, however, is that lexical item has a highly structured relationship with word order and tense: if a given verb appears in the data only (or almost only) in a single formula, it will overwhelmingly appear in the tense and word order

Table 25. 1pl middle endings

Ending	Variants	Examples
-umz	<-omps>, <-omptz>, <-oms>, <-omss>, <-omz>, <-opms>, <-umdz>, <-umps>, <-ums>, <-umss>, <-umz>, <-umzm>, <-vmps>, <-wmss>	<bekennoms> 'acknowledge' (DN XIV.743, 1535) <fannomss> 'found' (DN I.598, 1404)
-az	<-as>, <-azs>	<næmpnas> 'are named' (DN XIV.64, 1444) <kennazs> 'acknowledge' (DN IX.199, 1403)
-iz	<-edz>, <-ens>, <-es>, <-ess>, <-esz>, <-is>, <-iss>, <-isz>, <-ys>, <-yss>	<bekennes> 'acknowledge' (DN I.595, 1402) <kennisz> 'acknowledge' (DN IV.757, 1405)
-iz/-az	<-æs>, <-æss>	<kiennæs> 'acknowledge' (DN XIV.54, 1439) <bekænnæss> 'acknowledge' (DN V.1081, 1535)
-uz	<-o[m]ps>, <-os>, <-oss>, <-oz>, <-us>, <-uz>	<kennoz> 'acknowledge' (DN III.655, 1420) <kannus> 'acknowledge' (DN XI.143, 1424)

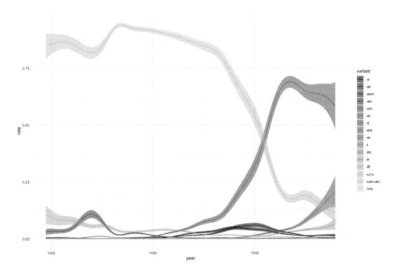

Figure 24. Kernel smoothed rates of orthographic variants of the 1pl/1du. active ending with Gaussian kernel and 10 year bandwidth [Colour figure can be viewed at wileyonlinelibrary.com]

dictated by that formula. For example, *setja* 'set' occurs in VERB-SUBJECT order in 1,519 out of 1,531 instances (99.22 per cent) compared with a rate for the whole dataset of 44.66 per cent; *heyra* 'hear' occurs in the past tense in 2,219 out of 2,225 instances (99.73 per cent past) and *biðja* 'ask' in the present tense in 560

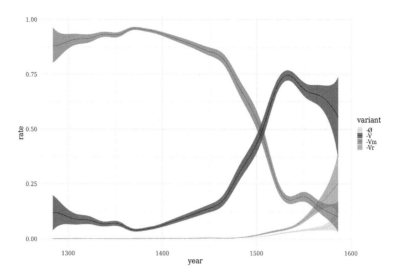

Figure 25. Kernel smoothed rates of morphological variants of the 1pl/1du. active ending with Gaussian kernel and 10 year bandwidth [Colour figure can be viewed at wileyonlinelibrary.com]

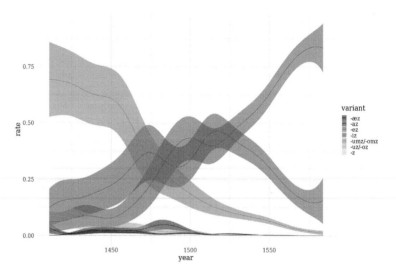

Figure 26. Kernel smoothed rates of orthographic variants of the 1pl/1du. middle ending with Gaussian kernel and 10 year bandwidth [Colour figure can be viewed at wileyonlinelibrary.com]

out of 581 instances (96.39 per cent present) compared to a rate in the whole dataset of 46.07 per cent present to 53.93 per cent past. As a result of these interactions, it would not be possible to use these data to investigate lexical effects.

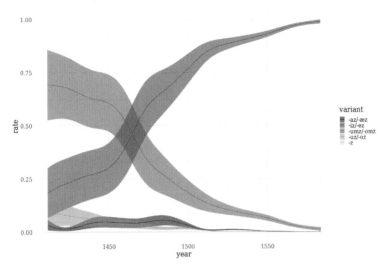

Figure 27. Kernel smoothed rates of morphological variants of the 1pl/1du. middle ending with Gaussian kernel and 10 year bandwidth [Colour figure can be viewed at wileyonlinelibrary.com]

4.3.3.2.5. Editorial intervention. Transcription practices are not a major concern for this variable. There are two common relevant abbreviations: the vowel of -*um/-om* can be abbreviated, typically with a nasal bar (as in <høyrdm5> for <høyrdum> in DN XXI.184); or the entire -*um/-om* ending can be abbreviated, typically with a nasal bar (as in <sett5> for <settum> in DN XXI.103). In both cases, as the nasal bar is used only when there is a nasal consonant and we are not distinguishing between unstressed vowels, these abbreviations never result in any ambiguity as to which ending is intended.

4.4. *Syntactic variables*

4.4.1. *Loss of lexical genitives*

4.4.1.1. *Background*

4.4.1.1.1. Introduction. Old Norse distinguished four cases: nominative, accusative, genitive and dative. All had both structural and lexical functions. Modern Nordic varieties have moved different distances along the path to losing case: at one end of the spectrum, modern Icelandic retains most of the case marking and usage patterns of Old Norse; Faroese has largely lost the genitive but retains the other three; Norwegian and Swedish varieties have mostly lost lexical genitives and show varying patterns of loss of structural genitives; most Continental Nordic varieties have lost all datives, with certain Norwegian and Swedish dialects retaining some; all Continental Nordic varieties have lost the nominative on all nominals but retain it on pronouns. Here, we will examine the

Table 26. Common protocol formulae with 1pl and 1du. verbs

Verb	Examples	
vilja, 'wish'	**meer wilium** yder kungera	DN VIII.274, 1425
	'we wish to make known to you...'	
	wer vilium yder kunnikt gøre	DN XI.155, 1434
	'we wish to make known to you...'	
	Wer Audhun medher guds naad biscuper j Stawangre **vilium** þet ollum monnum viterlight væra 'We[,] Audhun with god's grace bishop of Stavanger[,] **want** all people to be aware of it...'	DN II.693, 1427
gera 'make, do'	**Wy** Erich meth guths nathe Danmarks Suerighes Norghes Wendes oe Gothis konung oc hertugh j Pomern. **gøre** witerlicht alle the thette breff see eller høre, at 'We[,] Erich with god's grace king of Denmark[,] Sweden[,] Norway[,] Wends and Gots and lord of Pomerania, **make** all those [who] see or hear this charter aware that...'	DN V.645, 1434
	Þat **gerom mid** [...] suornir logreto menn ollum godum monnum kunnikt med þesso ockro brefe at 'We two[,] [...] sworn magistrates[,] **make** all good people aware with this our charter that...'	DN IX.275, 1439
kunngera 'make known'	Ollom monnom þeim seem þette breff see æller høyre **kwngerom wi** [...] swarnæ logretthes men j Ringgæsakær sokn 'We[,] [...] sworn magistrates in Ringsaker parish[,] **make known** to all those people who see or hear this charter...'	DN XII.207, 1443
	kiennomps **vi** oc **kungiørom** med tessæ varæ vpnæ brewe oc fwlkomlica til stam vm 'we acknowledge and **make known** with this our open charter and fully confess that...'	DN XIV.76, 1448
kennast 'acknowledge'	Thet **kennoms mit** [...] at 'We two[,] [...] acknowledge that...'	DN VIII.347, 1452
	Ollom monnom them som thetta bref se eller høra **kennis wi** [...] ok fulleghe till stahom thet 'We[,] [...] **acknowledge** and fully confess to all those people who see or hear this charter that...'	DN XIV.89, 1460

(continued)

Table 26. (continued)

Verb	Examples	
bekennast 'acknowledge'	Ollum monnum som thette breff se eller høre **bekenis vy** effter skriffne lorettis men pa Nes som er [...] at	DN IX.379, 1470
	'We[,] [the] following magistrates in Nes who are [...] **acknowledge** to all those people who see or hear this charter that...'	
	Bekennomps vy medh tesse vare nærwarandhe vpne breffue och fulleligh til standom at	DN III.967, 1489
	'We acknowledge and fully confess with this our present open charter that...'	
heils(an)a 'greet'	Ollom monnom theim som thettæ breff see æller høra **helse vij** efftherscriffnæ [...], kærlega med warum herræ, kwnnokt gørande ath	DN I.960, 1489
	'We [the] following[,] [...] **greet** all those people who see or hear this charter warmly with our lord, making known that...'	
	Allom mannom them som thetta breff see eller høra **helsom wii** æptherscrifne men [...] kerlige med gudh och sancte Olaff konungh	DN III.1009, 1499
	'We [the] following people[,] [...] **greet** all those people who see or hear this charter warmly with god and holy king Olaff	
senda 'send'	Ollum monnum þeim sem þetta bref sea æder høyra **sendom mit** [...] q. g. ok sine kunnikt gerande at	DN V.573, 1425
	'We two[,] [...] **send** to all those people who see or hear this charter g[od's] g[reetings] and our own[,] making known that..'.	
	Ollom godhom monnom them som thetta bref see ædher hœra **sendom meer** [...] q. g. ok wara. kunnigt gœrande. at	DN VIII.284, 1429
	'We[,] [...] **send** to all those good people who see or hear this charter g[od's] g[reetings] and ours, making known that...'	
vera 'be', sjá 'see', heyra 'hear'	kunnikt gørande ath **meer warom** a Hwame j nørdre gardenom j Æftaløythe sokn a Halwarssoko afthan anno domini mcdxl octauo **sagom** ok **hørdom**	DN VII.436, 1448
	'making known that **we were** in Hwame in the northern farm in Æftaløythe parish on Halwarssoko eve AD 1448 [and] **saw** and **heard**...'	
	kunnikt gerandes at **mith warom** a Gammæ som ligger j Grana sokn a sancte Nicholai dagh anno domini mcdlxxx nono **sogom** oc **hoyrdom** a at	DN I.964, 1489
	'making known that **we two were** in Gammæ which is located in Grana parish on saint Nicholai day AD 1489 [and] **saw** and **heard** that...'	
	kunnuckt gørendis thet **vj varom** oppa Helleland i fførne dal oc i Øslebø sokn anno domini mdxxx die anunciacionis **hørdom** a oc **sagom** a att	DN VI.708, 1530
	'making known that **we were** at Helleland in [the] farther valley and in Øslebø parish AD 1530 Annunciation day [and] **heard** and **saw** that...'	

Table 27. Common body formulae with 1pl and 1du. verbs

Verb	Examples	
gefa 'give'	Thy **geffwe wy** *wy honu*m quith frii ock allunng*is* aakærelousan for*e* oss ock waarom effth*er* koman*dom* for*e* forne*m*pde ~~breff~~ vmbod.	DN XXI.716, 1514
	'Therefore **we make** him free from prosecution and entirely under no obligation before us and our descendants regarding [the] aforementioned charter's instruction'.	
	þui **gefuir wer** han þær vm allungis kuittan.	DN I.558, 1397
	'Therefore **we make** him entirely free from prosecution concerning this'.	
dœma 'judge, adjudge'	**domdom wer** efter þy profwe som þa firir kom at	DN I.755, 1436
	'**we judge** according to this evidence which then came before [us] that...'	
	dømdom vj engom manne tel skuld heller skadha ther fore dømdom wj førnemdh	DN II.747, 1442
	'**we adjudge** to no person debt or damage therefore we judge [the] aforementioned...'	
vita 'know'	som **mit vithum** firir gudj sannast vera	DN VI.433, 1430
	'which **we know** before god to be truest'	
	at **mith vitom** firi gudhi sat vara at	DN III.768, 1441
	'that **we two know** before god to be true that...'	
	jtem **vitum mith** oc þet firj gudj sat vara oc manghe adhre godhe men medh okker at	
	'and **we two know** also that to be true before god and many other good people with us that...'	
kunna 'know, be able'	ok **kwnnu vij** þa eintidh sannarra fiinna.	DN I.643, 1415
	'and **we could** then find nothing truer...'	
	kunnum wi ey ytther meer pprof fa ath	DN III.710, 1431
	'**we could** get no more evidence that...'	

progression of just one small component of the history of the loss of case in Norwegian: the loss of lexical genitives.

4.4.1.1.2. Functions of the genitive before the change. As a structural case, the Old Norse genitive marked possessives and partitives; a reflex of one Old Norse genitive marker, -*s*, survives as a possessive marker in some varieties of Modern Norwegian. Lexical genitives in Old Norse were selected by certain adjectives, nouns, verbs and prepositions; adnominal lexical genitives were far more numerous than adverbal (2,550 known types compared with 278 adverbal) (Toft 2009: 60; cited in Berg 2015a: 7, 2015b: 181). Just a handful of prepositions selected genitives: *til* 'to', *millum* 'between', *útan* 'without',

Table 28. Common eschatocol formulae with 1pl verbs

Verb	Examples	
hengja 'hang'	tyll vijdnis byr **hynge vy** vore inde seghell for thette breff (och bede) [...] om theris indzegell for thette breff 'in testimony **we hang** our own seals on this charter [and ask] [...] for their seals for this charter'	DN XIV.26, 1407
	Ok til mere biuisning her vm **hænghdum wi** vaar jncigle ffore thetta breff 'and for more evidence hereof **we hung** our seals on this charter'	DN III.665, 1422
	ok ytarmeire stadhfesto her om þa **hengdo vi** var insigle firir þetta bref 'and in stronger affirmation hereof **we** then **hung** our seals on this charter'	DN II.684, 1425
biðja 'ask'	til ytermere witnisbyrd **bidhiom wi** godha manna incigle som ær [...] . ... for thetta breff 'in stronger testimony **we ask** for [the] seals of good men who are [...] ... on this charter'	DN VI.481, 1440
	Och til stadhelika witnisbyrdh **bidhiom wi** godhra manna incigle som ær [...] for thetta breff 'And for firm testimony **we ask** for [the] seals of good men who are [...] on this charter'	DN III.816, 1451
þrykkja 'print'	thil yttermer windesbyrd **tricker wi** wore yndzegler neden for thette wort obffne breff 'for stronger testimony **we print** our seals down on this our open charter'	DN III.1015, 1499
	tiill Saninden thaa **trycke wij** wore insigle ffore thetta breff 'in affirmation **we** then **print** our seals on this charter'	DN XV.142, 1512
setja, 'set'	herom **settha vy** vore insigla for thette bref 'therefore **we set** our seals on this charter'	DN X.619, 1530
	Ok till sannynda **settom meer** woor jncigli firir þetta bref 'And in affirmation **we set** our seals on this charter'	DN III.596, 1410

innan 'within' and the adposition-like phrases (*fyrir*) ... *sakar/skyld* 'because of' and *af vegna* 'on behalf of'. Despite their low number, prepositional genitives are relatively frequent in connected text, yet do not survive into Modern Norwegian. This study of the loss of lexical genitives concentrates on one preposition: *millum* 'between'.

4.4.1.1.3. The nature of the change. At the beginning of the period covered, *millum* consistently takes genitive objects. In Modern Norwegian dialects which retain a distinct dative case, *mellom* can take a dative (Aasen 1965: 276, 278); otherwise it takes the object case which is a reflex of accusative and dative (and the *s*-form reflex of the genitive only in certain fossilised phrases). This is in keeping with the general development of lexical genitives in Norwegian: where Modern Norwegian and Swedish dialects have reflexes of verbs which took genitive objects in the medieval languages, they take now take dative objects, dative/accusative objects, or prepositional phrase objects, depending on the survival of the case system in the dialects in question (Reinhammer 1973: 158–64; cited by Berg 2015a: 7, 2015b: 180).

We might expect, then, to see *millum* shift from taking a genitive to taking a dative in Middle Norwegian. In actuality, the picture is more complex. The evidence for case is difficult to interpret in later Middle Norwegian, especially regarding distinguishing accusative from dative and accusative from zero-marked; this is discussed in more detail below. However, there is unambiguous evidence that *millum* did not shift directly or solely to taking the dative.

Many examples in the corpus show that *millum* sometimes took an accusative in Middle Norwegian. In Extract (9), two of the three objects of <mellom> are unambiguously accusative: <min brodhor Christofor fornempdan>[14] and <mic>;[15] the other object, <arua> 'heir', is ambiguous between accusative, genitive and dative. In Extract (10) we see a mixed picture: the first object of <mellom>, <fyrnæmfdan Helgha henna husbonda>, is unambiguously accusative,[16] but the second, <hennar>, is genitive.[17] These accusatives are unambiguous because they include a form with explicit acc.sg. *-an*. More common are examples with zero-marked accusatives; we might question whether these really offer evidence that *millum* shifted to taking the accusative or whether they simply show the rise of forms not marked for case at all. In Extract (11) we might take <Fiskæim> as an accusative, but, as it has no suffix, it could simply be unmarked for case; likewise definite <garden> in Extract (12).

---

(9) Example of millum governing the accusative
DN X.78, 30th of August 1381

vm alt thet til thenna dagh hauer varit	about everything which had
mellom min brodhor Cristofor	happened until this day between my
fornempdan hans arua oc mic	aforementioned brother Cristofer[,]
	his heir and me

---

(10) Example of millum governing the accusative and the genitive
DN V.404, 26th of February 1401

huat retter kaupmale var mellom	what legal contract there was
fyrnæmfdan Helgha henna husbonda	between her husband [the]
ok hennar	aforementioned Helghi and her

---

[14] We might expect <mins brodhor Christofors fornempz> in the genitive or <minum brodhor Christofore fornempdom> in the dative.

[15] Rather than genitive <min> or dative <mer>.

[16] The genitive would be <fyrnæmfz Helgha henna(r) husbonda>, the dative <fyrnæmfdom Helgha henna(r) husbonda>.

[17] Although note that the preceding instance of the same word lacks the genitive final /r/: <henna>.

(11) Example of millum governing the unmarked accusative and the dative
DN V.316, 21st of February 1380

skipti war a komit milliom Rodhone ok Fiskæim	[the] boundary ran between Rodhonn and Fiskæim

(12) Example of millum governing the unmarked accusative
DN VII.352, 4th of October 1410

tunæt, er sameign ok wskipt mellom kirkiu lutæn ok Huams nørde garden.	the meadow which [is] common and undivided between [the] church's allotment and the northern Huam estate

There are also many examples of objects of *millum* marked for dative throughout the period covered. In Extract (13), <þeym> is unambiguously dative: we would expect <þeyra> for the genitive and <þa> for the accusative. In Extract (14), <gardhom> has the distinctive dat.pl. -*um*. In Extract (15) we see a typical example with equivocal evidence: the first object <os> could be accusative or dative; in the second, unambiguously dative <ærwingom> is accompanied by the possessive adjective <vare> which resembles an accusative (from Old Norwegian *vára*) or genitive (from Old Norwegian *várra*) but cannot be a reflex of dative *várum*.

(13) Example of millum taking the dative of a pronoun
DN II.574, 5th of February 1403

om alt þet þeym foor j melliom	about everything that happened between them

(14) Example of millum taking the dative of a noun
DN I.804, 7th of April 1449

gengho deilis ghongho gardhom jmellum	the boundary runs between [the] estates

(15) Example of millum taking the dative of a pronoun and noun
DN III.379, 1372

os j mellom oc vare ærwingom	between us and our heirs

Note that we often see different case marking on different objects of a single instance of *millum*, as in Extract (10) and Extract (11). This is particularly common with longer objects, as exemplified in Extract (16). The first object, <Angrims j fullu wmbode brœðranna a Ælghisætre>, is genitive-marked. The second, <Siuguurder Ottars son>, is probably genitive marked: <-er> is probably genitive -*ar* (although this is a little unexpected as this text otherwise preserves the distinction between -*ir* and -*ar*), but <Ottars son> lacks genitive marking; alternatively this NP could be read as nominative (*sonr* 'son' in patronymics loses nominative -*r* particularly early). The third object, <Viglæikr a Lyngi>, presents similar problems for interpretation: names in -*leikr* typically have genitives in -*s* rather than -*ar*, but this could be a hypercorrect spelling of an irregular genitive *Vígleikar*; alternatively, the NP could be nominative. The fourth and fifth objects, <erfuingium fru Rangdiðar> and <ollum odrum þæim sæm þi malle æighu at suara j Lyngi> are both unambiguously dative.

Conflicting case marking on co-ordinated objects occurs even with very simple objects as in Extract (17): the first object, <Sanda>, is genitive or accusative; the second, <Pukastadom>, is unambiguously dative.

---

(16) Example of millum taking genitive and dative objects
DN V.186, 1st of March 1346

millium brodor Angrims j fullu wmbode brœðranna a Ælghisætre ok Siuguurder Ottars son Viglæikr a Lyngi ok erfuingium fru Rangdiðar ok ollum odrum þæim sæm þi malle æighu at suara j Lyngi.	between brother Angrim as fully empowered representative of the brethren at Ælghisætr and Siuguurder Ottarsson[,] Viglæikr of Lyng and [the] heirs of lady Rangdiðr and all those others who are obliged to answer the case in Lyng

---

(17) Example of millum taking a genitive and dative object
DN VIII.330, 8th of October 1446

i bekkenom þen som renner mellom Sanda oc Pukastadom	in the stream which runs between Sandar and Pukastadir

---

Thus describing the entire change is challenging. It is likely that different innovations competed at different times, with accusative, dative and zero-marked objects of *millum* all probably occurring in speech. Ambiguous forms present a substantial challenge for studying these interacting options. Genitive case marking, especially in the masculine/neuter singular, presents the fewest ambiguities: the -*s* ending resembles no other nominal suffix. It is often possible to determine whether a form could be genitive-marked, even if it is ambiguous in other respects. Accordingly, the change studied here is not specifically the rise of dative, accusative or zero-marked objects of *millum*, but the decline of genitive objects without reference to what replaced them.

An additional minor change should be noted: the phrase *sín á millum* 'between them' and its variant *sín í millum* (which constitute formulaic phrases) seem to have been reanalysed as *sína/síni millum*. The result was a new, plural reflexive pronoun that could have been analysed as genitive (by analogy with forms like gen.pl reflexive possessive *sinna*), accusative (by analogy with forms like reflexive possessive masc.acc.pl *sína*) or perhaps even dative (by analogy with fem.dat.sg. forms like *sinni*). These forms occur fifteen times with *millum* in the corpus, including three instances where the full form of the preposition has been analogically restored (like <sina jmellom> in DN X.218). Norde (1997: 156) notes the same change for Swedish.

Finally, note that although *millum* is referred to as a preposition, its objects can precede or follow it. Full NP objects typically follow (as in Extracts (9)–(12), (15)–(17)) and pronoun objects precede (as in Extract (13) and Extract (15)). However, NP objects can precede *millum* (as in Extract (14)) and pronoun objects can follow it (as in Extract (18)).

---

(18) Example of millum with a following object pronoun
DN VI.529, 26th of September 1448

then owilia ok misthycke som	the ill will and discord which had
mellom them war vpresen	arisen between them

4.4.1.1.4. Earlier research. There is substantial scholarship on the loss of genitives with prepositions in the history of Norwegian. The change is mentioned in most standard histories of the language and one detailed study has been undertaken. The earliest evidence for the loss of lexical genitives in Continental Nordic is in runic inscription U395, a Viking Age inscription from Sigtuna in eastern Sweden with <firþi til sihtunum> for *førði til Sigtúnum*, seemingly showing *til* taking the dative; however, Åneman (1989) suggests that this placename is a loan from Celtic and the apparent dative ending is actually part of the stem. No evidence for loss of lexical genitives is known from Danish and Norwegian runic inscriptions (Åneman 1989).

Seip (1955: 307–9) suggests that genitive-governing prepositions and verbs became accusative-governing late during the Old Norwegian period, with early examples in the context of two co-ordinated objects. Haugen (1976: 294) mentions that over 1350–1550 the function of the genitive was progressively restricted, especially with verbs and prepositions (although 'literary Da and Sw expanded the use of the gen. in response to Lat and Ger influence'). Skard (1973: 103–4) states that 'Classical Old Norwegian' genitive-governing prepositions are found more and more often with the accusative over the Old Norwegian period, a development that continued in Middle Norwegian (Skard 1973: 155). Indrebø (1951: 250–1) states that by the end of the Middle Norwegian period, the spoken language had gone a long way towards losing the genitive entirely, although it was preserved better in writing; it was replaced partly by the dative, but more often by the accusative, and eventually by zero-marking. Larsen (1993) investigates the loss of the genitive in the DN, finding it is lost earliest of all the cases: there is decline already in the early-fourteenth century, despite a countervailing tendency to regularise genitive marking by spreading the *-s* suffix. Larsen (1993: 60) suggests that the decline of the genitive was caused by phonological and morphological factors: weak and feminine genitives in *-a*, *-u* and *-ar* merged with nominative and accusative endings by sound change and so were replaced by other constructions; such constructions then spread also at the expense of other genitives. Landrø (1975: 127; cited in Berg 2015a: 15), investigating the identity of fifteenth-century Icelandic scribe Jón Egilsson, uses datives with *millum* among other evidence to conclude that Egilsson was a Norwegian from the south-east, on the basis that the change was diagnostic of Norwegian at this point.

Berge (1974) investigates genitive nouns in Nordic-language charters dated 1424–1425, dividing up the data by geographical region into: central west (Bergen), peripheral west, central east (the lowlands around Oslofjord), peripheral east, Trondheim and Jämtland and Härjedalen (Berge 1974: 7–8). There are 242 nouns governed by prepositions in her data (194 *til*, fourteen *mellom*, seven *skyld*, eighteen *utan*, eight *vegna* and one *sakar*): the genitive has receded further with these prepositions than when governed by adjectives or nouns, with 72.33 per cent (175/242) of nouns governed by prepositions marked for genitive compared with 89.53 per cent (1,249/1,395) of possessives and nouns governed by nouns and 85.71 per cent (12/14) of those governed by adjectives; genitives governed by verbs have also receded substantially (6/12 instances with genitive marking) (Berge 1974: 69–77). Berge does not break her data down by both syntactic context and region, but taking all syntactic contexts together she finds the rates of genitive use in Table 29 (Berge 1974: 149–52).[18]

Discounting the conservative position of Trondheim (based on just a handful of examples), only the innovative position of Jämtland and Härjedalen stands out as a major regional effect.

Enger (2013: 6–7) summarises existing research on the loss of the genitive, highlighting the seeming contradiction that masculine/neuter gen.sg. *-s* is the single most distinctive case marker and expands at the expense of other genitive markers from 1200 onwards, yet the genitive is lost relatively early. Enger argues the loss of the genitive was not phonologically but morphologically motivated.

Berg (2015a) undertakes a more substantial investigation into the loss of lexical genitives in Norwegian, focusing particularly on genitives with *millum* in the DN over 1350–1450; he finds examples in 864 charters (of which 504 have

---

[18] These figures emerge after philological analysis of various forms where sound and morphological changes disrupt the expected genitive-marking patterns of Old Norse; taking the raw figures for rates of retention of Old Norse endings, there are larger differences between regions (Berge 1974: 144,150).

Table 29. Rates of genitive retention by region from Berge (1974)

Region	Use of genitive	%	Non-use of genitive	%	Total
West Norway (Bergen)	273	85.58	46	14.42	319
West Norway (peripheral)	183	88.41	24	11.59	207
East Norway (central)	676	87.11	100	12.89	776
East Norway (peripheral)	235	85.14	41	14.86	276
Jämtland & Härjedalen	53	82.81	11	17.19	64
Trondheim	24	96.00	1	4.00	25
Total	1444	86.67	223	13.38	1667

only examples of *millum* with the adverb *þar* 'there', offering no evidence about case) (Berg 2015a: 5). His approach is qualitative and philological (Berg 2015a: 6). He identifies late-fourteenth century examples of accusative objects of *millum*, sometimes with conflicting forms side-by-side; in the same period he identifies dative objects of *millum* (Berg 2015a: 11–12). Datives with *millum* remain common through the fifteenth century, but genitives are found occasionally even in the late-sixteenth century, specifically in the formula *millum þeira* / *þeira millum* 'between them' (Berg 2015a: 13). Berg concludes that lexical genitives fell out of use around 1400 in written Norwegian and presumably a little earlier in speech; they were first replaced by accusatives and later, as the accusative merged with the nominative to leave a two-case system, datives (Berg 2015a: 30).

Norde (1997: 145–66) examines the loss of lexical genitives in Old Swedish. After the preposition *til*, she finds variation between genitive and accusative[19] from the earliest texts and substantial change in Old Swedish towards accusatives and occasionally datives; the change is led by feminine nouns and pronouns lag behind (Norde 1997: 147–55).[20] When *til* governs multiple co-ordinated nouns one sometimes remains uninflected (or is marked accusative) while the other takes genitive; either order is possible (Norde 1997: 152–3). Patterns with *mællom* seem to be similar, although there are less data; there are less data again for the adposition-like phrase *fore ... skuld/sakir* 'for the sake of' and too little to quantify for *innan* 'within', *utan* 'outside' and *bland* 'among' (Norde 1997: 155–8). These patterns largely continue in Middle Swedish (Norde 1997: 158–66) although the genitive with prepositions is increasingly restricted to fixed expressions and was perhaps no longer productive (Norde 1997: 158). The figures found by Norde alongside the text and manuscript dates she gives (Norde 1997: 18–21) are given as proportions of genitives among objects of *til*,

---

[19] Or zero-marking (Norde 2001: 117).

[20] Although note that Delsing (1999: 87) argues that the change from *-a(r)* to *-Ø* in strong feminines after genitive-governing prepositions is a morphological change in the exponence of genitive, not a shift in the case-governance of the preposition. If we accepted this, the leading position of feminine nouns would presumably disappear and the timing of the change would appear slightly later. Norde (2001: 114) rejects this.

mællom and *fore … skuld/sakir* in Figure 28. Despite some unexplained variability, the trajectory of the loss of the lexical genitive can clearly be seen, especially against manuscript date.

Substantial work has been done on internal conditioning in the Continental Scandinavian loss of case, particularly the different chronologies in different classes of nominals. Grøtvedt (1970: 157) and Pettersen (1991: 505–14) observe that personal names and placenames seem to lead the loss of case in Norwegian and Wetås (2003; 2008) presents a detailed and perceptive study of this pattern. Hellberg (1960: 59) and Brylla (1987: 166) observe the same for Swedish. These observations apply most straightforwardly to the nominative and dative; there is some indication that they apply to genitives (Pettersen 1991: 514); whether they apply to lexical genitives is an open question, but is not the main object of study here.

Overall, then, we have a good understanding from Berg (2015a) of the language-internal developments: lexical genitives are replaced first by accusatives (or perhaps competing accusatives and datives), which are later replaced by datives as the accusative merges with the nominative. We have less idea, however, of how these changes spread, in terms of specific timing, social groups or geography. The evidence from Berge (1974) suggests the change reached around 25 per cent in 1425 (if we can assume genitives with *millum* behaved like genitives with other prepositions) and that Jämtland and Härjedalen were innovative, with little regional variation within the rest of Norway (if we assume genitives with *millum* behaved like genitives in all other syntactic contexts); this is, however, only a synchronic snapshot.

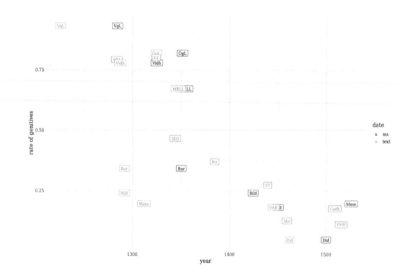

Figure 28. Rates of prepositional genitives in Middle Swedish texts from Norde (1997) [Colour figure can be viewed at wileyonlinelibrary.com]

It should be noted that in Norwegian, as in Swedish, Danish and English, other changes also affected the genitive: the -(V)s masculine/neuter strong gen.sg. spread to other classes and to the plural; case agreement within the NP disappeared; the -(V)s ending came to be marked only on the final element of the NP; this ending was reanalysed as a phrasal clitic. The loss of lexical genitives, of which the loss of genitive objects of prepositions is one element, is part of this larger story. Other aspects of this progression, particularly the apparent 'degrammaticalisation' implied by the change from affix to clitic, have been subject to detailed study, particularly in the histories of Swedish and English. The reader is referred to Norde (1997; 2001; 2006), Delsing (1999; 2001), Börjars (2003), Perridon (2013) and Trousdale & Norde (2013) for a view of this topic.

4.4.1.2. Data collection

4.4.1.2.1. Method of data collection. All 3,565 tokens of *millum* in original texts were identified. For each, each of its objects (a total of 5,144 NPs) and every case-markable element within these NPs was identified. The loss of the genitive presents a particular challenge defining unambiguous 'changed' and 'unchanged' forms. Even in Old Norse, many nominals are ambiguous between genitive and other cases:

- all weak nouns have accusative-genitive-dative syncretism in the singular; e.g. <kyndiuls mœsso> 'Candlemass' (DN I.213, 1331);
- masculine *a*- and *wa*-stems have accusative-genitive syncretism in the plural; e.g. <hornstadha> 'corners' (DN VI.270, 1369); and
- feminine *jō*- and *ō*-stems have syncretism between genitive singular and nominative-accusative plural (although context typically disambiguates).

Sound changes merging unstressed vowels and writing practices that did not consistently distinguish unstressed vowels even if they were distinct in speech created more ambiguities:

- weak singular nouns become ambiguous between all cases; e.g. <eyghen konnæ hans> 'his own wife' (DN VIII.422, 1489);
- genitive singulars in -*ar* become ambiguous with other endings in -*r* and -*Vr*; and
- genitive plurals in -*a* become ambiguous with other endings in -*V*.

In addition to these morphological sources of ambiguity, there are lexical sources: certain nouns (like *herra* 'lord') do not decline for case even in the earliest texts. The writing system can create more ambiguities still, as with words which are typically abbreviated (like <Mt> 'majesty'). In late Middle Norwegian, adjectives increasingly fail to mark case, making case governance ambiguous in a larger proportion of instances. Finally, in late Middle Norwegian, a pattern develops in which only one element in each NP is explicitly case-marked.

For these reasons, most potential tokens (elements in NPs which are objects of *millum*, could be case-marked, and thus would be expected to be genitive-marked) are not individually reliable indicators of whether *millum* is taking a genitive. Accordingly, only NPs which contained either an unambiguously genitive-marked element or an element which was unambiguously not genitive-marked were included in the study.[21, 22] Texts were categorised by whether they contained at least one unambiguously genitive-marked element among these NP objects of *millum*. In total, these comprised 692 texts with evidence that *millum* still took a genitive object (i.e. in which at least one element in at least one object of *millum* was genitive-marked) and 773 texts with evidence that *millum* no longer took a genitive (i.e. in which there were unambiguously non-genitive-marked elements and no unambiguously genitive-marked elements in objects of *millum*).

4.4.1.2.2. Formulae. Many tokens occurred in formulae. Two are worth noting:

1. <fiughurra stafstœda j millum> 'between four corners' (DN IV.167, 1325), with lexical variants <fiughura hornstadha j millum> 'between four corners' (DN VI.270, 1369) and <fiure honstafue i miellom> 'between four corners' (DN VII.345, 1406) (206 occurrences); and
2. <millim fial ok fioru> 'between fell and foreshore' (DN IV.506, 1377) (15 occurrences).

These present the familiar problem that they might be more conservative than surrounding text (and language use in other contexts) due to being directly copied from exemplars or being preserved as fossilised formulae in speech. However, they do not represent a large proportion of the data.

All other common formulae involving *millum* do not present the same problem because the objects of *millum* in them are non-formulaic. The most obvious is a protocol formula reporting that signatories witnessed a transaction between other parties. Examples of two variants of this formula are given as Extracts (19) and (20). The objects of *millum* in this formula are the names of specific individuals with whom the charter is concerned and accordingly are non-formulaic: even if the

[21] Thus, elements which were ambiguous for case but nevertheless could not be genitive *were* included. A typical example is <Hegliidt>, a placename mentioned in DN XVI.361 (1521). The second element is *hlíð* 'mountainside', a feminine i-stem with syncretism between accusative, dative and potentially nominative singular in -Ø in Old Norse, contrasting with genitive singular in -*ar*. Accordingly, the case marking of this example is hardly 'unambiguous'. However, it *is* unambiguously not genitive: <Hegliidt> cannot reflect Old Norse -*ar* or later Norwegian -*s*.

[22] Wetås (2003: 291–2) argues that placenames should not be included uncritically in studies of case loss in Middle Norwegian since the reflexes of many placenames in modern Norwegian dialects are in fact fossilised datives; accordingly, it is not possible to tell whether an individual dative placename in a text is really dative or a fossilised form synchronically unmarked for case. However, this does not present a problem when studying the loss of the genitive: whatever the correct synchronic analysis of such a form, it cannot be a genitive.

formula was copied from some unknown exemplar, the names of the parties are specific to this charter and so cannot have been. Thus case usage should not be especially conservative in this and similar formulae.

---

(19) Witness formula
DN I.454, 20th of February 1379

hørdum ord ok saghom handerband þeire millium. af æinni halfuu Wlfuer Þosteins son. en af annere Anunder Biornsson.	[we] heard [the] words and saw [the] handshake between them[,] on [the] one hand Wlfuer Þosteinsson and on [the] other Anunder Biornsson

---

(20) Witness formula
DN II.795, 21st of January 1452

sagom iaa oc handerband þeira a mellom Solfue Olafsson oc Gudrun Borgarsdotter eigin kona hans af eyno halfuo, en af andro halfuo Eiuinder Þorgyulsson oc i ombode Ældrid Bryniulfs dotter eigyn kona hans,	[we] saw [the] 'yes' and handshake between them[,] Solfue Olafsson and Gudrun Borgarsdotter his own wife on [the] one hand, and on [the] other hand Eiuinder Þorgyulsson as [the] representative of his own wife Ældrid Bryniulfsdotter

---

5

I<small>NDIVIDUAL CHANGES</small>

5.1. *Introduction*

The methods presented in this book allow us to explore the spatial distributions of linguistic features over the course of language histories, but this does not mean that their use is limited to linguistic geography. Different predictions about spatial patterning may be entailed by different understandings of individual instances of language change, by different understandings of the overall course of language history, and even by different understandings of the phenomenon of language change in the abstract. By testing these predictions with kernel smoothing, we can thus test different theories about language change at various different levels of abstraction. In the following three chapters I will explore some different uses that kernel smoothing can be put to in our case studies from the history of Norwegian, moving progressively from a narrow to a wider scope. In this chapter I will use spatial evidence to reflect on how we should think of two specific sets of changes in Middle Norwegian: the stopping of the dental fricative /θ/ and the loss of the *-um* 1pl active ending. In chapter 6, I will show how spatial findings can offer evidence for a theory about the history of the language as a whole, the Trudgill conjecture on the effects of intensive contact (as applied to the history of Norwegian). Finally, in chapter 7 I will explore a more general issue in our understanding of language change: that of different spatial models of linguistic diffusion.

5.2. *The loss of the dental fricatives*

As discussed under sections 4.2.2.1 and 4.2.3.1, Old Norwegian had only one dental fricative phoneme /θ/ whose voicing was predictable from stress and position in the syllable. The fact that Old Norwegian had two orthemes, <þ> and <ð>, which in context do usually correspond to the voiceless and voiced phones [θ ð] respectively, might be taken to imply that these were distinct phonemes, but this would be misleading. The rules governing when <ð> was used for /θ/ and when /θ/ was realised [ð] were not identical: specifically, in syllable onset in the initial syllable of function words /θ/ was written <þ> (since it was syllable initial) but seems to have been realised [ð] (since function words were usually unstressed). Moreover, if we look at neighbouring related languages, we do not see the same patterns. In Old Swedish and Old Danish, the rules governing the voicing of /θ/ seem to have been the same as in Old Norwegian and yet <þ> (later <th>) is generally used in all positions. In Old English, from which the <þ ð> orthemes had been inherited, the rules governing fricative voicing were very similar and yet <þ ð> were used largely interchangeably; early Middle English, again with a similar system of predictable voicing, had an orthography more like that of Old East Nordic, favouring <þ> in all positions. Thus we can see that, in spite of the distinct orthographies, there is no real reason to think that [θ ð] were distinct phonemes in Old Norwegian.

Given that we have a single phoneme /θ/ that undergoes what is schematically the same change, shifting from a fricative to a stop, regardless of voicing, it is reasonable to ask: do we really have two sound changes here or only one? It is perfectly possible to imagine that a single change in which /θ/ lost a [+continuant] feature might have progressed blind to position, stress and predictable voicing, causing /θ/ to merge with /t/ or /d/. Occam's Razor suggests we should prefer an account with a single change rather than two structurally similar changes which occurred independently, encouraging us to take this possibility seriously. Yet it is also possible to imagine that two quite separate changes took place, one which affected only the voiceless allophone in stressed onset and caused it to merge with /t/ and one which affected only the voiced allophone in other positions and caused it to merge with /d/; in principle these could have occurred in either order and would have left a phoneme /θ/ or /ð/ with relatively restricted distribution in the period between the two changes. It is possible also to imagine an intermediate scenario, in which there was a single structural change affecting the phoneme in its entirety, but in which voicing (or the same factors by which voicing was predictable) was a conditioning factor, so that [ð] > /d/ lagged or led [θ] > /t/ by a detectable margin.[23] Finally, we might imagine scenarios in which there were two separate changes in some kind of causal relationship: the alternation implied by the first change in progress might have represented an analogical model for the innovation of the second; or the unbalanced phonological system resulting from the first change going to completion might have been a factor in the innovation of the second.

The proposal here is that these scenarios can be distinguished by looking at the evidence of timing and spatial patterning. If the stopping of [θ] and [ð] were truly a single, unconditioned structural change then there should be no significant differences between their timings and the courses by which they diffused through the country – the only differences we would see would be those small enough to be the result of random noise in the record. If the two represented a single sound change with phonetic conditioning that distinguished the voiced and voiceless allophones, or if the changes were separate but causally linked, then we would still expect them to have broadly similar spatial patterning but we would find that their timing was different but overlapping. Finally, if they were truly independent sound changes, then a much wider range of findings would be possible: they might have taken place at quite different times, with

---

[23] Another scenario which would be indistinguishable from this in the written record is that the stopping of /θ/ might have progressed as a single change without any phonetic conditioning, but that there might have been differences in the speed with which scribes adapted the orthography: <ð> might have felt to have been a better or worse ortheme for /d/ than <þ> for /t/, creating a lag for one change in the record but not the other. However, given that there is no particularly obvious reason this should have been the case and that it would be impossible to distinguish it from a real, phonetic conditioning effect anyway, it will not be explored further.

little overlap, and with completely different points of origin and spatial patterning.

5.2.1. Timing

Firstly, kernel smoothing in time alone was used to explore the relative timing of the two changes. Figure 29 shows the kernel smoothed estimates for the different orthographic variants of the voiceless dental fricative and Figure 30 shows the estimates for the different orthographic variants of the voiced dental fricative. Figure 31 gives the estimates for <t> excluding <th> for the voiceless dental fricative and for the decline of <ð> for the voiced dental fricative (that is, one minus the rate for <ð>), the two most relevant orthographic changes to signal the phonological changes we are interested in. As can be seen from the figures, for the voiceless dental fricative we see a sharp and steady rise in <t> from the beginning of the fifteenth century which is close to completion by 1500, whilst <th> shows less definitive patterning over time. For the voiced dental fricative, the earliest data in the corpus reveals that <d> was already replacing <ð> in the final decades of the thirteenthth century, a change which was close to completion by 1400, although later changes in the use of <dh> and <th> in the same contexts complicate this picture.

Figure 31, directly comparing the two orthographic changes most diagnostic for the sound change, paints a very clear picture. These data suggest that the two changes are almost completely separated in time, with the tail end of [ð] > /d/ overlapping only slightly with the beginning of [θ] > /t/. The year that the

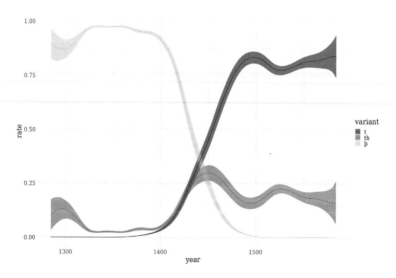

Figure 29. Kernel smoothed estimates of rates of orthemes for /θ/ [θ] [Colour figure can be viewed at wileyonlinelibrary.com]

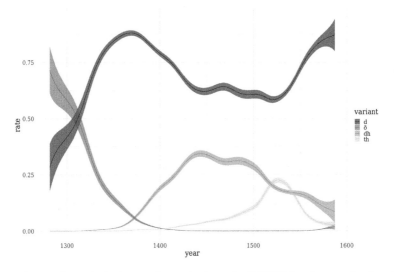

Figure 30. Kernel smoothed estimates of rates of orthemes for /θ/ [ð] [Colour figure can be viewed at
wileyonlinelibrary.com]

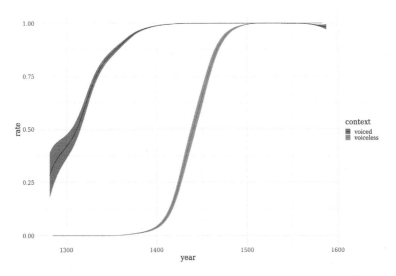

Figure 31. Kernel smoothed estimates of rates of the loss of the distinctive orthemes <þ ð> for /θ/ by
voicing [Colour figure can be viewed at wileyonlinelibrary.com]

replacement of <þ> by <t> first passes 1 per cent is 1379, and at this point <ð> >
<d> is already at 96 per cent. Clearly we cannot think of these as a single,
unconditioned change, and this degree of separation makes it a stretch even to
imagine them a unified change with phonetic conditioning.

Nevertheless, it is possible to conceive of ways in which these two changes could be causally related in spite of this wide temporal separation. It seems likely that a 'defective' phoneme /θ/ with a quite restricted distribution would be more vulnerable to being lost, and the presence of even infrequent variation between another fricative and stop might provide the analogical model to generate a new sound change with the same pattern. If we were to find clear relationships between the spatial distributions of these two changes, that could provide evidence for such an account.

5.2.2. Spatial distribution

The spatial distributions of the changes can offer further evidence for what relationship we should posit between them. A single, unified sound change, with or without conditioning, might be expected to have followed a single identifiable pathway of diffusion through the country regardless of phonological context, whereas two completely distinct changes could have unrelated spatial distributions.

It is harder to make unequivocal predictions about the spatial distributions of two distinct changes in some kind of causal relationship with one another. If the innovation of the stopping of the voiceless dental fricative was partly prompted by variation between [ð] and [d] providing a model for new variation between [θ] and [t], we might expect [θ] > /t/ to first occur and spread from one of the relic areas where [ð d] variation survived longest. On the other hand, if the innovation of the stopping of the voiceless dental fricative was made more likely by the fact that it had become a phoneme with a highly restricted distribution (occurring only in the onset of stress syllables), we might predict that the innovation would take place somewhere where the loss of [ð] had progressed furthest or started earliest. The fact that these two hypotheses entail precisely contrary predictions demonstrates the difficulty in teasing out the idea of more complex causal relationships between the changes.

With these various possibilities in mind, Figures 32–34 show kernel smoothed estimates for the two changes at various points in time. Figure 32 shows the progression of <ð> > <d> from 1270 (the earliest point we can make any meaningful estimations, given the available data) to 1390 (when the change is largely complete). Figure 33 shows the progression of <þ> > <t> from 1400 to 1490. Finally, Figure 34 shows a direct comparison of the extents of the two changes in 1380, around the beginning of the period when change affecting the voiceless fricative.

From Figure 32, we can see that the stopping of the voiced dental fricative seems to have spread outwards from south eastern Norway. In 1270 we see stark dialectal differentiation, with charters from Østlandet, even as far inland as upper Gudbrandsdalen, already showing <d> at rates of 70 per cent and over whilst the west and north lag behind; at this early point Stavanger seems to be most conservative, with rates of <d> still below 50 per cent. Over the course of the

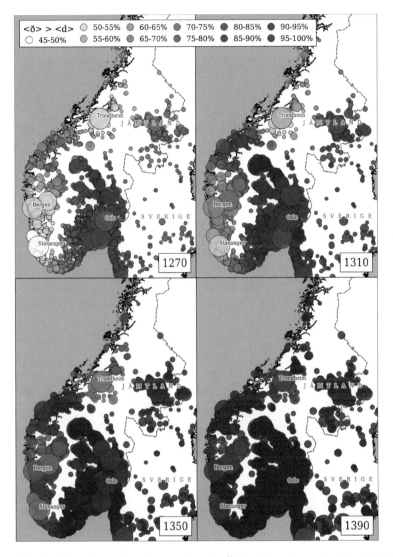

Figure 32. Spatial kernel smoothed estimates of loss of <ð> for /θ/ in voiced contexts for 1270-1400
[Colour figure can be viewed at wileyonlinelibrary.com]

change it appears to spread around the south coast as well as diffusing through Gudbrandsdalen and Romsdalen into the northerly half of the west coast. At many points these differences appear to be greater than the 30 per cent (i.e. twice the 15 per cent maximum margin of error for these kernel smooths) implying that the differences are statistically significant. This is confirmed if we examine Figure 35, which shows the individual estimates and margins of error for the cities of Oslo, Bergen, Stavanger and Trondheim.

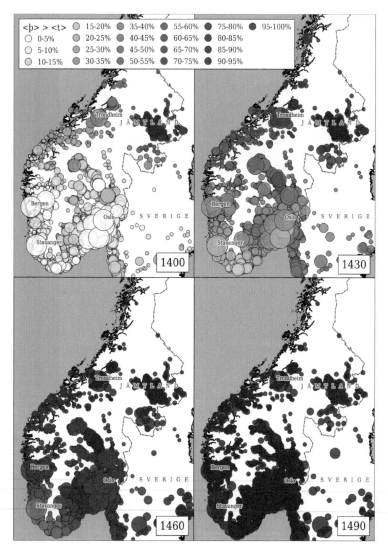

Figure 33. Spatial kernel smoothed estimates of loss of <þ> for /θ/ in voiceless contexts for 1400-1490 [Colour figure can be viewed at wileyonlinelibrary.com]

Although Oslo is far from the most innovative location in the south east, it leads the change compared with the other major cities by an amount greater than the 95 per cent confidence margins of error.

From Figure 33 we can see that the diffusion of the stopping of the voiceless dental fricative followed a very different pathway indeed. The most innovative localities are in the north east of the area for which we have enough data,

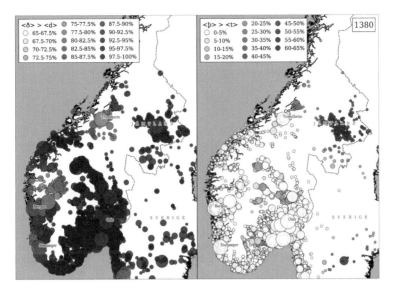

Figure 34. Spatial kernel smoothed estimates comparing the loss of <ð þ> for /θ/ in voiced and voiceless contexts in 1380 [Colour figure can be viewed at wileyonlinelibrary.com]

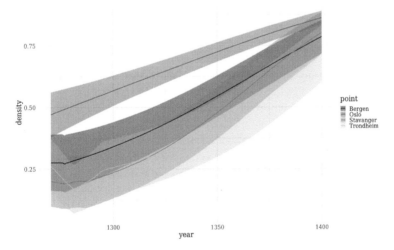

Figure 35. Spatial kernel smoothed estimates of the loss of <ð> for /θ/ in voiced contexts for Bergen, Oslo, Stavanger and Trondheim [Colour figure can be viewed at wileyonlinelibrary.com]

Trøndelag and Jämtland. Over the fifteenth century we see a relatively straightforward pattern in which the change diffuses southwards and westwards, leaving Stavanger, Rogaland and Agder as the most conservative region. Again, we can confirm that these differences are greater than the margins of error by examining Figure 36, which shows the exact degree of change with error

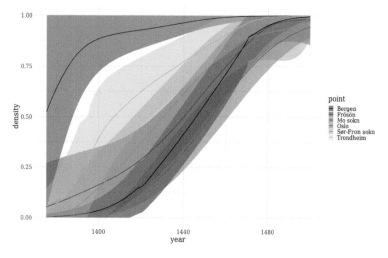

Figure 36. Spatial kernel smoothed estimates of the loss of <þ> for /θ/ in voiceless contexts for Bergen, Frösön, Mo i Telemark, Oslo, Sør-Fron and Trondheim [Colour figure can be viewed at wileyonlinelibrary.com]

margins for Trondheim, Frösön in Jämtland, Oslo, Bergen, Sør-Fron in Gudbrandsdalen, and Mo i Telemark. Frösön leads all other localities by a substantial margin most of the time; Trondheim is also generally ahead, enough so that it is outside the error margins at least for Oslo and Bergen.

These completely different pathways of diffusion seem to put a nail in the coffin of the idea that [ð] > /d/ and [θ] > /t/ could in any sense be a *unified* change. It was already a stretch to imagine that phonetic conditioning could be so strong for a single change that there would be a gap of a century between its completion in different contexts; it seems impossible to imagine that a such a conditioned change would also have completely different prevalence in different dialects according to phonological context. This is confirmed if we examine Figure 34, comparing the two changes in 1380. We can see that the two changes really only co-existed at all in a limited number of dialects: in most localities, [ð] > /d/ had probably already gone to completion when /θ/ > /t/ began.

The exception, which is relevant for considering the possibility that the two changes had some causal relationship, is Jämtland and Trøndelag. Trøndelag is relatively conservative for the voiced fricative in 1380, with almost a quarter of tokens still written <ð> in areas south of Trondheim and in the city itself; at the same time, Jämtland and rural Trøndelag are the most innovative areas for the loss of the voiceless fricative. This raises the possibility that variation between [ð] and [d] provided a relevant model for the innovation of remaining /θ/ > /t/, with a point of innovation somewhere in Jämtland or Trøndelag. However, this is a relatively weak argument that we should not put much weight on. The conservative areas for the voiced fricative and innovative areas for the voiceless fricative do not match perfectly; if this hypothesised relationship were correct, we might expect Trondheim itself to be more innovative for /θ/ > /t/. Our data for Jämtland is quite problematic, with a real dearth of charters from the first half of the fourteenth century; as a result, we should be more cautious of estimates for this area in this time frame, where estimates might be skewed by the disproportionate weight of later charters. Finally, the involvement of Jämtland at a time when Jämtland was gradually moving from the Norwegian to Swedish sphere of influence (and accordingly from West to East Nordic written norms) raises the question of the role of contact with Swedish – and our corpus does not allow us to explore this in more detail.

Thus evidence from timing and spatial distributions, both illuminated with kernel smoothing, has allowed us to determine definitively that we should regard the stopping of [θ] and [ð] as fully independent changes, in spite of their structural similarity. We have also come up against the boundaries of what we can say from these data, however: a causal relationship between the two changes seems unlikely, but is impossible to reject from this evidence alone.

5.3. *The loss of 1pl active -um*

The second case study I will examine here is the loss of the 1pl active ending -um. This is a substantially more complex change than the loss of the dental fricatives just discussed; the background to this change and the dataset gathered to explore it is detailed under section 4.3.3. The relevant facts for this investigation are that, in principle, we have several surface changes, given schematically in Table 30. The 1pl ending *-um* loses its coda consonant to create an ending *-u*. There is very good reason to believe that this was neither an instance of sound change nor an analogical change within the paradigm of person-number agreement suffixes, but the product of a reanalysis of the word boundary between the suffix and subject pronoun in sequences VERB-*um vér* and VERB-*um vit*. In the preterite this would have created a merger between the 1pl

Table 30. Changes affecting verb person-number agreement suffixes in later Middle Norwegian excluding the 2nd person

		I			II			III			IV
present	sg.	-ir/-ar/-r	→	sg.	-ir/-ar/-r	→	sg.	-ær/-r	→	pres.	-er/-r
	1pl	-um		1pl	-u		1/3pl	-æ			
	3pl	-a		3pl	-a						
preterite	sg.	-i/-a/-Ø		sg.	-i/-a/-Ø		sg.	-æ/-Ø		pret.	-e/-Ø
	1pl	-um		1/3pl	-u		1/3pl	-æ			
	3pl	-u									

and 3pl endings, since the 3pl was already *-u*, but in the present these two should have remained distinct as *-u* and *-a* respectively. In practice, though, changes in the orthography for unstressed vowels in the same period renders this distinction very difficult to trace: the main thing we see in the record is a direct replacement of *-um* by *-e/-æ*.[24] For this reason, here I will not attempt to distinguish among the unstressed vowels, and instead consider the change from 1pl *-Vm* to 1/3pl *-V*.

Putting aside the issue of the unstressed vowels and differences between the present and preterite, an implication of this account is that the nature of the change from *-Vm* to *-V* was different depending on the relative positions of the subject pronoun and the verb. In the sequence VERB-SUBJECT, the loss of the final consonant reflects a reanalysis which introduced a new 1pl ending to the paradigm; in the sequence SUBJECT-VERB and all word orders in which other elements intercede between the two elements we must instead posit an analogical change, either spreading this new 1pl *-V* ending to verbs in other syntactic contexts, or (in the case of the preterite) directly merging the 1pl and 3pl endings.

A further factor to consider is that the simplification of the plural agreement paradigm also occurred elsewhere in Nordic and may have taken place earlier in Danish than in Norwegian (Skautrup 1968: 273). We can be confident that the reanalysis in VERB-SUBJECT contexts must be internal to Norwegian since it generated the *m-* pronouns which do not occur in Swedish or Danish, but the analogical changes which resulted in *-V* endings in other syntactic contexts could in principle be the result of contact with East Nordic varieties where the paradigm was already levelled.

Thus in the remainder of this chapter I will try to use timing and spatial evidence, as illuminated using the kernel smoothing method, to explore both of these questions: can we confirm that there are two distinct changes from 1pl *-Vm* to *-V*, one in the sequence VERB-SUBJECT and one elsewhere? And, assuming that these two changes can be distinguished, can we find any evidence to bear on the question of whether the analogical change in non-pre-subject positions was an internal development or the result of contact?

5.3.1. Timing

Figure 37 shows kernel smoothed estimates for the rates of the four morphologically distinct endings over time. We can see that the broad pattern is that *-Vm* and *-V* are in a relatively stable relationship from the beginning of the

---

[24] In at least some dialects, these changes were not purely orthographic. In fifteenth century manuscripts we find <æ> replacing both <u o> for unstressed /U/ and <a> for unstressed /a/ at a greater rate than it replaces <i e> for unstressed /I/; this suggests that unstressed /U a/ may have merged, leaving a two-vowel system in unstressed positions /æ I/. Certainly in Modern Norwegian dialects we find a variety of different unstressed vowel systems which do not necessarily maintain all the distinctions of Old Norwegian. However, the fifteenth century is also the period of increasing literary and orthographic influence from Middle Danish where all unstressed vowels had already merged as schwa, written <e>. As a result, it is impossible to know how for sure to interpret changes in unstressed vowel orthographies in Middle Norwegian in this period.

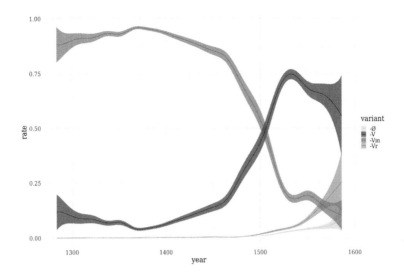

Figure 37. Kernel smoothed estimates of rates of 1pl endings [Colour figure can be viewed at wileyonlinelibrary.com]

period covered until the mid-fifteenth century, with -*V* representing around 10 per cent of tokens; -*V* begins to rise in frequency, replacing -*Vm* over the course of the fifteenth and the first quarter of the sixteenth centuries, before the historically singular endings -*Vr* and -*Ø* begin to rise and replace both -*Vm* and -*V* towards the end of the period covered.

Starting with our first research question, if we should regard this as two distinct changes reflecting different mechanisms of change, a reanalysis in the sequence VERB-SUBJECT and an analogical change in other syntactic contexts, we might expect the two to have quite different timing. The reanalysis is likely to have happened earlier than the analogical change, since the availability of the reanalysed -*V* 1pl ending in the paradigm may have played a part in the analogy. Beyond absolute timing, as independent changes the two might have qualitatively different time courses or quite different rates of change. To test these predictions, we can separate the data into two datasets according to word order and explore them separately. Figure 38 shows the kernel smoothed estimates for the morphological variants in VERB-SUBJECT order and Figure 39 shows the same for SUBJECT-VERB order. Figure 40 directly compares just the loss of -*Vm* (i.e. 1 minus the estimate for -*Vm*) for the two datasets.

As we can see from these figures, there are some striking differences between the change in the two contexts. The main rise in frequency for both occurs between around 1425 and 1525, but, as predicted, this change begins earlier in VERB-SUBJECT position and this context leads until the very end of the period covered; the difference between the two is well outside the margins of error until

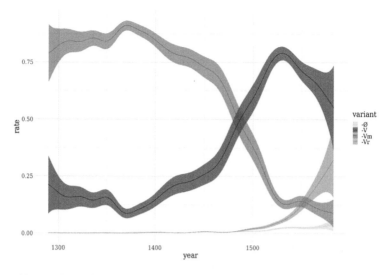

Figure 38. Kernel smoothed estimates of rates of 1pl endings in VERB-SUBJECT order [Colour figure can be viewed at wileyonlinelibrary.com]

the volume of data drops off in the late sixteenth century. This observation alone might still allow an analysis that this is a single, unified change with stochastic conditioning by word order. However, the more striking difference between the two is that for the whole of the fourteenth century -*V* represents a minority variant in VERB-SUBJECT position but is basically not found in SUBJECT-VERB position; again, the difference between the two is always far greater than the margins of error. This is entirely in keeping with the two-changes account sketched out above, in which a reanalysis took place in VERB-SUBJECT position at an earlier point in time and an analogical change spreading the -*V* ending to other syntactic contexts occurred only later. The very similar timing of the drop in frequency of the -*Vm* ending in both contexts in the fifteenth and sixteenth centuries suggests that the two changes are intertwined: we should perhaps think of the analogical change operating both to spread the -*Vm* ending to new contexts and to increase its frequency in its original context. Nevertheless, the idea that these are two separate changes is very well supported.

We noted above that there is also reason to think that the change might have operated differently in the present and preterite paradigms: in the preterite, the reanalysis would have had the effect of merging the 1pl and 3pl, whereas in the present the two would still have had distinct vowels. This might mean that further change would have been disfavoured in the preterite due to merger avoidance. With this in mind, it is worth applying the same method to this change in the different tenses. Figure 41 shows the kernel smoothed estimates for the morphological

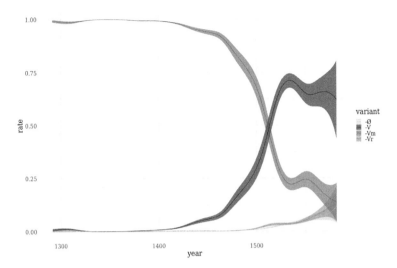

Figure 39. Kernel smoothed estimates of rates of 1pl endings in SUBJECT-VERB order [Colour figure can be viewed at wileyonlinelibrary.com]

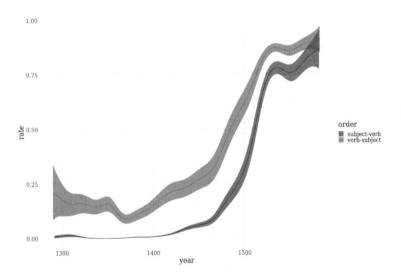

Figure 40. Kernel smoothed estimates of loss of 1pl -*Vm* by word order [Colour figure can be viewed at wileyonlinelibrary.com]

variants on present tense verbs and Figure 42 shows the same for preterite verbs. Figure 43 directly compares the loss of -*Vm* for these two datasets.

Again, we do find some substantial differences between the two contexts. As expected, the present leads the change by a substantial margin compared with the preterite: -*V* becomes the majority variant in the present around 1487,

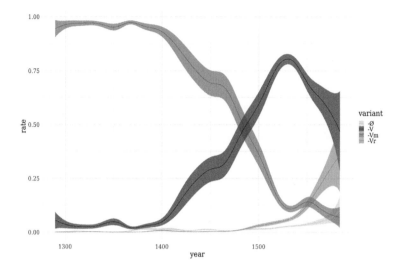

Figure 41. Kernel smoothed estimates of rates of 1pl endings on present verbs [Colour figure can be viewed at wileyonlinelibrary.com]

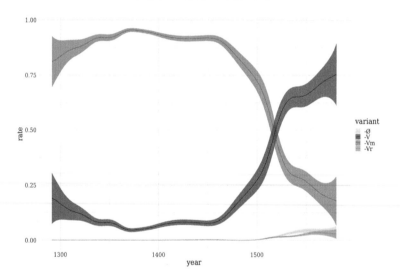

Figure 42. Kernel smoothed estimates of rates of 1pl endings on preterite verbs [Colour figure can be viewed at wileyonlinelibrary.com]

approximately three decades earlier than in the preterite. Nevertheless, this is entirely consistent with an account in which we are looking at a single change with conditioning by tense. In both contexts we see an overall similar trajectory, with a long period of near-stability in the fourteenth century followed by steady

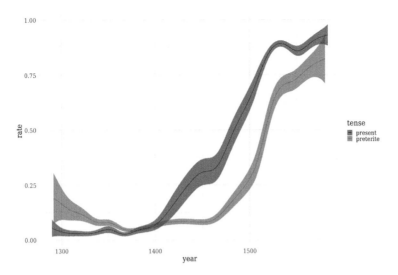

Figure 43. Kernel smoothed estimates of loss of 1pl *-Vm* by tense [Colour figure can be viewed at wileyonlinelibrary.com]

change in the fifteenth and sixteenth centuries.[25] It is also reasonable to expect that there might be interaction between the two sets of contexts, especially given the highly formulaic nature of the data (discussed in section 4.3.3.2.4). To check this possibility, we can examine the effect of tense and word order together: Figure 44 compares the loss of *-Vm* by tense in VERB-SUBJECT position (orange, yellow) with SUBJECT-VERB position (black, purple).

This reveals some clear interactions:

- putting aside fluctuations for verbs in VERB-SUBJECT order in the first quarter of the fourteenth century when the dataset is small, the patterns in the fourteenth century broadly seem to show effects of order and not any effects of tense;
- there is little or no difference in the course of the change between present and preterite tense in VERB-SUBJECT order;
- present-tense verbs in SUBJECT-VERB order pattern with verbs in VERB-SUBJECT order for the sharp rise in frequency in the fifteenth century; and
- preterite verbs in SUBJECT-VERB order lag far behind the other three contexts.

[25] We do see that the later change, by which the distinctive plural endings were lost and historically singular endings came to be used in all person-number combinations, shows quite different patterning in the different tenses. However, this is at the edge of the period for which we have reliable data and outside the scope of this investigation.

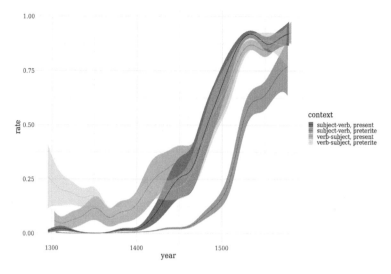

Figure 44. Kernel smoothed estimates of loss of 1pl -*Vm* by word order and tense [Colour figure can be viewed at wileyonlinelibrary.com]

The obvious interpretation is that the reanalysis took place at some point before the beginning of the period covered by the corpus and (as expected) was not affected by tense. Analogical change began to drive up the rates of the levelled ending in the syntactic context it already existed in the early fifteenth century, and at the same time to spread it to other contexts. This spreading of levelling was disfavoured in the preterite, where it would create a merger between the 1pl and 3pl, creating a conditioning effect so that the change was slowest (but concurrent) in that context. In short, this supports the hypothesis that we have two distinct changes: a reanalysis in VERB-SUBJECT order, with no other conditioning, and a later analogical change in SUBJECT-VERB order with synchronic conditioning by tense.

5.3.2. Spatial distribution

Spatial evidence could support or undermine the account we have developed so far and can also bear on our second research question: whether the later analogical levelling should be thought of as an internal development or the result of contact with Middle Danish. If we are really dealing with two independent changes in the two syntactic contexts, that allows for the possibility that they might have had quite different points of innovation and have diffused through the country by different routes. If the analogical change resulted from contact with Danish, we might expect to find it most and earliest in localities where mobility and contact was concentrated: urban areas, and particularly the coastal cities. There is also a possibility that contact with Middle Low German played a

role in these changes, since, as noted above (section 4.3.3.1.4), it had lost person
distinctions in the plural and had a similar pattern of plural ending reduction
before personal pronouns (Lasch 1974: 224–7). This might lead us to expect the
change to start in localities with more Low German contact: Bergen, Oslo and
Tønsberg.

Figure 45 shows the kernel smoothed estimates for the change in VERB-SUBJECT
order and Figure 46 shows the same for SUBJECT-VERB order. Figure 47 compares

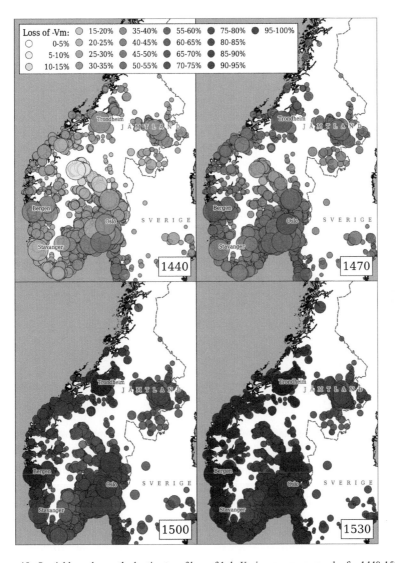

Figure 45. Spatial kernel smoothed estimates of loss of 1pl -*Vm* in VERB-SUBJECT order for 1440-1530
[Colour figure can be viewed at wileyonlinelibrary.com]

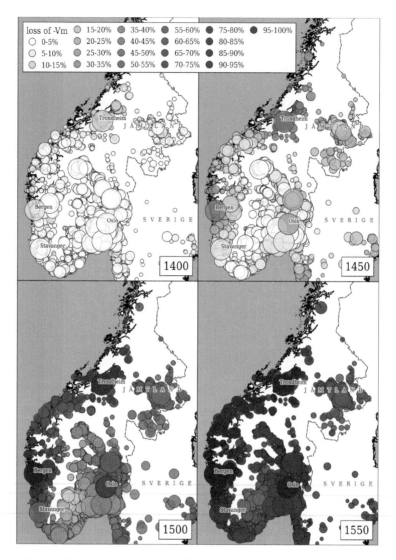

Figure 46. Spatial kernel smoothed estimates of loss of 1pl -*Vm* in SUBJECT-VERB order for 1400-1550
[Colour figure can be viewed at wileyonlinelibrary.com]

estimates for the two word orders in 1370. Two main observations should be made from these visualisations. Both broadly show cities leading the change, but this pattern is far from identical across the two datasets. In VERB-SUBJECT order it is a weak effect and is found almost exclusively with Bergen and Trondheim; if Oslo is ever an innovative centre for this change, it is only marginally and inconsistently. By contrast, in SUBJECT-VERB order this is a much stronger pattern that also extends to Oslo (and perhaps very weakly Hamar).

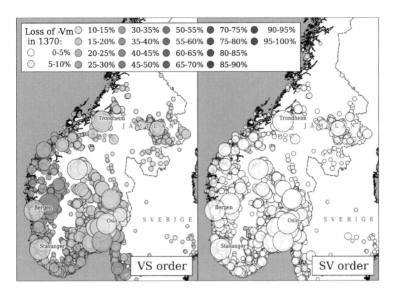

Figure 47. Spatial kernel smoothed estimates of loss of 1pl -*Vm* by word order for 1370 [Colour figure can be viewed at wileyonlinelibrary.com]

It is also worth exploring what these visualisations tell us about the consistent low rates of -*V* in VERB-SUBJECT order we found throughout the fourteenth century. In principle, such a pattern might reflect dialectal differentiation. A change could have gone to completion in VERB-SUBJECT order in a minority of dialects but not spread elsewhere; in such a case, the stable low frequency of the innovation in the corpus as a whole would reflect the stable position of an isogloss. Examining our spatial kernel smoothed estimates, however, reveals that this is clearly not the case for 1pl -*V* in VERB-SUBJECT order. Instead, we see a variant which has successfully diffused throughout the language area but remains at a consistently low frequency everywhere.

On the other hand, we see that the change in SUBJECT-VERB order behaves quite differently. It begins as a low frequency variant exclusive to the cities – its likely places of innovation, at least in a Norwegian context – but immediately diffuses outwards and becomes more frequent. There is no equivalent period as a stable minority variant. Instead, as can be seen from the map for 1370, the initial stable period shows close to no evidence for this change anywhere.

These observations are largely confirmed when we examine the estimates and error margins in the figures comparing specific localities. For the change in VERB-SUBJECT order, the observation that the cities lead the change is largely too subtle to confirm with confidence. Comparing Bergen, Oslo and Hamar to the smaller settlements of Vossevangen, Haug and Hobøl, and Fåberg respectively (Figures 48–50), we find that the difference is only greater than the margin of error in the case of Hamar and Fåberg; indeed, the estimated value for Oslo is not even the highest in its vicinity in the early part of the change. By contrast, for the

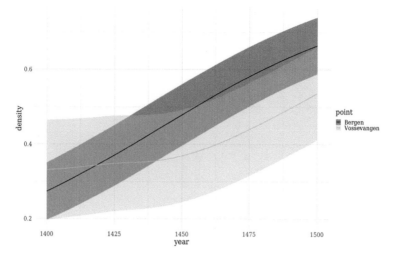

Figure 48. Spatial kernel smoothed estimates of the rise of 1pl -*V* in VERB-SUBJECT order for Bergen and Vossevangen [Colour figure can be viewed at wileyonlinelibrary.com]

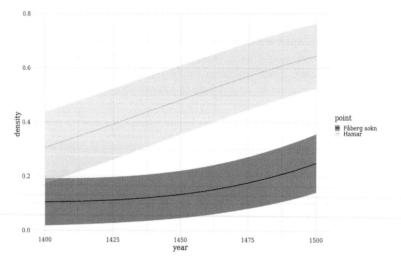

Figure 49. Spatial kernel smoothed estimates of the rise of 1pl -*V* in VERB-SUBJECT order for Hamar and Fåberg [Colour figure can be viewed at wileyonlinelibrary.com]

change in SUBJECT-VERB order, all three cities tested lead the smaller localities in their vicinities by wide margin (Figures 51–53). The difference is smallest in the case of Oslo and its neighbours (Figure 53) but is nonetheless well outside the margins of error over a long period. We can also see that the differences between the cities is statistically significant for the change in SUBJECT-VERB order (Figure 54), with the cities of Bergen and Trondheim leading compared with Stavanger, Oslo and Hamar.

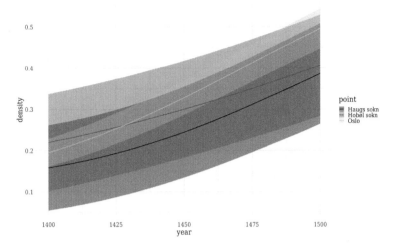

Figure 50. Spatial kernel smoothed estimates of the rise of 1pl -*V* in VERB-SUBJECT order for Oslo, Haug and Hobøl [Colour figure can be viewed at wileyonlinelibrary.com]

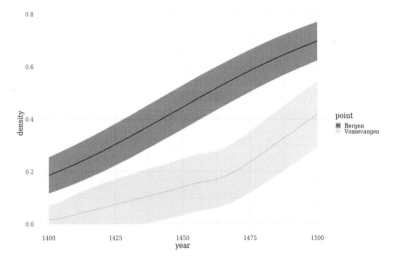

Figure 51. Spatial kernel smoothed estimates of the rise of 1pl -*V* in SUBJECT-VERB order for Bergen and Vossevangen [Colour figure can be viewed at wileyonlinelibrary.com]

These spatial findings speak very clearly to our research questions. The convincingly different spatial distributions and pathways of diffusion for the change in the two different syntactic contexts confirm the idea that we are dealing with two fundamentally different changes. The reanalysis of the sequence -*um vér* (and similar) to -*u mér* had diffused all across the country (in keeping with the observation that the *m*- pronouns are found in Middle Norwegian documents from all regions) without 1pl -*V* agreement becoming the

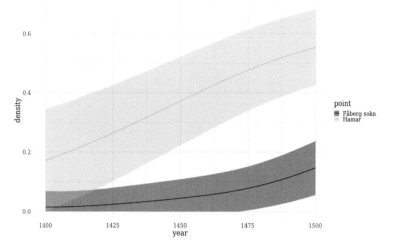

Figure 52. Spatial kernel smoothed estimates of the rise of 1pl -*V* in SUBJECT-VERB order for Hamar and Fåberg [Colour figure can be viewed at wileyonlinelibrary.com]

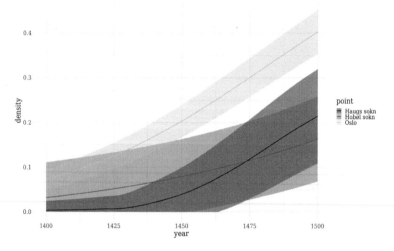

Figure 53. Spatial kernel smoothed estimates of the rise of 1pl -*V* in SUBJECT-VERB order for Oslo, Haug and Hobøl [Colour figure can be viewed at wileyonlinelibrary.com]

majority variant in any dialect. The analogical levelling by which the -*V* ending then expanded from a minority variant in a restricted context to entirely replace -*Vm* was a continuous, rapid process of diffusion outwards from the cities.

Not only do the differences between these two patterns suggest that we are dealing with two distinct changes, they also fit the idea that the reanalysis was an internal development and the analogy external. The conditions for the reanalysis in VERB-SUBJECT order were equally present in all dialects and so it is unsurprising

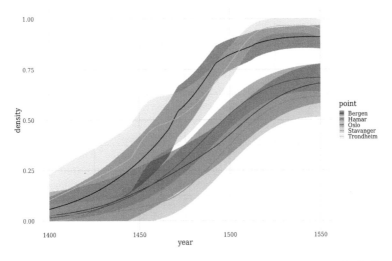

Figure 54. Spatial kernel smoothed estimates of the rise of 1pl -*V* in SUBJECT-VERB order for Bergen, Hamar, Oslo, Stavanger and Trondheim [Colour figure can be viewed at wileyonlinelibrary.com]

to find that -*V* represented a minority form everywhere in this context. Its later rise in frequency did not reflect a major structural change in any dialect since it was already grammatical everywhere. The rise of -*V* in SUBJECT-VERB order, on the other hand, was a more significant structural change, and the conditions for that change seem to have been more present in the cities – particularly Bergen and Trondheim. An obvious factor that distinguishes the cities from rural areas is that their populations were more diverse and more mobile, and so they tended to be the sites of language and dialect contact. Thus this spatial evidence is consistent with the suggestion that contact with Danish played a role in the levelling to -*V*.

5.4. *The Constant Rate Effect*

There is already a widely-used diagnostic used to explore the independence of observed changes suspected to be related: the Constant Rate Effect (CRE). It is worth checking to see whether the conclusions we have come to here, in part from spatial evidence, are in line with this approach, which works only with evidence of timing and speed.

The Constant Rate Hypothesis (CRH; Kroch 1989) states that multiple surface changes which reflect the same underlying change in the grammar[26] will display the same rate of change, even if they are time-shifted relative to one another. In the

[26] The Constant Rate Hypothesis is most often invoked in the context of theories of syntax which postulate a set number of discrete parameters, so that the type of relationship between two surface changes in question is that they are the product of the same change of parameter setting. However, as part of a competition of grammars framework, the idea is basically theory-neutral (Pintzuk 2003: 511; Kauhanen & Walkden 2018: 484) and has been used in many other contexts.

usual implementation, a logistic curve is fitted to each of the different changes.[27] If the slopes of these curves fall within a reasonable confidence interval of each other they can be assumed to be the same, and the change can instead be modelled by fitting logistic curves for every context whose intercepts are allowed to vary but whose slopes are kept constant. Kauhanen & Walkden (2018) try to address two problems with this approach: firstly that it allows for changes separated by arbitrarily large time intervals to be seen as the same; and secondly that it leaves the observed pattern under theorised – why should the slope be kept constant but intercept be allowed to vary across contexts? They present a more fully worked-out model which incorporates different contextual biases which moderate the trajectory of the change, referred to as the 'bias model' in contrast to the traditional 'logistic model'. The bias model has a number of interesting behaviours that go beyond the scope of the discussion here; the curves it predicts are not necessarily logistic (especially at extreme parameter values), so slopes and intercepts are not directly comparable with those of the logistic model. We can, however, use it to test for Constant Rate Effects by comparing normalised errors to those from the logistic model and an unconstrained logistic model (i.e. allowing slopes to vary). The bias model also has the particular advantage that it predicts a maximum time separation between the occurrence of a change in different contexts ('Theorem 4', Kauhanen & Walkden 2018: 501):

$$\Delta(s) = \frac{2}{|s|} \log\left(\frac{1}{\sqrt{2}-1}\right) \approx 1.76 \frac{1}{|s|},$$

where s is the slope of the approximated logistic curve. If a change is separated by more than $\Delta(s)$ across contexts, this suggests it is not a unified change.

The R package 'cre' (Kauhanen 2020) was used to fit the bias and logistic models to the datasets. For the dental fricatives, we see a substantially higher normalised error for the bias model (0.0780) than for logistic (0.0245) or unconstrained logistic (0.0246) models. This is due to the fact that the change in the two contexts is separated by a larger gap than the bias model predicts to be possible. With fitted $s = 0.0499$ for the bias model, $\Delta(s) = 35.41$, yet we can see from the logistic model that the changes in the two contexts are separated by as long as 122.30 years ($k_{(voiced,voiceless)} = (1317.52, 1439.82)$). This is entirely in line with our conclusions above: there is no sign of a Constant Rate Effect and so evidence from timing alone suggests that these are independent changes; the spatial evidence confirms this.

For the loss of 1pl -Vm on the other hand, the largest gap across our four contexts is *not* greater than the maximum predicted by the model ($\Delta(s) = 53.64$, whereas the largest time separation is only 42.40 years) and the normalised error for all three models is almost identical. This might seem to suggest that we *do* see a Constant

---

[27] The choice of a logistic curve was originally a relatively arbitrary decision, but it has since been shown that reasonable models of language acquisition and change might well be expected to generate something like logistic curves across a population (Niyogi & Berwick 1997; Yang 2002; Ingason, Legate & Yang 2013; cited in Kauhanen & Walkden 2018: 486).

Rate Effect here and so is compatible with the analysis that this is a single change across the four contexts, contradicting the arguments made above. I would make two comments on this. Firstly, the normalised error for all three models is very high (0.1067–0.1079) compared with the models fitted to the dental fricatives data (0.0245–0.0780) and *much* higher than for the datasets reported in Kauhanen & Walkden (2018) (although this may be a product of their analysing extremely small datasets). It seems likely that this is a result of the fact that, in VERB-SUBJECT contexts, the change does not progress from 0 to 100 per cent here but has a stable initial period at closer to 10 per cent; as a result, these simply are not very good models of this change. This is confirmed by modelling the data for the two word orders separately: we find that the bias model has a normalised error almost twice as high for the VERB-SUBJECT than SUBJECT-VERB data (0.1361 and 0.0781 respectively). One possible interpretation of this, then, is that we have evidence for a CRE and so a single underlying change across tenses, but given the nature of the dataset we do not have a good model to test for a CRE across word orders. This is thus potentially consistent with the arguments we have made from spatial distributions. Alternatively, if we accept the suggestion of a CRE across word orders as well, then we have a conflict between the evidence of timing alone and the evidence of geography. This is not necessarily a problem: the CRH predicts that two instances of the same change in different contexts should progress at the same speed, but there is nothing to say that two changes (especially changes which interact) might not happen to progress at the same speed in spite of being independent. In this case, adding evidence from spatial distribution gives us a further tool to differentiate between coincidence and real relatedness.

5.5. *Conclusions*

In this chapter I have explored how evidence for spatial distributions and timing can bear on our analyses of individual changes in the history of a language, and so the kernel smoothing methods presented in this book can be useful tools for the analysis of individual linguistic variables. Chronological and spatial evidence has confirmed what is suggested by the orthography for dental fricatives in Middle Norwegian, that, perhaps contrary to our a priori expectations from the phonology, there were two completely independent changes stopping [ð] and [θ]. More subtly, similar evidence has demonstrated that we should regard the shift from -*Vm* to -*V* endings in 1pl verbs as two distinct changes in two different syntactic contexts, and that one of these changes was probably an internal development where the other may well have been the result of contact.

In these cases, with the possible exception of distinguishing internal and external change in the verbal agreement paradigm, we could generally have arrived at our conclusions from the evidence of timing alone. Geography has played only a supporting role. In the next chapter we will examine a research question with a larger scope, testing hypotheses about the history of the language writ large, and in this context spatial evidence will come much more to the fore.

6

The Trudgill conjecture

6.1. *Introduction*

In the previous chapter we explored two sets of changes, phonological developments affecting the dental fricatives and morphological developments in 1pl subject-verb agreement, to exemplify how the methods presented in this book can help answer research questions about individual instances of language change. In this chapter, I expand my scope to a question which deals with trends in the history of a language as a whole: that of the effect on Norwegian of intensive contact with Low German. The effects on the development of the Continental Nordic languages of contact with Middle Low German has been the subject of much study over the past one and a half centuries, and many questions remain to be answered about how this contact operated, which changes should be ascribed to it, and why it had such extensive consequences. Here, however, I will restrict myself to testing one particular theory which has been applied to this case concerning the systematic effects of different types of contact.

Much work on language contact documents the ways in which specific features have been transferred between languages, or attempts to infer the situations in which classes of features can or cannot be transferred. There is a rich vein of scholarship exploring the ways in which sociolinguistic factors – the context in which contact takes place – moderate these possibilities for change, with seminal works such as Weinreich (1953), Thomason & Kaufman (1988) and Winford (2005). Recent decades have seen a strain of scholarship which goes one step further, going beyond the categorisation of feature transfer and trying to identify an abstract typology of *all* kinds of change which can result from contact or lack of contact. An important synthesis and a unified account is found in the work of Peter Trudgill (2011), whose thesis is presented most completely in his book *Sociolinguistic Typology*. Trudgill's proposal, hereafter the 'Trudgill conjecture', is that different social contexts favour different types of language change independently of the existing features of the particular languages involved. Abrupt, high-intensity contact between communities speaking different varieties, involving high levels of adult language acquisition, results in 'structural simplification' (Trudgill 2011: 33–4) and disfavours spontaneous 'structural complexification' (Trudgill 2011: 67). Long term, low-intensity contact involving child acquisition and balanced bilingualism leads to structural complexification as marked structures spread between varieties via 'additive borrowing' (Trudgill 2011: 34). Finally, long-term isolation favours 'spontaneous complexification' (Trudgill 2011: 62). Similar ideas have occurred in the literature over a long period of time (note, for example, Werner 1984: 64) and in recent years a similar programme of research has been pursued by several scholars, significantly Dahl (2001) and McWhorter (2011). However, Trudgill's theory is especially complete and, since his work cites the history of Nordic as evidence (Trudgill 2011: 6–8, 19–20, 56–8, 118–19), it offers a clear series of hypotheses to explore in the context of Middle Norwegian. In this chapter, I will first give a more detailed account of Trudgill's ideas and how they apply to the broad sweep of Norwegian language history in the late Middle Ages, before going on to show how the methods explored in this book can offer us new evidence to test the theory.

6.2. *Theoretical background*

6.2.1. *Trudgill, Dahl and McWhorter*

Before discussing the Trudgill conjecture and related theories in detail, an aside on the notions of 'complex' and 'simple' languages is required. Linguists have long shied away from the labels 'simple' and 'complex', a legacy of the harmful ends these concepts had been put to in racist analyses of language variation and typology in colonial contexts. Indeed, it has been normal to go so far as to assert the idea that all languages are equally complex as fact (e.g. Hockett 1958: 180–1; Cipollone et al. 1998: 2; and Akmajian & Demers 2010: 9). In recent years more serious work has been done to challenge this assertion, explore possible definitions of language complexity and map out resulting typologies (Romaine 1992; Maddieson 2006, 2007; Shosted 2006; Kusters 2008; Parkvall 2008), but the area remains contentious and definitions hard to operationalise. This issue is given close attention by Trudgill and by the other scholars who propose related theories. For our purposes, however, the precise definition is not important. What is relevant is that there exists a set of features which might colloquially be referred to as 'complex' and which are defined as those which present a particular difficulty to adult second language learners. These include large phoneme inventories with distinctions relying on subtle acoustic cues; highly permissive phonotactics with very large number numbers of possible syllable types as a result; large morphological paradigms with the mandatory expression of many morphosyn-tactic or semantic features; agreement systems which necessitate a great deal of redundant expression; and suppletive and irregular paradigms which require a learner to memorise a great deal of unpredictable morphological material. If we accept the idea that such features might cluster in certain historical-sociolinguistic contexts and might have a common aetiology, ideas at the core of Trudgill's theory, then we need not worry about whether 'complex' is the best choice of term.[28]

We turn now to the three hypotheses which make up the Trudgill conjecture. First, and most relevant for this chapter, is the hypothesis that high-intensity contact involving adult language acquisition results in structural simplification. The proposal here is that the poor language-learning abilities of adults compared with children results in imperfect learning of the complex features of a language,

---

[28] For a more detailed discussion and literature review of the notion of linguistic complexity, see Blaxter (2017b: 14–20).

and these imperfectly learnt features are then passed on to future generations (Trudgill 2001: 372–3); Dahl uses the term 'abnormal transmission' to describe this imperfect acquisition (Dahl 2001: 375). A basic objection to this idea is that, typically, L2 features do not spread within a language community to L1 speakers. However, Trudgill argues that such transfer does occur when a sufficiently high proportion of the population are L2 speakers (Trudgill 2011: 57–8). This idea has some history in the literature; Thomason & Kaufman (1988: 47) suggest that 'if the shifting group is so large numerically that the [target language] is not fully available to all its members, then imperfect learning is a probability, and the learners' errors are more likely to spread throughout the TL speech community'. Some researchers maintain that there is a simple, direct relationship between the proportion of L2 speakers and the rate of simplification, rather than some specific threshold; for example Bentz & Winter (2012: 4) write that 'the more L2 speakers exist in a population, the more case should be eroded'..

An important element of this hypothesis is that languages *only* undergo systematic simplification through such abnormal transmission. McWhorter (2011: 1–2) writes that 'the difference in complexity between languages' grammars is determined significantly by the extent to which second-language acquisition has played a role in their histories [...]. Under this analysis, languages that have not maintained this [high] level have always been interrupted in their normal accumulation of complexity'. If this condition is absent, then the other two components of the Trudgill conjecture (for which see further below) will instead result in increase of complexity.

Similar ideas in a different tradition are put forward by Meisel (2011), who reviews studies of successive and simultaneous acquisition of multiple varieties by children and finds that parameter mis-setting and imperfect acquisition occur only when acquisition begins after around four years of age. This highlights the fact that when we talk about L2-acquisition and abnormal transmission, we need not necessarily be speaking of acquisition by adults, merely by speakers past the critical period for the acquisition of the features in question, substantially expanding the range of historical scenarios which might produce the necessary social conditions at scale.

The second component of the Trudgill conjecture is the hypothesis that long-term contact involving child language acquisition and balanced bilingualism results in structural complexification through 'additive borrowing', the spread of complex features between varieties (Trudgill 2011: 26–32, 34). Of the three hypotheses, that make up the conjecture this is perhaps the least controversial. The phenomenon of Sprachbünde in regions of long-term stable contact has long been observed, where cross-linguistically marked features can be shared and so accrue across a series of neighbouring languages over time. Comparison with genetically related languages outside the Sprachbund which lack the marked features can then demonstrate that this increased complexity is a consequence of contact. Perhaps the best-known example is the Baltic Sprachbund, in which languages like Aromanian and Bulgarian are characterised by shared features such as a postposed definite article which are not found in related languages outside the Sprachbund like Italian and Slovene.

Note that both of the hypotheses discussed thus far concern the results of contact. In the theory, what determines whether language contact results in complexificatory or simplificatory change is not the degree of contact but the sociolinguistic conditions in which change takes place, with child bilingualism resulting in complexification and adult second language learning resulting in simplification. The third and final component of the Trudgill conjecture concerns what happens in the absence of contact. This hypothesis states that long-term isolation also results in complexification, in this case the spontaneous development of complex features (Trudgill 2011: 62–5). 'Traditional dialects' often provide examples of this tendency. The speech communities of such varieties, which represent highly connected and stable social networks with little external contact, both generate new linguistic complexity and are especially able to maintain complexity (Trudgill 2011: 66, 71–3). Trudgill argues this on the basis of data from World Englishes (cited from Kortmann & Szmrecsanyi 2009), concluding that it does indeed make sense 'to look for cases of spontaneous, non-additive complexification in relatively isolated, low-contact, nonstandard-ized varieties of modern European languages [. . .] in comparison with their respective standard and urban varieties' (Trudgill 2011: 71).

The mechanism behind spontaneous complexification is a slight point of contention between researchers in this paradigm. McWhorter sees it as the result of drift (in the biological sense: random change that usually fails to completely erase evidence of previous random change, thus adding to the complexity of the whole) (McWhorter 2001: 126, 131; Dahl 2001: 375; Wurzel 2001: 381). Some complexity is lost in the normal course of language change, but new complexity is developed, with the result that high complexity is maintained overall (McWhorter 2011: 2). Dahl (2001: 375) argues instead that the central process involved is grammaticalisation, and that this is a definable process leading directly to complexification. Wurzel (2001: 381), also arguing against McWhorter, suggests that the parallel with biological evolution is mistaken: languages are not natural systems in the proper sense but are changed by more directly intentioned action than natural systems. Trudgill (2011: 93–4, 96) argues in less abstract and general terms, suggesting that accruing phonological changes and grammaticalisations without intervening morphological simplification operate to increase opacity and irregularity, but also that small, isolated communities may favour typologically marked phonological changes which make increase of morphological irregularity particularly likely Trudgill (2011: 98–9). Trudgill also suggests that the development of new morphosyntactic categories and greater syntagmatic redundancy requires many generations of uninterrupted native-speaker acquisition, and thus is more likely in isolated speech communities (Trudgill 2011: 107–8, 114–15). Schreier (2009), while problematising a simplistic notion of isolated vs. high-contact communities, suggests that isolated speech communities can act as historical linguistic 'laboratories', rapidly incubating contact effects or internally motivated developments.

Unlike simplification through intensive L2-contact, it is not argued that spontaneous complexification occurs only in low-contact varieties (nor, indeed, that it inevitably occurs in low-contact varieties): what is proposed here is a tendency rather than a rule (Trudgill 2011: 72). Nevertheless, an important corollary to the idea that simplificatory change is typical only of languages undergoing high levels of adult second-language acquisition and that other normal social contexts tend to encourage complexification is that languages which have undergone significant simplification must be seen as historically atypical (Trudgill 2011: 187–8). McWhorter (2011: 1) writes: '[t]he normal state of language is highly complex, to an extent that seems extreme to speakers of languages like English', maintaining 'extensive marking of fine shades of semantic and syntactic distinctions, plus rampant allomorphy and irregularity'. This provides an explanation for certain instances of 'drift' in the sense used by Sapir, the slow convergence towards analyticity, strict word order and phonological simplicity in Modern European and Modern Arabic varieties compared with their predecessors (McWhorter 2011: 4–5).

6.2.2. Other proposals regarding relationships between complexity and social factors

Various researchers have worked on similar proposals concerning the relationship between social factors and language change or linguistic structures. It is useful for our purposes to survey some of these to identify contrasting hypotheses that we might see confirmed or contradicted in the Middle Norwegian data.

Wray & Grace (2007) discuss a relationship between esoteric and exoteric communication and linguistic structures. The esoteric-exoteric distinction, based on Thurston (1987; 1988; 1994; cited in Wray & Grace 2007: 549), characterises contrasting contexts for communication and so contrasting properties of that communication. Esoteric communication takes place 'in the domain of familiars [. . .] who share a culture and environment, general knowledge of the community and its activities, and who have a unified identity. Within such a context, communication [. . .] need not be explicit with regard to generally known facts' (Wray & Grace 2007: 550). Cultural homogeneity and strength of in-group identity tend to perpetuate group and membership continuity. 'The language, consequently, will be defined by features that are acquirable by babies, with rather few influences from adult learners'. (Wray & Grace 2007: 550).

By contrast, exoteric communication is outward-facing, involving people with whom some amount of sociocultural context is not shared. Accordingly, less information may remain implicit and linguistic structures must be more transparently compositional and more easily learnable by adults (Wray & Grace 2007: 551). Wray & Grace focus particularly on compositionality, suggesting that 'certain kinds of social and cultural pressures can counteract the psycholinguistic pressures [towards unnecessary explicitness], requiring and sustaining an augmented compositional engagement [...]. Where literacy or certain kinds of oral tradition form part of the culture, these may even provide a platform for reducing the natural potency of the psycholinguistic pressures, by providing additional means for handling complex linguistic constructions' (Wray & Grace 2007: 553). However, they caution that 'there is not a direct correlation between any single social, geographical or cultural factor and Language Type' (Wray & Grace 2007: 555).

Also working with the exoteric-esoteric distinction, Lupyan & Dale (2010) propose a continuum between the exoteric niche, where languages are likely to serve as media of communication between strangers and speakers are more likely to be non-natives or have learned from non-natives, and the esoteric niche, where they are not (Lupyan & Dale 2010: 2–3). It is these 'niches', rather than modes of communication, that then correlate with language complexity. Lupyan & Dale undertake statistical analysis using language data from WALS and Ethnologue. In addition to linguistic features, they look at speaker population, geographic spread of languages, number of neighbouring varieties and geographic co-ordinates of languages. They demonstrate that compared to languages in the esoteric niche (those with low population, low geographic spread and low number of linguistic neighbours), languages in the exoteric niche are more likely to share a laundry list of grammatical features (Lupyan & Dale 2010: 3). Relevant for our purposes, such languages are more likely:

- to be isolating;
- to lack case marking (and, where they have case marking, distinguish fewer cases and have more syncretism);
- to mark fewer categories on the verb;
- to have less verb-argument agreement (and, where they have it, tend to have more syncretism); and
- to lack morphological expression of pronominal subjects.

They argue that this is because complex morphological paradigms present problems for adult learners; by contrast, such paradigms are typified by overspecification which facilitates child language acquisition by providing more cues for categories. Thus, where languages are often learned by adults, they will tend to change towards morphological simplicity, whereas where languages are learned only by children, they will acquire and maintain overspecification (Lupyan & Dale 2010: 7).

Bentz & Winter (2012) test Lupyan & Dale's hypothesis by examining the relationship between the number of L2-speakers a language has and morphological case. Taking into account effects of language family and area, they find a significant negative correlation between number of cases and ratio of L2 to L1 speakers (and no effect of total number of L1 speakers) (Bentz & Winter 2012: 60–1). Bentz & Winter (2013) present a more detailed test of the same hypothesis, framed also as a test of Trudgill and McWhorter's proposals (2013: 2–3). Examining the presence of case marking using mixed-effects regression, they demonstrate that languages with a greater proportion of second language speakers are more likely to have no case marking; examining number of cases distinguished they demonstrate that languages with a greater proportion of second language speakers exhibit fewer cases (Bentz & Winter 2013: 8–10). They show that these results are robust when the effects of clustering within language families and areas are taken into account (Bentz & Winter 2013: 9–11). A significant problem with this kind of research is that it assumes uncritically that there is a strong relationship between the number of L2 speakers a language *currently* has and the number of L2 speakers it had at earlier points in history when the features in question developed. Finally, Bentz & Christiansen (2013) argue that development from Proto-Indo-European to Proto Germanic and Proto Romance and thence to the modern Germanic and Romance languages, involving loss of case, is related to exoteric communication and the influence of adult learners.

As can be seen, the approaches of Lupyan & Dale (2010) and Wray & Grace (2007) making use of the esoteric-exoteric distinction have much in common with Trudgill, McWhorter and Dahl. Both emphasise the relevance of differences between the language-learning abilities of the child and those of the adult for identifying how different social contexts condition language change and linguistic structures. However, there are differences in detail. Wray & Grace's focus on transparent compositionality as the main property associated with exoteric communication coincides only partially with definitions of simplicity discussed by Trudgill, McWhorter and Dahl. Lupyan & Dale fail to propose convincing unifying generalisations concerning the long list of linguistic features they associate with the exoteric niche, and these features are still only a subset of those covered by definitions of 'simplicity' used by Trudgill and others. Most importantly, the three sociolinguistic contexts relevant for the Trudgill conjecture – intensive contact involving adult L2 acquisition, stable contact involving child bilingualism and long-term isolation – do not map directly onto the exoteric and esoteric niches. Descriptions of the exoteric niche imply that dialect contact has the same importance as language contact: what is relevant is contact between people of different communities with different cultural and communicative norms in a very general sense, rather than something strictly defined in linguistic terms. It is easy to imagine situations with long-term, stable contact involving child bilingualism but also mobility and diversity where the Trudgill conjecture might predict additive borrowing but Wray & Grace or Lupyan & Dale would predict loss of complexity. Equally, situations with a great deal of dialect contact but little language contact clearly represent the exoteric niche, but sit in ambiguous place in Trudgill's theory.

A related family of proposals within sociolinguistic typology suggests relationships between linguistic features and population sizes. Within this paradigm, writers including Hay & Bauer (2007) and Atkinson (2011) have proposed a positive correlation between population size and phoneme inventory. Atkinson (2011: 346) suggests that smaller populations of speakers favour reduction in 'phoneme diversity'. However, this study, which also aims to connect phoneme diversity with distance from Africa, has come under significant criticism. Maddieson et al. (2011: 268) criticise the 'phoneme diversity' measure which Atkinson uses, pointing out that Atkinson ignores phonemic differences in vowel length, nasalisation and phonation, differences in phonotactics, and in the number of underlying contrasts. They state that '[t]he phoneme diversity variable Atkinson calculates is thus neither a true measure of the size of the phoneme inventory, nor of the phonotactic possibilities in the languages concerned, but a hybrid touching on some aspects of these properties' (Maddieson et al. 2011: 268). Many different effects, including strong patterns related to climate, are found in the data, and these may subsume the effects central to the paper's argument (Maddieson et al. 2011: 274–277). The claim regarding population size is criticised for several reasons: the population size data is problematic for historical reasons; the statistical evidence seems to be equivocal; and it is unclear what real-world mechanism could cause smaller populations to favour lower 'phoneme diversity' (Maddieson et al. 2011: 271–4). Both Dahl and Atkinson find that there is a stronger correlation with total speakers of a language family than of a language (Dahl 2011: 173); this seems to undermine the idea that the number of speakers of the language is the relevant factor.

Hay & Bauer (2007: 390–1) find significant positive correlations between population size and inventories of monophthongs, obstruents, sonorants, consonants and phonemes. They use regression analysis and bootstrap validation to show the result for total phoneme inventory size is robust when language family is taken into account (Hay & Bauer 2007: 391–5). In explanation they suggest that speakers of languages with larger total populations tend to be exposed to greater linguistic variation. Citing experimental work showing that phonemic distinctions are acquired more quickly and robustly through exposure to greater variation in realisation, they suggest that larger populations are thus capable of maintaining a greater number of finer distinctions (Hay & Bauer 2007: 397–8). However, Hay & Bauer's work too has been criticised on methodological grounds. Moran et al. (2012: 881–2) point out that they may not have taken sufficient steps to account for the non-independence of data points in their sample, especially regarding the effects of language families and the overrepresentation of Indo-European. Indeed, they conclude that Hay & Bauer's 'sample was simply too small and too biased to yield reliable results' (Moran et al. 2012: 883) regardless of the statistical tools. In a larger and somewhat less biased sample, Moran et al. (2012: 883–8) demonstrate that the effects identified by Hay & Bauer (2007) are too weak and vary too much between language families and genera to be generalised to 'language writ large'.

Furthermore, the findings of Atkinson (2011) and Hay & Bauer (2007) have been challenged by Donohue & Nichols (2011: 62), who find no significant correlation between phoneme inventory size and population size in a relatively large sample. This finding is based on data which treats speech communities 'as though they still had the sizes reported for them in the early to mid-twentieth century' (Donohue & Nichols 2011: 161) by examining census figures for ethnic groups instead of languages. Although they do find differences in phoneme inventory sizes between large areal groupings of languages on a rough scale from east to west, they argue that this is an artefact of the economic and political histories of different continents over the historical period (Donohue & Nichols 2011: 162–9). Dahl also criticises their approach, pointing out that some unidentified factor in the 'long-term socio-cultural history of the community speaking the language' is probably the factor affecting both population size and linguistic features (Dahl 2011: 172).

It is also worth noting that Atkinson and Hay & Bauer's proposal is diametrically opposed to much of the other work discussed here (since large phoneme inventories constitute a form of complexity and larger groups are more subject to contact). It seems particularly counter-intuitive in light of the negative correlation identified between population size and morphosyntactic complexity identified by other typologists (e.g. Sinnemäki 2009; Nichols 2009 cited in Dahl 2011: 173, Lupyan & Dale 2010 discussed above), although Dahl accepts these as real differences between sociolinguistic typological patterns in phonology and morphosyntax (Dahl 2011: 176). Thus, although these proposal regarding relationships between numbers of speakers and complex or simple features might offer contrasting predictions we could test across Middle Scandinavian, they are too internally contradictory and too much criticised for this to be an avenue worth pursuing here.

The final proposal I will consider here comes from variationist sociolinguistics. In his influential 2007 paper, Labov discusses the two distinct means by which linguistic structures can be passed between individuals: transmission, in which structures are acquired natively by children from adult speakers within their own speech community, and diffusion, in which structures are transferred between speech communities. Transmission is associated with the Stammbaum model of language change, which assumes an unbroken chain of native acquisition by children from parents (Labov 2007: 345–6). It is characterised by its high degree of faithfulness and accuracy: children are very good at replicating the variety of their elders in great detail (Labov 2007: 346). Nevertheless, change does occur through transmission. Such change, resulting from the interaction of social, cognitive and physiological factors, is typically change from below, and once initiated is characterised by incrementation, by which native learners advance age-structured patterns beyond the inherited model (Labov 2007: 346).

By contrast, diffusion is associated with the Wave model of language change[29] by which features are spread between adult speakers and between speech

---

[29] In the sense that the Wave model involves both diffusion (where features are transmitted rapidly through space between adults) and transmission (where features are transmitted more gradually through space by children) whereas the Stammbaum model is focused on transmission.

communities (Labov 2007: 347). It is more limited than transmission: 'structural features' are relatively unlikely to diffuse, excepting the loss of structural categories (mergers) (Labov 1969: 348–9, 370). Where variables with complicated systematic conditioning are spread by diffusion, their structural constraints tend to lose detail and become less categorical (Labov 2007: 353–9). This has been demonstrated for several cases, including: the conditioning of (a)-tensing spreading from New York City English (Labov 2007: 353–63); the conditioning of quotative be like spreading from American English to English English and New Zealand English (Buchstaller & D'Arcy 2009: 308–22); and the conditioning of quotative be like spreading from younger to older speakers within the same communities (Tagliamonte & D'Arcy 2007: 205–13). Labov (2007: 349–50) argues that these tendencies result from the impoverished language-learning abilities of adults compared with children. This is not the only possibility: Britain (2009: 140) argues that loss of structural detail in borrowed features can instead be the result of interaction with structures in the native system.[30]

Labov's proposal offers some important similarities and points of comparison with the Trudgill conjecture. Both proposals suggest that the differential language-learning abilities of adults and children lead to simplifications wherever adults are especially implicated in language change. However, where Trudgill's focus is on the extreme case in which non-native speakers constitute a large proportion of the population, Labov's account suggests a path by which structural simplification may be favoured in much less extreme scenarios, when, through geolinguistic diffusion, adult speakers encounter new features or structures in their native variety. In this way, although Labov's account builds on the same basic mechanism as the Trudgill conjecture, it makes predictions more in line with approaches in the esoteric-exoteric communication paradigm: it would predict simplification not only in cases of intensive language contact but in a wider range of social contexts with high mobility and a high frequency of dialect contact.

6.2.3. The case of Nordic

Trudgill (2011: 6–7) and McWhorter (2011: 2) cite the development of the Continental and Insular Nordic languages as a clear example of pressure exerted by adult learners in language change. This echoes earlier work: O'Neil (1978) suggests that intensity of contact (in Scandinavia of Middle Nordic with Middle Low German, in England of Old English with Old Norse) is a good predictor of morphological simplification within Germanic; Werner (1984: 219) compares the Insular Nordic languages with other Germanic languages to make a similar point. The Continental Nordic languages (Norwegian, Swedish and Danish) have reduced their phoneme inventories and ranges of possible syllable structures,

---

[30] Similarly, Buchstaller & D'Arcy (2009: 317–21) note that losses and changes in distributional detail when an innovation diffuses are conditioned by the details of the recipient system.

largely lost case, in many varieties reduced from a three- to a two-gender system, lost subject-verb agreement and reduced the flexibility in possible word orders. By contrast, the Insular Nordic languages (Faroese and Icelandic) have retained the case and verbal inflection of Old Norse with relatively little change. Trudgill (2011a: 3–5) argues these changes in Continental Nordic were due to contact with Middle Low German through the Hanseatic League. This contact fits the scenario predicted to cause structural simplification, as a third to half the population of the Scandinavian Hanseatic cities are believed to have been transient, Low German-speaking migrants (Trudgill 2011: 57–8, see section 3.2.2 for extensive discussion).

Norwegian represents a particularly simple test case for this theory. Unlike Denmark and Sweden, contact with Hansa was concentrated in a small number of sites in Norway: the Hansa kontor in Bergen and smaller presences in Oslo and Tønsberg (see section 3.2.2.2). Thus, if the hypothesis is correct, we would expect that simplifying changes were innovated in and spread from these three towns. Some broad observations concerning the modern Continental Nordic languages and their dialects seem to fit this explanation. Trudgill (2011: 6–7) notes that the most innovative Norwegian dialects are found in 'well-trafficked' South-Western coastal areas, whereas the most conservative are found in remote inland valleys. This fits a picture in which simplificatory changes spread outwards from centres of Hansa contact, particularly Bergen. Hansa merchants represented a somewhat lower proportion of the population of Bergen than of the Swedish and Danish Hansa cities (Trudgill 2011: 58; cf. section 3.2.2 above), matching the status of Norwegian as the most conservative of the Continental Nordic languages. However, examining the distribution of features among Norwegian dialects is not the best way to test Trudgill's proposal for Norwegian. A more direct approach is to examine structurally simplifying changes which spread throughout Norwegian and identify the role of the contact centres in their innovation and diffusion. For this it is necessary to explore the Middle Norwegian sources with our statistical methods for illuminating spatial and temporal patterns.

6.3. *Predictions*

On the basis of the Trudgill conjecture, we can predict that structurally simplifying changes were more likely to be innovated and more likely to spread throughout the population in Bergen, where there was a high proportion of L2 speakers, than other cities. Thus we expect to find that many of the simplifying changes which characterise the history of Norwegian started life in Bergen. Secondarily, we might expect to see structurally simplifying changes emanating from the smaller centres of Hansa presence, Tønsberg and Oslo.

Other possibilities should also be considered. There was more of the type of intensive contact between Nordic and Low German on which Trudgill focuses in Sweden and Denmark than in Norway. Thus we should acknowledge the possibility that some or all of the simplificatory changes in question were innovated in East Nordic and entered Norwegian through dialect contact. Since the cities – particularly the larger cities which represented centres of ecclesiastical and administrative power – were the sites of a great deal of mobility and dialect contact, this scenario might also result in simplificatory changes spreading outwards from the cities, making it hard to distinguish from a direct confirmation of the Trudgill conjecture operating in Norwegian. However, in this case we would expect direct points of contact with Swedish (Østfold, Bohuslän, Jämtland) and Danish (the south coast) to be equally innovative.

The esoteric-exoteric paradigm, with its broader definition of the sociolinguistic conditions which favour simplificatory change, offers accordingly broader predictions about where simplificatory change might have arisen. Travel was easier and more rapid by sea than inland, especially in mountainous regions, and communities in which fishing represented a major part of the economy would naturally travel more widely as part of everyday subsistence. As a result, we might see not only urban areas but all coastal areas as characterised by the 'exoteric niche', at least as compared with inland areas. If we were to find that simplificatory changes consistently arose around the coasts and never inland, this would seem to offer evidence for this explanatory framework. The writers who have worked in this paradigm have given narrower definitions of the features involved than Trudgill, so we might limit our investigation to morphological features when evaluating it.

These three scenarios could offer confirmatory evidence in favour of sociolinguistic-typological accounts of simplificatory change in Nordic. On the other hand, if we found that changes arose in many localities all across the language area, with no consistently recurring points of innovation and no strong tendency for urban areas to play a special role, this would undermine the idea that sociolinguistic conditions played an important role in determining the type of change which Norwegian underwent in the late Medieval period.

6.4. *Variables*

To make arguments about the broad, external history of the language we need evidence from multiple separate instances of language change: effectively, the three scenarios outlined above are hypotheses about tendencies across many changes over time. Many of the variables detailed in chapter 4 for which we have gathered data are simplificatory in Trudgill's terms and so can contribute evidence here. In the morphology, the changes in subject-verb agreement paradigms all constitute morphological levelling. In each case, the innovative systems have more syncretism or mark fewer categories than the systems they replaced, meaning that there are fewer distinct forms for learners to acquire. These changes are given schematically in Tables 31–34; note that in each, fewer cells are needed to describe the innovative system than the conservative system.

Some of the changes affecting the 1pl and 1du. pronouns can also be seen as structurally simplifying. The overall change to the morphological system of

Table 31. Loss of 1sg. agreement in the active voice in Old Norwegian

Conservative	
1sg.	-i/-a/-Ø
2/3sg.	-ir/-ar/-r

→

Innovative	
sg.	-ir/-ar/-r

Table 32. Loss of 1pl agreement in the active voice in Middle Norwegian

	Conservative	
present	1pl	-um
	3pl	-a
preterite	1pl	-um
	3pl	-u

→

Innovative	
1/3pl	-æ
1/3pl	-æ

Table 33. Loss of 1pl agreement in the middle voice in Middle Norwegian

Conservative	
sg., 2pl	-iz/-az/-z
1pl	-umz
3pl	-az

→

Innovative
-ez

Table 34. Loss of number agreement in the active voice in Middle Norwegian

	Conservative	
present	sg.	-ær/-r
	1/3pl	-æ
preterite	sg.	-æ/-Ø
	1/3pl	-æ

→

Innovative
-er/-r
-e/-Ø

which these form a part, by which the distinct category of the dual was lost altogether, clearly constitutes a loss of structural complexity. Whether each individual change should be seen as simplificatory depends on whether it effected this structural change. Whichever of the spread of *mit* into plural contexts, the spread of *mér* into dual contexts and the borrowing of *vi* (not marked for dual vs. plural because East Nordic had already lost this distinction) happened first in a given variety would be structurally simplificatory, while following changes would be structure neutral. For example, if a particular dialect first merged *mit-mér* into *mit* and only later replaced *mit* with borrowed *vi*, only the former change would be simplificatory, whereas if a dialect borrowed *vi* to replace both *mit* and *mér* at a point when the number distinction was still being maintained then this change *would* be simplificatory. It would be prejudging the data to assume one of these accounts before exploring the spatial distributions, so all three of these changes will be included in the analysis (see Tables 35–37).

Of the phonological changes, the two changes affecting the dental fricatives are also clearly simplificatory. Both of these are mergers and so result in smaller phoneme inventories. They also involve the loss of cross-linguistically marked sounds which may be harder for non-native speakers to acquire. The rise of svarabhakti vowels represents a somewhat more complex case. If our phonology is defined in terms of phonemes and phonotactic rules, then we have either the same number of elements after the change as we had before, or potentially more, if more restrictive phonotactics require more rules to describe. However, crucial from the point of view of L2 acquisition are the range of syllable types and the marked nature of the syllable types that are lost. The number of possible syllables is larger with the more permissive phonotactics of Old Norwegian than the more restrictive phonotactics of Middle Norwegian. The syllable types which were lost were those with coda clusters with rising sonority, primarily syllables ending in Cr, which are highly cross-linguistically marked and relatively difficult to produce for non-natives. Accordingly, this sound change too will be included in our analysis as a simplificatory change.

Finally, the loss of case in broad terms is the paradigm example of structural simplification. The loss of case in the history of Norwegian refers to many changes over a period stretching from Proto Germanic through to Modern Norwegian, and it is not automatically obvious that each individual change in the case system resulted in a loss of complexity. Nevertheless, I argue that the particular change for which we have data here, the loss of genitive objects of *millum*, can be considered simplificatory. Lexical case clearly presents more of a challenge to second language learners than does structural case, since it

Table 35. Merger of mit and mér into mér

Conservative		
1du.	mit	→
1pl	mér	

Innovative: mér

Table 36. Merger of mit and mér into mit

Conservative		
1du.	mit	→
1pl	mér	

Innovative: mit

Table 37. Replacement of mit and mér by *vi*

Conservative		
1du.	mit	→
1pl	mér	

Innovative: vi

necessitates the memorisation of arbitrary material. Most prepositions took accusative or dative objects in Old and Middle Norwegian, and so prepositions which took genitive objects represented both exceptions to the general rule of case governance for prepositions and a deviation from the structural functions of the genitive. If, instead of looking at the context of the loss of case as a whole, we examine the development of the genitive in particular, we see a change from an Old Norwegian genitive case with variable exponence and multiple functions to a single -s suffix with a single, predictable function in Modern Norwegian; this clearly represents a loss of structural complexity, and the loss of genitive objects of *millum* is a step in this process.

In total we have identified thirteen changes which can be seen as reducing structural complexity and so together represent a test for the Trudgill conjecture and related theories in the history of Norwegian. These changes are summarised in Table 38. In the following sections I will examine the spatial distribution of each change separately, asking whether it is consistent with the predictions outlined in section 6.3 above. The changes will be dealt with in roughly chronological order.

6.5. *Spatial distributions*

6.5.1. *Loss of 1sg agreement in the present active*

As a consequence of the fact that it is at the very earliest edge of the period covered by the corpus, the loss of a distinctive ending for the 1sg in the present

Table 38. Summary of structurally simplifying changes to be examined

Change	Domain	Midpoint
loss of 1sg. agreement on present tense verbs: $-V_{1SG} > -Vr_{1/3SG}$	morphology	1298
loss of the voiced dental fricative: [ð] > /d/	phonology	1312
rise of svarabhakti vowels: /Cr/ > /CVr/	phonology	1345
loss of the voiceless dental fricative: /θ/ > /t/	phonology	1440
merger of 1du. pronoun into 1pl pronoun: *mit* > *mér*	morphology	1457
merger of 1pl pronoun into 1du. pronoun: *mér* > *mit*	morphology	1464
replacement of 1pl pronoun with loanword: *mér* > *vi*	morphology	1464
loss of 1pl middle verbal agreement: $-Vmz_{1PL} > -Vz$	morphology	1467
loss of genitive objects of *millum*	morphosyntax	1471
replacement of 1du. pronoun with loanword: *mit* > *vi*	morphology	1476
loss of 1pl verbal agreement in VERB-SUBJECT order: $-Vm_{1PL} > -V_{PL}$	morphology	1485
loss of 1pl verbal agreement in SUBJECT-VERB order: $-Vm_{1PL} > -V_{PL}$	morphology	1510
loss of number agreement on present tense verbs: $-V_{PL} > -Vr_{PRS}$	morphology	1586

Notes: For changes in which the innovative variant did not pass 50 per cent at any point, the year with the highest rate is given. For changes where the midpoint would fall outside the period covered by the corpus, the date given is the year in which the estimation falls closest to 50 per cent for which we have a sufficient density of data, defined as one charter per year. In effect, this means that for the loss of number agreement on present tense verbs, the date is simply the end of the period covered by the corpus, and for the loss of 1sg. agreement on present tense verbs, the date is simple the beginning of the period covered by the corpus.

active is one of the least well-evidenced changes we explore here. Not only is the dataset very small as a whole, but the most interesting part of the change for the purposes of answering our research question is the early part where we have less data still. As a result, we must be cautious about making stronger claims than the evidence can support.

Figure 55 shows the kernel smoothed estimates for the change over time from the distinctive 1sg. endings -Ø/-i/-a to -r/-ir/-ar, syncretic with the 2/3sg. Note that the small size of the dataset results in very wide error margins before 1300 (these kernel smoothed estimates were calculated with a 10 year bandwidth). Figure 56 shows the spatial kernel smoothed estimates for the same change for the years 1275–1350. A much higher temporal bandwidth is needed in order to achieve separation between relevant points in space, and this has the effect of making the change appear much slower than in Figure 55.

Figure 56 shows a consistent pattern throughout the change: there are very large innovative areas centred on the cities of Oslo, Bergen and Trondheim, and there are conservative areas in Oppland (covering Valdres and lower Gudbrandsdalen) and on the south-west coast centred on Stavanger. This pattern by which the three leading regions do not obviously form a single connected region makes it difficult to infer where the change was innovated (if indeed it started at a single point). The fact that Oslo appears to be a little ahead of the other regions in the earliest estimates might seem to suggest that we should imagine a change starting in the south-east, perhaps in Oslo itself, and thence spreading to Bergen and Trondheim.

However, when we examine the estimates and error margins for individual locations, we find that we cannot be confident in any of these differences.

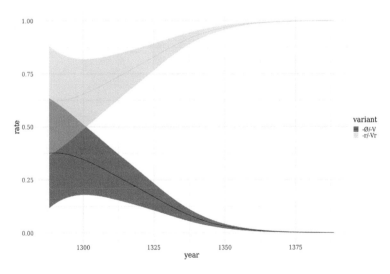

Figure 55. Kernel smoothed estimates of rates of morphological variants for the 1sg. present active
[Colour figure can be viewed at wileyonlinelibrary.com]

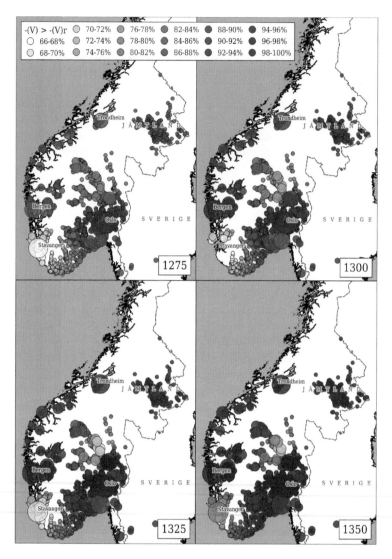

Figure 56. Spatial kernel smoothed estimates for the loss of the distinctive 1sg. present active ending for 1275–1350 [Colour figure can be viewed at wileyonlinelibrary.com]

Figure 57 shows the contrasts between the three major cities for the kernel smoothed estimates corresponding to Figure 56; it is clear that although Oslo is slightly ahead of the other two cities before the year 1300, this difference is always far smaller than the margins of error. Figure 58 instead contrasts kernel smoothed estimates for Bergen, Stavanger, Oslo and Gausdal in lower Gudbrandsdalen, four locations chosen as the largest possible contrasts implied

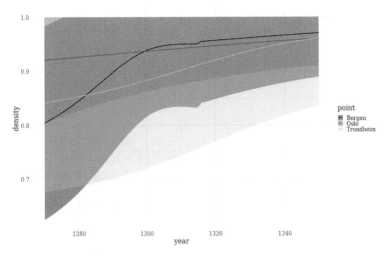

Figure 57. Spatial kernel smoothed estimates of the loss of the distinctive 1sg. present active ending for Bergen, Oslo and Trondheim [Colour figure can be viewed at wileyonlinelibrary.com]

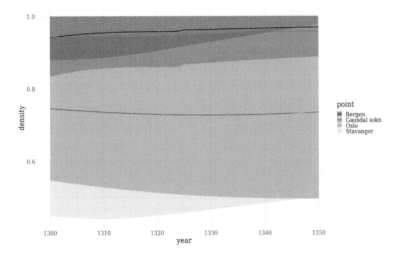

Figure 58. Spatial kernel smoothed estimates of the loss of the distinctive 1sg. present active ending for Bergen, Gausdal, Oslo and Stavanger [Colour figure can be viewed at wileyonlinelibrary.com]

by Figure 56, here calculated with a higher temporal bandwidth in order to allow comparison of smaller localities. Again we see that even the largest differences are well within the error margins.

This exploration of the loss of the 1sg. present active ending can teach us a useful lesson. An uncritical examination of the kernel smoothed estimates in Figure 56 might have led us to draw conclusions about how the evidence of this change relates to our research question (a change spreading from the cities, and perhaps specifically from the south-east, could certainly be in keeping with some of our hypotheses). However, the reality is that the dataset is too small to have confidence that the differences between localities we see are real, and not just the result of random noise.

6.5.2. Loss of the voiced dental fricative

The changes affecting the voiced dental fricative were explored in section 5.2 and we will not repeat that analysis here. Referring in particular to Figure 32, we can see that the change is already well underway at the earliest point in time for which we have enough data sufficiently well-distributed across the country to get an impression of spatial distribution. In principle, this makes identifying a point of innovation more difficult. However, the fact that the pattern we see at this early point is relatively simple makes our task easier. What we see in Figure 32 is a change spreading outwards from south-eastern Norway. Within Østlandet the most innovative areas are actually far inland: Oppland, and in particular the northern part of Gudbrandsdal stand out as leading localities. The difference between these localities and more southerly parts of Østlandet are well within the margins of error, however, so we should not take this as strong evidence that the change was innovated there. Rather, the evidence allows for the possibility that that the loss of the voiced dental fricative had its roots in Norway, anywhere within a region stretching from Bohuslän in the south-east to Vågå in the north-west.

In terms of relating this to the hypotheses, this very large area leaves open a lot of possibilities. Densely populated and highly trafficked Viken, including the urban areas of Oslo and Tønsberg, represents an area with much language and dialect contact that clearly fits in the exoteric niche. In particular, if we took Oslo or Tønsberg to be the point of innovation, this would be very in keeping with the Trudgill conjecture, since these represented the locus of the second major presence of Hansa merchants in Norway after Bergen, and therefore a major site of contact with Middle Low German. However, there is no evidence that the cities led this change: if this was innovated in Oslo, it spread so rapidly to the countryside that no gradient can now be detected in the record, and it did not preferentially spread from the cities of the south east to cities and towns elsewhere in the country.

The other possibility that this distribution leaves open is that this change spread from Swedish. Since Bohuslän and Østfold are innovative areas, it is perfectly plausible that what we see in Figure 32 is the legacy of a Swedish variant following a natural pathway of diffusion from southern Sweden northwards into Norway. However, the evidence from the history of Swedish is not straightforwardly consistent with this: the use of the ortheme <ð> fell out of use at an earlier point than in Norwegian sources, but the phoneme /ð/ may have remained until a much later point.

6.5.3. The rise of svarabhakti vowels

The next change among our datasets is the intrusion of svarabhakti vowels into coda /Cr/ clusters. Like the previous two, this change had already begun at the earliest time period for which we have data. However, unlike them, it is still only at the beginning of its period of steady increase at the turn of the fourteenth century and so we have somewhat better evidence for the crucial early stage.

Figure 59 shows kernel smoothed estimates for the different orthographic variants which occur in svarabhakti vowel contexts. In the Old Norwegian of the late thirteenth century we most commonly find no vowel written in these contexts, but a variety of vowels are beginning to appear; of these, <e> becomes by far the most common, so that by the end of the period covered by the corpus the vast majority of tokens have a svarabhakti vowel written <e>. For the remainder of the analysis we focus only on the presence or absence of the svarabhakti vowel rather than precisely which vowel ortheme is used (i.e. degree of change in subsequent figures is equivalent to the inverse of the zero variant in Figure 59).

Figure 60 shows the spatial kernel smoothed estimates for the rise of the svarabhakti vowel from 1270 to 1390. As with the loss of the voiced dental fricative discussed above, we see a change spreading out from Østlandet. A region stretching from Østfold to inner Telemark in the south and as far north as Lesja in upper Gudbrandsdalen is consistently innovative compared to the south and west coasts and to Trøndelag. We see svarabhakti vowels rising in frequency in all locations across the period covered, but the border of this region with relatively higher frequency also expands, so that we see the innovation spreading

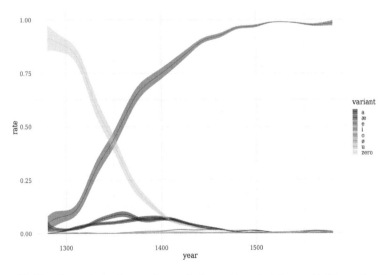

Figure 59. Kernel smoothed estimates of rates of orthographic variants in svarabhakti vowel contexts
[Colour figure can be viewed at wileyonlinelibrary.com]

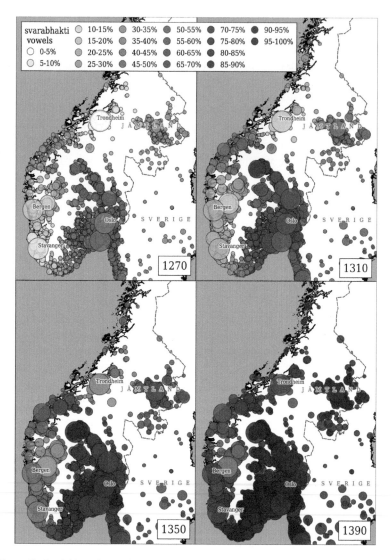

Figure 60. Spatial kernel smoothed estimates for the rise of svarabhakti vowels for 1270–1390
[Colour figure can be viewed at wileyonlinelibrary.com]

north- and then westwards through Romsdalen as well as westwards and then northwards along the coast in the south. As a result, the last conservative locality is Vossevangen in inland Hordaland, representing the endpoint where these two separate pathways of diffusion meet. Figure 61 demonstrates that some of the differences between the cities we observe here are greater than the sizes of the margins of error: we can be confident that Oslo and Hamar lead compared with Stavanger, Bergen and Trondheim. However, although there are apparent

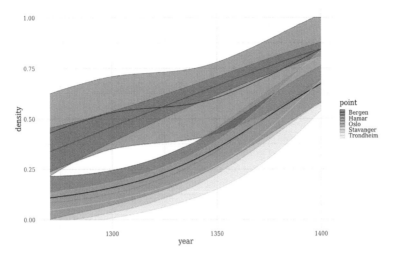

Figure 61. Spatial kernel smoothed estimates of the rise of svarabhakti vowels for Bergen, Hamar, Oslo, Stavanger and Trondheim [Colour figure can be viewed at wileyonlinelibrary.com]

differences among localities in the innovative eastern region, these are all too small to state with confidence that they are real.

How does this fit into our various hypotheses? Firstly, the most direct prediction from the Trudgill conjecture would be that the change was innovated in Bergen, the location of the greatest concentration of contact with Low German. Clearly these data are not line with that prediction: Bergen is a consistently conservative locality in a consistently conservative region, so it is hard to imagine it could be the point of innovation. Within this paradigm, if Bergen is not the point of innovation, we might instead expect to find Oslo or Tønsberg are. What we see here certainly is consistent with that possibility, although we cannot confidently place the point of innovation in one of these localities in particular. Again, these data would also be consistent with a Swedish innovation entering Norwegian in the south-east.

A framework of analysis which puts a wider emphasis on mobility and contact of all types rather than intense language contact in particular would lead us to expect a change spreading more easily around coasts and between cities. We do perhaps see some evidence for this: certainly in the west, we see the change spreading around the coast before it then spreads inland. However, some of the clearest leading areas for most of the change are uplands far from the coast, and there is no evidence whatsoever that urban areas play a leading role.

6.5.4. Loss of the voiceless dental fricative

The changes affecting the voiceless dental fricative were explored in section 5.2 and so, as with the voiced dental fricative above, we will not repeat that analysis here; instead, we refer back to Figure 33 and Figure 36. From these visualisations, we can see that the change appears to have begun in the north-eastern part of the region our corpus covers: Jämtland is a leading area from the earliest point, followed later by Trondheim and Trøndelag, Møre og Romsdal, and the northern parts of Oppland. Had we found that Jämtland alone was a highly innovative region we might be concerned that this reflected not a linguistic difference but was instead due to differences in the writing systems, with charters in Jämtland showing more influence in drafting and orthography from Swedish literary norms. However, the relatively consistent north-to-south gradient we see within the rest of Norway offers reassurance on this point. The differences between the cities, Frösön and Sør-Fron appear to confirm that the contrasts we see between different areas of the country are real and very unlikely to be the result of random noise. As a result, we can be relatively confident in this pathway of diffusion.

This very clear narrative is not obviously consistent with any of our hypotheses. The change cannot have been innovated in Bergen, Oslo or Tønsberg; it does not appear to have been innovated on the coasts, nor does it show a preferential tendency to spread around the coasts; it does not appear to have begun in an urban area, and the cities play no particular role in its spread. These distributions are consistent with a change entering Norwegian from Swedish, but for this to happen not in the well-trafficked south but instead at the Jämtland–Trøndelag border (or perhaps even further north) is surprising. It would certainly undermine the idea that the change arose first in Swedish *due to* intense contact with Middle Low German, since Swedish contact with Hansa was mostly concentrated much further south. One alternative way in which we might be able to relate this finding to contact is by bringing a different language contact scenario into consideration, that of contact between Nordic and Sámi. However, as mentioned in section 3.2.2.7, it is difficult to obtain good evidence on the nature of historical contact between Nordic languages and Sámi, and in general there is far more evidence for contact effects in the other direction. As a result, it is difficult to go further than to state that this is a possibility.

This finding does present a conflict with the observation that this change happened earlier in Old Danish written sources than in West Nordic. Had this change spread from Danish (whether directly or via Swedish), we would expect it to have entered Norwegian in southern Norway, contrary to what we see here. The most obvious interpretation of the distributions in these data is that the loss of the voiceless dental fricative was innovated (at least) twice in Nordic. Although this is not the most parsimonious account and so should be disfavoured in principle, it is not especially implausible. /θ/ is cross-linguistically marked and seems to be a diachronically unstable phoneme. It must have been lost many times independently across Germanic as a whole, taking into account examples like Continental West Germanic, dialects of English in England and Ireland, and many English-based creoles. Without further evidence on the diffusion of this change in medieval Swedish, this account of multiple independent innovation seems the best interpretation available to us.

6.5.5. Merger of 1du. pronoun into 1pl pronoun

Next we come to some of the changes affecting the 1pl/du. pronoun system. We see the replacement of the 1du. pronoun *mit* by the historical 1pl pronoun *mér*, with a loss of the du.-pl distinction in this context as a result, only for a brief period in Middle Norwegian sources. Although this change never goes to completion anywhere in the written sources of the time, we know from Modern Norwegian dialect evidence that *mér* (or more precisely its later phonological variant *me*) became the general 1pl pronoun, with no du.-pl distinction, across a great swath of spoken dialects in inland Norway, along the west coast and in parts of Trøndelag (Jahr 1990; Skjekkeland 2005: 110; Blaxter 2019: 7). The later rise of *vi* we see in the written sources, obscuring the continuation of this change, must at least in part have been a purely literary phenomenon, and so it is the changes affecting *mér* and *mit* that are more important for our research question here. Note that all of these changes are explored in more detail in Blaxter (2019).

Figure 62 shows the kernel smoothed estimates of rates of the different morphological and lexical variants of the 1st person subject pronoun for two referents. At the beginning of the fourteenth century we see that the Old Norwegian 1du. pronoun *vit* is rapidly being replaced by the reanalysed variant *mit*, a change which is largely complete by around 1360. This is then replaced by the borrowed East Nordic 1pl pronoun *vi* from around the beginning of the fifteenth century, going to completion in the mid-sixteenth century. However, beginning slightly earlier than this, we see a rise in the use of *mér*, historically the Middle Norwegian 1pl pronoun, which peaks around 21 per cent in 1457;

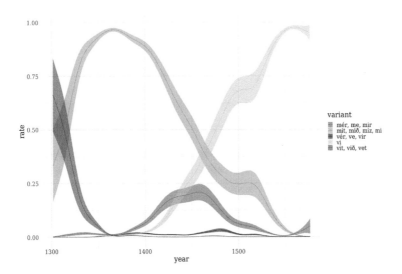

Figure 62. Kernel smoothed estimates of rates of morphological and lexical variants of the 1du./pl subject pronoun referring to two referents [Colour figure can be viewed at wileyonlinelibrary.com]

this is the change we focus on here. Figure 63 shows the spatial kernel smoothed estimates of this change for 1390–1510 (note that the scale for this map does not go to 100 per cent). We can see that there is a rise in the rate of *mér* for dual subjects first around the end of the fourteenth century in an area of the south-west coast with its centre on Vanse in Vest-agder. We then see more instances of *mér* in inland areas further east, with a high point around Lower Buskerud in the

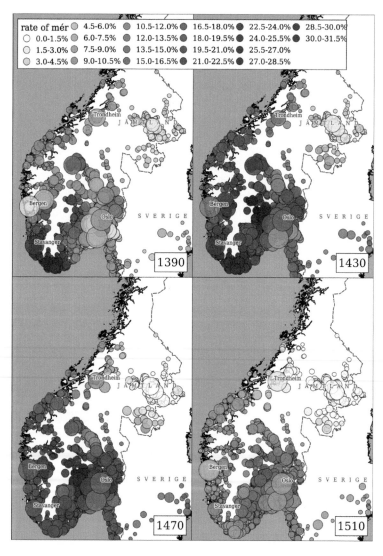

Figure 63. Spatial kernel smoothed estimates for the occurrence of mér for dual referents for 1390–1510 [Colour figure can be viewed at wileyonlinelibrary.com]

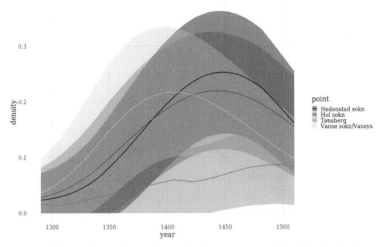

Figure 64. Spatial kernel smoothed estimates for the occurrence of *mér* for dual referents for Hedenstad, Hol, Tønsberg and Vanse [Colour figure can be viewed at wileyonlinelibrary.com]

mid-fifteenth century. Finally, as this variant disappears from the record it recedes earliest from the south-west, and remains longest in areas further inland such as Hallingdal.

However, we are coming up against the limits of the size of the dataset in trying to make these distinctions. The rate of dual *mér* is never very high compared with *mit* or *vi* and so the differences between the localities within the innovative zone are very small. What is more, all of the most interesting localities whose innovative status suggests they might be the sites of the innovation are rural, and have relatively few documents localised to them. As a result, we need a very high temporal bandwidth and relatively large error margins in order to get independent estimates at these locations. This has been done in Figure 64. Here we can see that we can distinguish between conservative Tønsberg, just outside the edge of the innovation region, and the other three localities examined. However, at no point can we say with confidence that the estimates in Vest-agder (Vanse), Lower Buskerud (Hedenstad) and Hallingdal (Hol) differ from one another.

What we can say relatively clearly from these data is that the merger of *mit* and *mér* into *mér* does not offer evidence in support of the Trudgill conjecture. There is really no way this change could have been innovated in one of the centres of contact with Middle Low German (Bergen, Tønsberg, Oslo); the cities, where contact was centred, play no particular role in the diffusion of the change; and there is no way this innovation could have spread from Danish or Swedish (since *mir* and *mér* do not occur in East Nordic). It is also not clearly consistent with a sociolinguistic-typological theory building on the esoteric-exoteric distinction. It is possible that it was innovated in a well-trafficked coastal region, but we do not have strong evidence for this: the innovative region where this variant seems to have originated includes a very large stretch of inland southern and eastern Norway.

6.5.6. Merger of 1pl pronoun into 1du. pronoun

Next we turn to the inverse change, by which historically dual *mit* begins to appear with 1pl subjects, potentially causing a merger of the dual and plural in this context. As with the case of *mit > mér*, *mér > mit* never goes to completion in late medieval sources as it is overtaken by the (partially purely literary) change of *mér > vi*, but we know that it must have gone to completion in speech in at least some varieties on the basis of evidence from Modern Norwegian dialects, where we find historically dual pronouns for the 1pl in a region including Agder, inland Buskerud, and parts of Rogaland and Hordaland. Figure 65 shows the kernel smoothed estimates for the different morphological and lexical variants of the 1st person subject pronoun referring to more than two referents. We see a broadly similar pattern to Figure 62, with a couple of notable differences: the reanalysed plural pronoun *mér* (red in Figure 65) rises later and falls earlier than its dual equivalent *mit* (orange in Figure 62); the rise of the historically dual form *mit* (orange in Figure 65) in plural contexts happens a little later than the rise of the historically plural form *mér* (red in Figure 62) in dual contexts, with the result that *mit* is actually more common in plural contexts than historically 'correct' *mér* in sources from sixteenth and late fifteenth centuries.

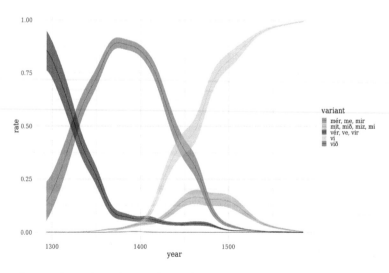

Figure 65. Kernel smoothed estimates of rates of morphological and lexical variants of the 1du./pl subject pronoun referring to more than two referents [Colour figure can be viewed at wileyonlinelibrary.com]

Figure 66 shows the spatial kernel smoothed estimates of rates of *mit* for more than two referents. We see here that there is an innovative zone for this change which seems to begin around Agder and Rogaland before expanding to cover inner Telemark and some of Buskerud, before shrinking from the coasts so that in the sixteenth century plural *mit* is mostly a phenomenon of inner Telemark. The innovative region seems to have a consistent border in the east at around

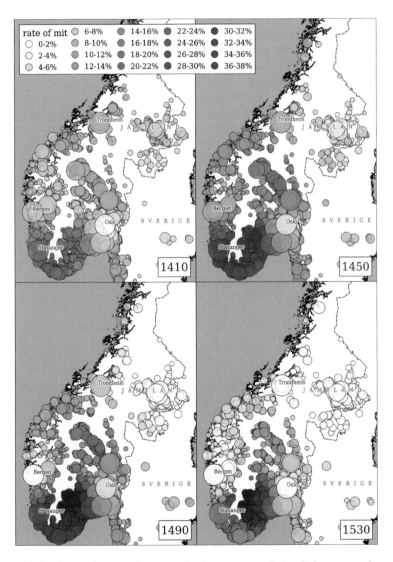

Figure 66. Spatial kernel smoothed estimates for the occurrence of *mit* referring to more than two referents for 1410-1530 [Colour figure can be viewed at wileyonlinelibrary.com]

the longitude of Skien: this is never a variant found much in charters from Tønsberg and Oslo. Examining the estimations and error margins for specific localities in Figure 67, note that we can be confident in this observation (Tønsberg has significantly lower levels than Vinje in inner Telemark for the whole course of the change, and than Vanse in Agder at its peak). We cannot, however, confidently make distinctions between the localities within the innovation region, since the error margins for these overlap. If we extend our analysis to include Hol in Hallingdal, necessitating larger error margins and a higher temporal bandwidth due to the small size of the dataset from Hallingdal (cf. Figure 68), we see that we can also have some confidence in the northern boundary for the innovative region: we can never confidently state that Hol has a rate different to Tønsberg, and we are confident it is lower than Vinje, at least in some periods.

Turning back to our research question, our findings here are very like those we identified for the reverse change, *mit* > *mér*, in section 6.5.5. These patterns do not seem consistent with any of our hypotheses: certainly not with the Trudgill conjecture (there is no obvious way that intense contact with Low German can be implicated here), nor in any straightforward way with sociolinguistic-typological theories based on the esoteric-exoteric distinction.

As an aside, however, it is interesting that the two contrasting simplifications of the 1du./pl pronoun system have such similar distributions, especially in their early years. In both cases we cannot pin down a place of innovation with any great specificity, but the regions in which they are likely to have been innovated overlap substantially in that they both include much of Agder. The differences we see are that plural *mit* is innovated a little later than dual *mér*, and that as the changes develop the two become regionally differentiated, with dual *mér*

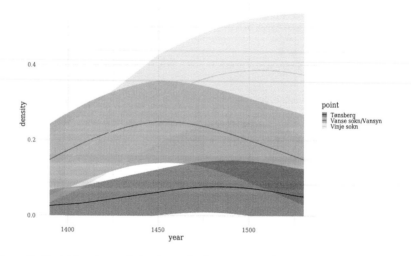

Figure 67. Spatial kernel smoothed estimates for the occurrence of *mit* referring to more than two referents for Tønsberg, Vanse and Vinje [Colour figure can be viewed at wileyonlinelibrary.com]

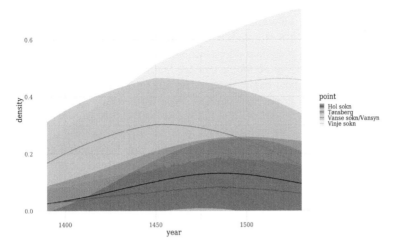

Figure 68. Spatial kernel smoothed estimates for the occurrence of *mit* referring to more than two referents for Hol, Tønsberg, Vanse and Vinje [Colour figure can be viewed at wileyonlinelibrary. com]

focusing in an area including Hallingdal and to a less extent Valdres, some distance further north than the area where *mit* becomes focused, in inner Telemark. The modern distribution of the two 1pl pronouns which descend from these, *me* and *mi*, do indeed occur in dialects in two complementary areas, with the *me* area north of the *mi* area (although the isogloss is somewhat further south), but without these data the most obvious assumption about how this came about would have been that the two simplifications of the pronoun system were independent innovations, with *mér/mit* > *mér* innovated somewhere north of *mér/mit* > *mit* and an isogloss forming between the two variants. Instead, what seems to have happened is that *mér/mit* > *mér* happened first and prompted *mér/mit* > *mit* in the same dialect region;[31] the two competed and *mit* succeeded in the south, whereas further north *mér/mit* > *mér* spread uncontested.

6.5.7. *Replacement of the 1pl pronoun by borrowed vi*

Following the changes to the subject pronoun used in 1pl contexts discussed in section 6.5.6, we see wholesale replacement of *mér* and *mit* by the borrowed East Nordic form *vi*. As mentioned above, the rise of *vi* as the merged 1du./pl pronoun goes nearly to completion in written sources, but since other forms survive into

---

[31] It is perfectly possible to imagine how the two could be causally linked. In a dialect in which the first innovation has happened but not yet gone to completion, *mit* remains marked for dual whilst *mér* can be used for dual or plural referents. If *mér* can always be used wherever *mit* can be used, then this pattern can be analogically extended to allow *mit* to be used wherever *mér* can be used. At this point, both variants would be grammatical in both contexts, and so could compete directly.

Modern Norwegian dialects we know that this must in part have been a literary phenomenon. This undermines its value as evidence for trends in language change. Nevertheless, it is possible that at least part of the rise we see in these sources does reflect a spoken phenomenon, as *vi* is a feature of many spoken dialects today. From Figure 65 we can see that the rise of *vi* when referring to more than two referents begins around the turn of the fifteenth century and is going to completion in the late sixteenth, towards the end of the period covered by the corpus (and, not incidentally, the end of the shift to writing Danish). From Figure 69 we can see that this change was not highly spatially differentiated. Jämtland leads, although this is unsurprising in this late period for a feature shared with Swedish. Within the rest of Norway there is a slight effect by which cities, particularly Bergen, Oslo and Trondheim, are ahead of surrounding areas, but this is very subtle; referring to the estimations and margins of error for individual localities in Figures 70–72, we see that we cannot confidently confirm this difference anywhere. In sum, in spite of the relatively large size of the dataset, there is relatively little we can conclude about the spatial distribution of the rise of *vi* for more than two referants. This might plausibly reflect its status as a primarily written phenomenon.

6.5.8. Replacement of the 1du. pronoun by borrowed vi

Finally among the changes affecting the 1du./pl pronoun system we come to the replacement of the Norwegian 1du. pronouns by the borrowed East Nordic form *vi*. As we can see from Figure 62, this change begins in the early part of the fifteenth century and is approaching completion by the mid sixteenth. The spatial kernel smoothed estimates are given in Figure 73. The pattern we see here is fundamentally similar to the rise of *vi* in plural contexts: Jämtland leads, but beyond this there are relatively few clear patterns. If the cities have any differentiated role here it is even less clear than in plural contexts, and there are no obvious regional effects except a slight tendency for inland areas to lag compared with the coasts in the latter half of the change.

6.5.9. Loss of 1pl middle agreement

In spite of taking place roughly in the middle of the period covered by the corpus, the dataset for the loss of the distinctive 1pl middle ending -*Vmz* suffers from problems of data sparsity. 1pl middle voice verbs are simply extremely rare in thirteenth and fourteenth century charters, and only rise in frequency in the fifteenth century due to changes in drafting practices. At the point when we first have enough data to make robust estimates, the change is already well underway, making it difficult to infer its early distribution and thereby its place of innovation; this is clear from Figure 74, which shows smoothed estimates for the change for the period for which there is sufficient data. Figure 75 then gives the spatial kernel smoothed estimates. We can see a broad south-west-to-north-east

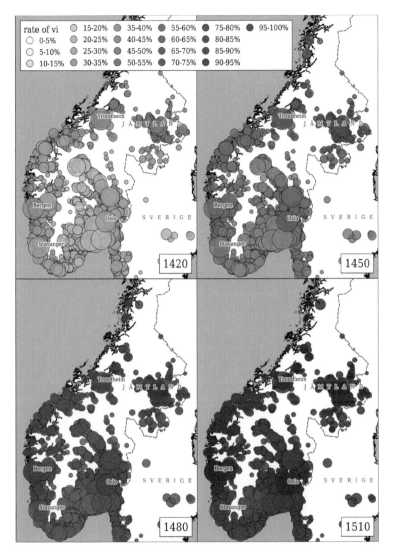

Figure 69. Spatial kernel smoothed estimates for the occurrence of *vi* for plural referents for 1420–1510 [Colour figure can be viewed at wileyonlinelibrary.com]

pattern of spread, with the most innovative region being a large area including the whole of Sørlandet, Rogaland and Hordaland and the most conservative area being Jämtland in the north-east and lower Gudbrandsdalen, deep inland. Examining the estimates and error margins for individual localities in Figure 76, we find that the small dataset means that we can only be confident in some of these impressions. The difference between Fröson and Bergen is greater than the margins of error, meaning we can be quite confident that Jämtland lags

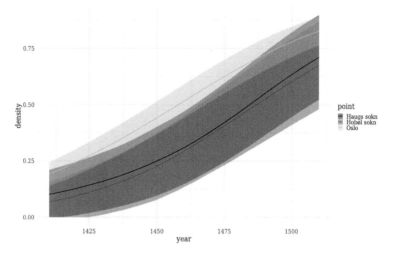

Figure 70. Spatial kernel smoothed estimates for the occurrence of *vi* for plural referents for Oslo, Haug and Hobøl [Colour figure can be viewed at wileyonlinelibrary.com]

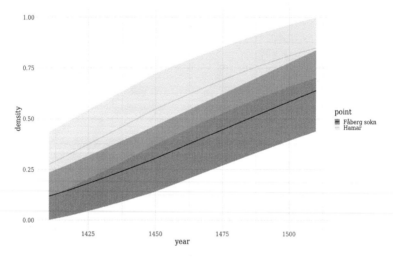

Figure 71. Spatial kernel smoothed estimates for the occurrence of *vi* for plural referents for Hamar and Fåberg [Colour figure can be viewed at wileyonlinelibrary.com]

behind the south-west. Estimates within the rest of Norway, however, tend to overlap.

This leaves a highly ambiguous picture: potentially consistent with our hypotheses, but too underspecified to be convincing. If we assume that the change could have started anywhere within the innovative southern region identifiable in the top-left panel of Figure 75 (and even this is pushing the

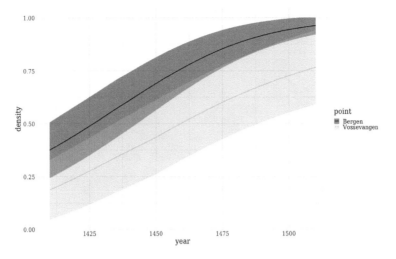

Figure 72. Spatial kernel smoothed estimates for the occurrence of *vi* for plural referents for Bergen and Vossevangen [Colour figure can be viewed at wileyonlinelibrary.com]

evidence to its limits), then this includes the possibility that this simplificatory innovation took place in Bergen, as the Trudgill conjecture predicts. It is also interesting to note that the change seems to spread around the west coast before spreading inland down through Gudbrandsdalen; this seems in line with theories which place general emphasis on areas with high mobility as opposed to language contact, but is too weak an observation to be given much weight. There is no indication of a special role for urban areas in the diffusion of the change.

6.5.10. Loss of genitive objects of millum

We do not have an especially large dataset for the loss of genitive objects of the preposition *millum* 'between', but that data is relatively evenly distributed across the whole period of change. Kernel smoothed estimates for the change are given in Figure 77; we start to see a rise in texts where *millum* takes objects in cases other than the genitive beginning in the late fourteenth century, a rise which seems to stabilise at a little below 90 per cent in the early sixteenth century.[32]

---

[32] Note that by this late period, genitive objects of *millum* tend to be restricted to fixed formulae and pronouns, implying that it is no longer a productive pattern by this point. It would be possible to make an argument that both of these types should be excluded from the dataset, or that pronouns and full nouns should be treated as separate datasets in which the change can be investigated separately. This has not been done here, in part simply because the dataset is not large enough to allow it. However, I would argue that although these are disfavouring contexts for the change (as would be expected for a syntactic change of this type), they do not represent truly unrelated contexts in which the change progressed entirely independently. From a practical standpoint, there is not enough data to separate out in this way and still get a view of spatial distribution.

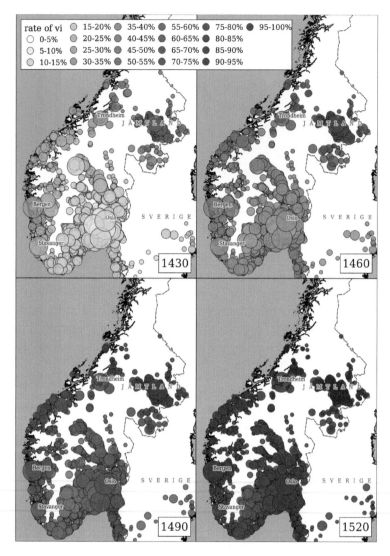

Figure 73. Spatial kernel smoothed estimates for the occurrence of *vi* for dual referents for 1430–1520 [Colour figure can be viewed at wileyonlinelibrary.com]

Figure 78 then shows the spatial kernel smoothed estimates for this change across the main period of rise, from 1400 to 1520. Three observations jump out from these visualisations.

Firstly, Jämtland is a leading area. Unlike in the case of the voiceless dental fricatives (section 6.5.4 above), this does not translate into a north-east-to-south-west gradient within the rest of Norway. This is taken to suggest that this does

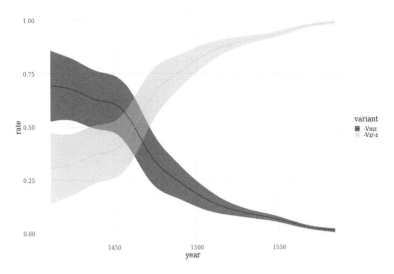

Figure 74. Kernel smoothed estimates of the loss of the distinctive 1pl middle ending [Colour figure can be viewed at wileyonlinelibrary.com]

not reflect a pattern of diffusion of the change outwards from the north east to the rest of the country, but rather is an artefact of Swedish influence on documents from Jämtland (putting aside the question of whether this implies that Jämtish speech had the change earlier than dialects in the rest of Norway or whether this is purely an artefact of Swedish documentary drafting norms). As mentioned above (section 4.4.1.1.4), we do have a prior study of the loss of lexical genitives in Swedish to which we can make a direct comparison. The dataset used by Norde (1997) is structured very differently to that used here, with a very small number of texts but a much larger number of tokens per text. Accordingly, if normalised by text (as has been done for all other datasets throughout this monograph), this would be a very small dataset and we would need very large bandwidths to achieve reasonable margins of error (cf. Figure 79). On the other hand, if we do not normalise by text (cf. Figure 80) we have a more reasonably sized dataset, but we see a large artefact in the estimation in the late thirteenth century as a result of three texts known only from much later manuscripts (a good example of the reason we should normalise by text wherever possible). Nevertheless, with either method we can see that the change happens almost a century earlier in written Swedish than in Norwegian. Thus our suspicion that the leading position of Jämtland in the estimates is due to Swedish influence is highly plausible.

Secondly, the cities appear to lead the change compared with immediately surrounding rural areas, an effect which becomes more pronounced as the change progresses. However, examining the estimates and error margins for individual cities and smaller settlements in their vicinities (Figures 82–84), we cannot state

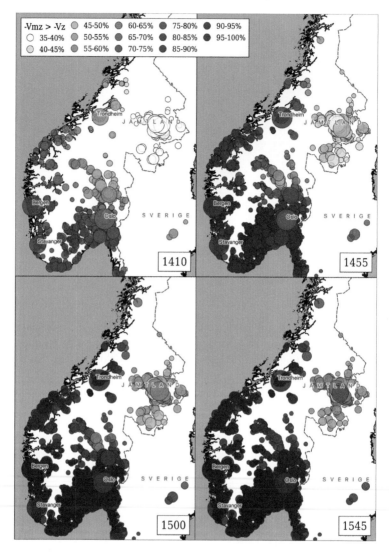

Figure 75. Spatial kernel smoothed estimates for the loss of the distinctive 1pl middle ending for 1410–1545 [Colour figure can be viewed at wileyonlinelibrary.com]

with confidence that any of these differences are real. This is a product of the fact that the dataset is relatively small, making it difficult to get large enough samples in low population density localities without overlapping with nearby cities.

Finally, there is some indication that the change reaches coastal dialects (especially moving along the west coast) earlier than inland dialects. This is not an especially strong effect, but we can note that Trondheim and Bergen lead

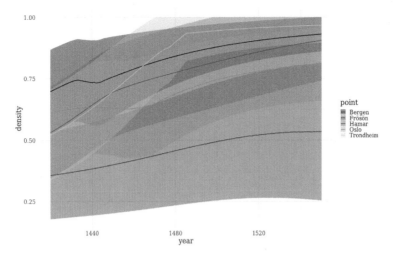

Figure 76. Spatial kernel smoothed estimates for the loss of the distinctive 1pl middle ending for Bergen, Frösön, Hamar, Oslo and Trondheim [Colour figure can be viewed at wileyonlinelibrary. com]

other cities by a margin which is significant at least for a brief period (cf. Figure 81), and that the area that remains conservative latest is in the inland south, covering parts of inner Telemark, Agder and Buskerud.

These observations are potentially in line with our hypotheses about sociolinguistic typological effects on change. It is relatively convincing that what we see in the data is a change which began earlier in Swedish and spread into Norwegian via contact in urban areas. This is consistent with the Trudgill conjecture, both because some of the urban areas with the highest populations of Middle Low German speakers (Oslo, Bergen) are leading areas, and because there was more of such contact in Sweden. What we see is also consistent with other, less focused theories, such as those which build on the esoteric-exoteric distinction: such approaches would predict a major role for cities and coasts, and we see (non-significant) indications of both of these in the data.

6.5.11. Loss of 1pl agreement in verb-subject order

The loss of the distinctive -*Vm* endings for the 1pl, initially replaced by -*V* endings which tended to result in merger with the 3pl, has already been discussed in section 5.3. I will not repeat that analysis here, but instead explore how those findings bear on our hypotheses.

Referring to Figure 47, this change was already widespread in VERB-SUBJECT order at a low but stable frequency at the beginning of the period covered by the corpus. Accordingly, we cannot usefully speculate on where it was innovated on the basis of these data. However, from the beginning of the fifteenth century we

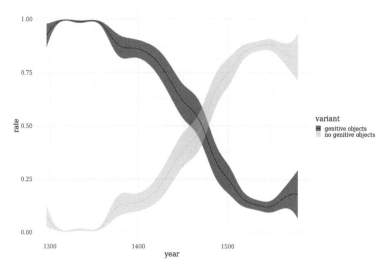

Figure 77. Kernel smoothed estimates for the loss of genitive objects with *millum* 'between' [Colour figure can be viewed at wileyonlinelibrary.com]

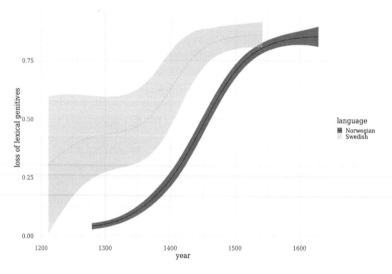

Figure 78. Spatial kernel smoothed estimates for the loss of genitive objects with *millum* 'between' for 1400-1520 [Colour figure can be viewed at wileyonlinelibrary.com]

see a steady rise in the simplified forms, and urban areas – particularly Trondheim and Bergen, but at times also Oslo, Hamar and Tønsberg – tend to lead this change compared to their immediate environs by a small margin. This can be demonstrated to be significant only for Hamar (cf. Figure 49). It is also

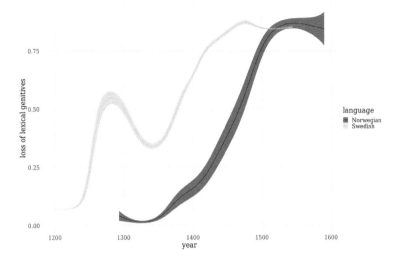

Figure 79. Comparison of kernel smoothed estimates for the loss of genitive objects with *millum* 'between' in the Diplomatarium Norvegicum and the loss of lexical genitives in Middle Swedish by text from Norde (1997) [Colour figure can be viewed at wileyonlinelibrary.com]

noticeable that the most conservative areas towards the end of the change are inland areas, although this effect too is subtle.

With all due caveats concerning the small magnitude of these effects and the fact that most of them do not fall outside the margins of error, this can be argued to be broadly in line with our hypotheses. Since the existence of the change appears to predate the period covered by the corpus, we have no evidence that intensive contact with Low German triggered its innovation; indeed, since it seems likely the change is internal to Norwegian (cf. section 4.3.3.1.4), it is likely it predated a major Hansa presence in the country altogether. However, the leading positions of the cities, particularly Bergen, raises the possibility of a role for this intensive contact in the later levelling process by which the innovative variant came to entirely replace -*Vm*. This would also be in line with a less focused theory in which mobility and contact more generally favour simplificatory change.

Standard histories of the language suggest that subject-verb agreement was lost earlier in Danish than Norwegian (cf. section 4.3.3.1.4). There are a small number of documents localised to Denmark in our corpus, especially in the sixteenth and late fifteenth centuries, and if we examine the kernel smoothed estimates of the distribution of the change including Denmark for 1500 in Figure 85 this does seem to confirm the impression of Danish leading the change compared with Norwegian. Given this, the leading position of cities could also be interpreted as evidence that contact with Danish among mobile urban elites helped drive the change forward; this is particularly in keeping with the observation that inland Hamar is one of the leading localities. If we accept this

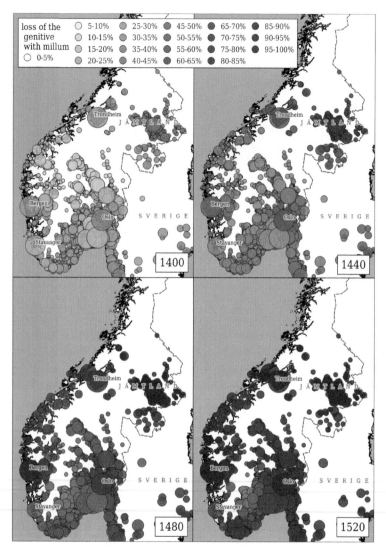

Figure 80. Comparison of kernel smoothed estimates for the loss of genitive objects with *millum* 'between' in the Diplomatarium Norvegicum and the loss of lexical genitives in Middle Swedish by token from Norde (1997) [Colour figure can be viewed at wileyonlinelibrary.com]

argument, it could be seen as consistent with the Trudgill conjecture, since contact with Middle Low German was even more extensive in Denmark, or as supporting a sociolinguistic-typological theory which puts weight on dialect contact rather than focusing exclusively on language contact in accounting for simplificatory change.

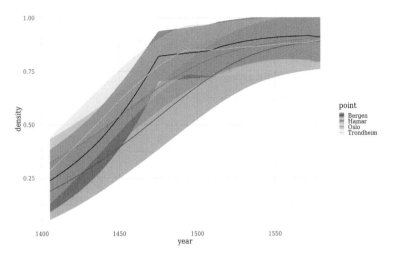

Figure 81. Spatial kernel smoothed estimates for the loss of genitive objects with *millum* 'between' for Bergen, Hamar, Oslo and Trondheim [Colour figure can be viewed at wileyonlinelibrary.com]

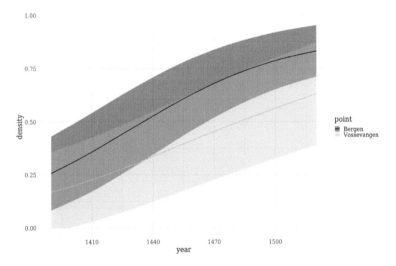

Figure 82. Spatial kernel smoothed estimates for the loss of genitive objects with *millum* 'between' for Bergen and Vossevangen [Colour figure can be viewed at wileyonlinelibrary.com]

6.5.12. Loss of 1pl agreement in subject-verb order

The loss of the distinctive 1pl ending *-Vm* in SUBJECT-VERB order has already been discussed in section 5.3 and I will not redo the analysis here. I will, however, expand on and consider how those findings bear on our hypotheses. Referring to Figure 39, we see that the innovation is virtually unknown in Norwegian before

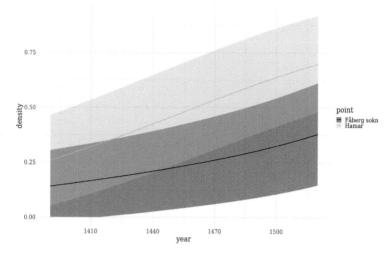

Figure 83. Spatial kernel smoothed estimates for the loss of genitive objects with *millum* 'between' for Hamar and Fåberg [Colour figure can be viewed at wileyonlinelibrary.com]

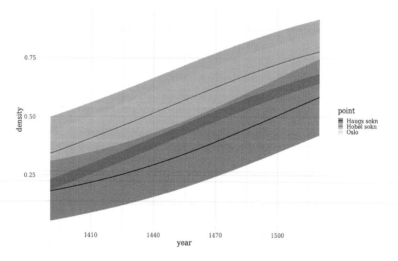

Figure 84. Spatial kernel smoothed estimates for the loss of genitive objects with *millum* 'between' for Oslo, Haug and Hobøl [Colour figure can be viewed at wileyonlinelibrary.com]

the early fifteenth century; in Figure 46 we can see that when it begins to rise it appears first in the cities of Trondheim and Bergen and that these two cities, along with Oslo and to a lesser extent Tønsberg, lead the change for the whole period covered. The tendency of the cities to lead compared with rural areas was conclusively demonstrated to be real and reliable in Figure 51–53, and the leading position of Bergen and Trondheim compared with other cities is

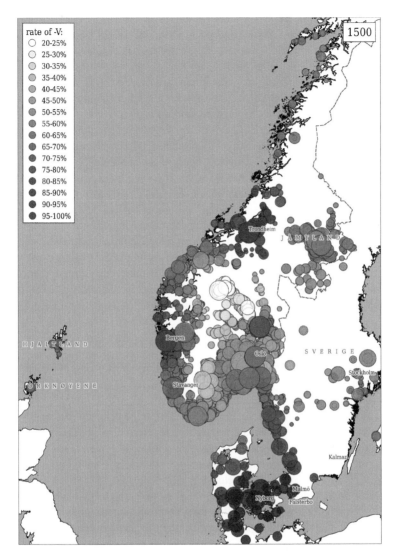

Figure 85. Spatial kernel smoothed estimates of loss of 1pl -*Vm* in VERB-SUBJECT order for 1500
[Colour figure can be viewed at wileyonlinelibrary.com]

confirmed in Figure 54. Broadly speaking, the rate at which the innovation appears in other areas is simply a function of distance from these three cities, implying that what we see is basically diffusion directly outwards from them to the surrounding countryside. One possible caveat to this observation is that the change seems to spread to the western coastline running from Bergen to Trondheim, including areas of Hordaland, Sogn og Fjordane, Møre og Romsdal and Sør-Trøndelag, faster than we might expect. Certainly, the gradient between these two western cities and the intervening coastline is far less sharp than the gradient between Oslo and the rural south east. This might be suggestive of the change spreading along coastlines with greater ease than inland. Alternatively it might simply be a product of the fact that these two cities are particularly advanced for this change and that there are far fewer data from northern Vestlandet than from the east, necessitating higher bandwidths and more smoothing here to achieve the required sample size.

The observation that – at least within Norwegian – this innovation appears to have been innovated in Bergen or Trondheim is clearly consistent with the predictions we have derived from the Trudgill conjecture. The leading position of cities throughout is consistent with any theory which centres mobility and contact as determinative of simplificatory change, whether putting focus on intensive language contact or taking a broader view. The slight tendency suggested for more rapid diffusion along the coasts might better fit such a less focused theory, but it is a much less certain observation. As with the same change in VERB-SUBJECT order discussed in section 6.5.11 above, it is also plausible that this change happened first in Danish and spread thence into Norwegian via urban contact; the distribution in Danish documents in this corpus (cf. Figure 86) is consistent with this suggestion.

6.5.13. Loss of number agreement on present tense verbs

The final variable I will examine in this section is the loss of subject-verb agreement for number. This change is only in its infancy in the final years covered by the corpus, so we can expect to have difficulty in mapping its spread with any certainty. Furthermore, it begins well into the period when most writing in Norway has shifted to Danish, and so it is far from clear that any changes we find in this variable really reflect a linguistic change in spoken Norwegian rather than some phenomenon occurring in the written standard. Finally, given different patterns of syncretism in the preterite and the present, we might expect this change to operate differently by tense – and indeed, this has already been noted that it is mostly a phenomenon of the present tense in these data (cf. Figure 41). Accordingly, we will only explore the change in the present tense, while bearing these caveats in mind.

Figure 87 shows the change over time, combining the two endings which represent a loss of number agreement ($-\varnothing$ endings occur on the preterite-presents, $-Vr$ endings elsewhere). We can see that this change is beginning around the turn of the sixteenth century and rising sharply in the last decades covered by the corpus, the 1550s and 1560s. Then turning to Figure 88, we see that this rise is strongly associated with the south, particularly Agder in the south-west and inner Telemark and Buskerud in the east, with an isogloss that separates out Oslo as relatively conservative. However, referring to the estimates and error margins for individual localities in Figure 89, we see that there is simply too little data at this extreme edge of the dataset to differentiate between localities with confidence

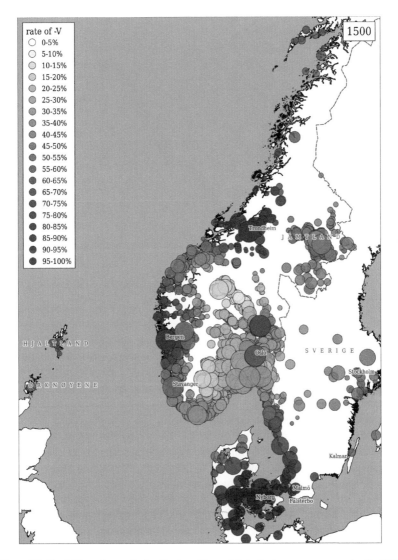

Figure 86. Spatial kernel smoothed estimates of loss of 1pl -*Vm* in SUBJECT-VERB order for 1500
[Colour figure can be viewed at wileyonlinelibrary.com]

(especially since the absolute differences in question are actually very small:
with the high temporal bandwidth used in these figures, the innovation is never
estimated at greater than 30 per cent for any individual location). The only
difference greater than the margins of error is the difference between the two
most extreme points tested, Stavanger and Trondheim, and that only briefly at
the very end of the period covered.

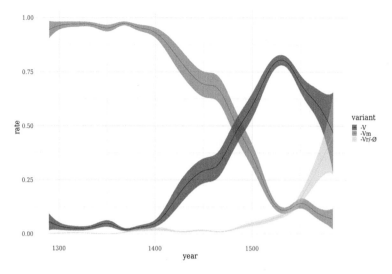

Figure 87. Kernel smoothed estimates of rates of 1pl endings on present verbs, combining -Vr and
-Ø [Colour figure can be viewed at wileyonlinelibrary.com]

As with the loss of 1sg. active agreement at the beginning of the period
covered by the corpus, it is difficult to draw strong conclusions from such thin
data. The fact that we can demonstrate that at least some spatial distinctions we
see here are (just) statistically significant does mean that we can infer that this
change originated somewhere in the south – and most likely the south-west – but
we cannot go much further than that. The fact that the cities of Oslo, Bergen and
Trondheim are in no way leading localities for this change speaks against the
possibility that it was spreading from East Nordic. Comparing the rate we see in
late charters localised to Denmark in this corpus in Figure 90, we see
confirmatory evidence for this: we only find high estimates of this change in
northerly parts of Denmark where the estimates are influenced by documents
from southern Norway (this finding should be taken with a grain of salt, since
this is not designed as a corpus of Danish). Overall, then this change is not
particularly supportive of any of hypotheses, but primarily simply because we
can say so little about it.

6.6. Conclusions

The results we have seen here are complex and require nuanced interpretation. In
the simplest understanding, the Trudgill conjecture implies a prediction about the
point of *innovation* of simplificatory change. After all, the proposed mechanism
concerns innovation: imperfect learning of the language by L2 speakers
generates new simplified variants which can then spread into the population of
native speakers. Applying this simple interpretation to the contact situation in
Norway in our period, we predicted that these simplificatory changes should

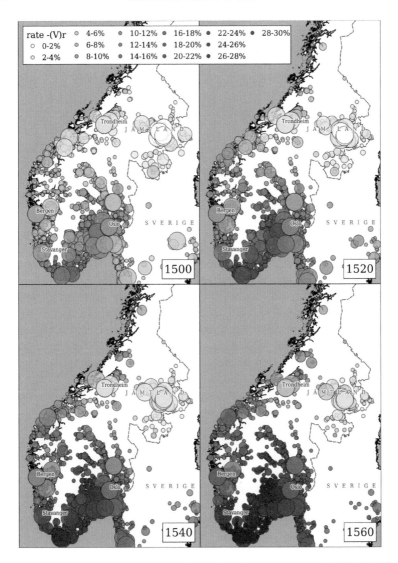

Figure 88. Spatial kernel smoothed estimates of loss of number agreement on verbs with 1pl subjects for 1500–1560 [Colour figure can be viewed at wileyonlinelibrary.com]

have been innovated in the cities with a major Hansa presence, primarily Bergen. Clearly, this prediction was not borne out. Indeed, of these changes, only for two do we find positive evidence that the earliest region in which they were used in Norway included Bergen: the loss of 1pl middle -Vmz, which we cannot localise with any more specificity than to the whole of the south-west, and the loss of 1pl active -Vm in SUBJECT-VERB order, which appears earliest in Bergen and Trondheim. Other changes seem most likely to have arisen first somewhere in

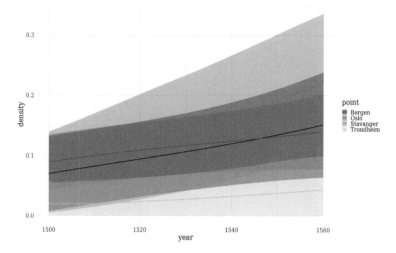

Figure 89. Spatial kernel smoothed estimates of loss of number agreement on verbs with 1pl subjects for Bergen, Oslo, Stavanger and Trondheim [Colour figure can be viewed at wileyonlinelibrary.com]

the south-east (loss of [ð], svarabhakti vowels) or specifically Oslo (loss of genitive objects of *millum*) – consistent with a role for Middle Low German influence, but not strong evidence for it. Still others (loss of plural -*V*, mergers of *mit-mér*) seem to have begun in the south-west but too far south to associate with Bergen; the loss of [θ] first appears in Norwegian in Jämtland and Trøndelag, nowhere near any major centre of Hansa activity.

However, restricting ourselves to this simplest reading of the theory, although it streamlines our analytical task, is a flawed approach. Language change happens in a vastly complex system, and to suggest that the proposed mechanism could have one and only one predictable signal undermines the validity of our conclusions. To this end, two points should be considered which substantially complicate the predictions we might draw from the theory; in both cases, the consequence is that our findings are more in line with the Trudgill conjecture than they might originally have seemed.

Firstly, although the mechanism by which intensive contact is proposed to operate on language change refers to innovation, this does not necessarily imply that it will only have an influence on innovation. Many changes are innovated multiple times independently. Certainly this applies to most simplificatory changes, which are in some sense 'natural' changes: all speakers produce 'erroneous' (in the sense that they are not consistent with community usage) phonemic mergers, morphological levelling and expansions of productive rules during the process of (both native and L2) language acquisition before later mostly shifting to L1 adult norms. With such changes, we might not expect to see simple patterns of spread in which an innovation occurs in a single locality and diffuses outwards from this locality alone. Such innovations might be said

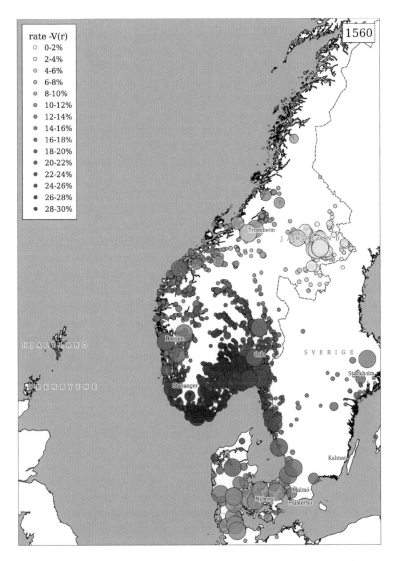

Figure 90. Spatial kernel smoothed estimates of loss of number agreement on verbs with 1pl subjects for 1560 [Colour figure can be viewed at wileyonlinelibrary.com]

always to exist at a very low frequency everywhere, and especially in communities with a high proportion of L2 speakers. When they take hold and begin to rise in frequency in one place, dialect contact will rapidly have the effect of transforming the 'error' into a recognisable variant, especially in those localities in which it was already more frequent. Thus we might expect to see a locality with intensive language contact become innovative in the early-to-mid stages of a change, even if it was not the site of the original innovation per se.

This might be a good fit for several cases we see in the data where cities, and particularly Bergen and Oslo, cannot be conclusively shown to be the point of innovation but do lead the change compared to other regions: the loss of lexical genitives with *millum*; the loss of *-Vm* in both contexts examined (although for some of these we cannot be highly confident in our result). The rise of *vi* for plural subjects shows similar patterning, and although it cannot (as a loanword) be given exactly the same explanatory account, we can nevertheless build a similar picture of multiple independent but mutually reinforcing innovation of a simplificatory change in centres of contact here.

Secondly, a prediction that these changes should have spread from Bergen ignores the fact that Norwegian was part of a dialect continuum with Swedish and Danish and that there was more contact with Middle Low German – some intensive, some more stable – in Sweden and Denmark. With this in mind, we might predict that simplificatory changes in Continental Nordic should often have started in Swedish or Danish before spreading into Norwegian. As it turns out, our results are very consistent with this prediction. Of these changes, only for two (the two different mergers of *mit* and *mér*) can we completely exclude the possibility that the change started in East Nordic. For four of the earlier changes (loss of [ð], rise of svarabhakti vowels, loss of [θ], loss of genitives with *millum*) it seems very plausible that they diffused from Swedish. One later change (loss of *-Vm* in SUBJECT-VERB contexts) seems likely to have spread from Danish, and it seems very likely that Danish contact played a crucial role in transforming the loss of *-Vm* in VERB-SUBJECT contexts from a stable low-frequency variant into a rising innovation. The rise of *vi* too in both contexts examined must have spread from East Nordic, and most likely specifically Danish.

As a result of this more nuanced reading of the evidence and the Trudgill conjecture, it becomes harder to disambiguate the predictions implied by the different theories. A sociolinguistic-typological theory which puts the same emphasis on dialect contact as on language contact in generating simplificatory change might in principle make different predictions about the locations of innovation. In such a theory, innovations should arise in cities and on well-trafficked coasts, since these are the likely sites of dialect contact regardless of whether they are the locations of intensive language contact. The problem for our purposes is that since these are also the sites of contact with Swedish and Danish, it would be very difficult to disambiguate such a phenomenon from a tendency for simplificatory change to begin in and spread from East Nordic. Furthermore, it is difficult to distinguish between an effect of coasts and an effect of urban areas in these data due to the geography of Norway. It is true that for many of these changes, the most conservative areas are deep inland. However, since most of the major cities of the period were on the coasts, this could simply be a side-effect of a tendancy for urban areas to be innovative.

However we parse the import of these results for particular theories of language change, it is clear that they offer confirmatory evidence for the sociolinguistic-typological approach more generally. If these changes were mostly driven by internal factors, we would not expect to see any recurring patterns in the external contexts of their innovation or in the spatial patterns which followed. We might see points of origin evenly scattered across the country, with each change taking a different pathway of diffusion to reach the rest of the language area as a result. Instead, there are some clear recurring patterns, both in points of innovation and pathways of diffusion. Tantilisingly, these recurring patterns seem to show clustering in time. We see:

- the rise of svarabhakti vowels and the loss of [ð] arising in the south-east and spreading both around the coasts and via Gudbrandsdal-Romsdal to the rest of the country in the early fourteenth century;
- the two mergers of *mit-mér* and the loss of 1pl middle -*Vmz* seemingly arising in the south-west and diffusing outwards relatively continuously in the mid fifteenth century (although the latter parts of the *mit-mér* changes are more complex); and
- the rise of *vi* in plural contexts, the loss of genitive objects of *millum*, and the loss of 1pl -*Vm* in both contexts spreading outwards from the cities in the late fifteenth and early sixteenth centuries.

Of the remaining changes, the loss of the 1sg ending, the rise of *vi* in dual contexts and the loss of subject-verb agreement for number are under-evidenced and the results rather equivocal. Only in the loss of [θ] do we find a well-evidenced change with a unique pattern of diffusion.

These patterns support the sociolinguistic-typological approach in the abstract simply because such an approach puts weight on language external (sociolinguistic, language-contact, social) factors in explaining when and where particular classes of successful change occur (i.e. in answering the actuation of problem of Weinreich et al. 1968). Such factors could be expected to vary over time and space but be consistent across different areas of grammar at a particular moment and in a particular place. The examples of such factors we have discussed all clearly fit this observation. Intensive language contact with Middle Low German was localised to a number of specific cities around Scandinavia, and rose and fell according to changes in relations with the Hanseatic League. Dialect contact was driven by mobility and would have been concentrated in cities and along coasts, but this could shift over time with the economic fortunes of those regions (and with the Black Death in the mid fourteenth century, which halved the Norwegian population and thereby drastically changed the motivations for migration, as discussed in section 7.1). The same sorts of patterns would also apply to any other features of social context we might invoke to explain why particular changes happened when and where they did.

From a methodological standpoint, it is clear that we could not hope to test the predictions of the Trudgill conjecture and other sociolinguistic typological theories without a robust statistical tool for describing and visualising the spatial distribution of language changes from historical sources: kernel smoothing. An earlier approach to answering these questions might simply have tried to identify the location of the earliest recorded instance of each innovation, but this approach is flawed in a crucial way. It is a relatively safe assumption that we never observe the true innovator of any new linguistic feature (certainly this must be true in the medieval period). Too few people were literate and too few texts survive for this to be remotely likely. This alone makes examining the first occurrence of a form somewhat suspect as a method of determining when and where the innovation occurred. The noisy reality of historical linguistic data contributes to making it highly uncertain that the first extant token will occur in a text anywhere near that point in time and space. In order to identify the most probable location we need to take a much wider view of the data and see where the earliest *consistent* rise in frequency happens. This can only be done with a statistical method like kernel smoothing. What is more, by using this method we have been able to illuminate facts not just about the point and moment of innovation of these instances of language change, but about the whole course of their diffusion through the language community. This, too, would be quite impossible without the methods described here.

Seen from another angle, we have here demonstrated how kernel smoothing can be put to uses which go beyond internal explorations of particular changes in the grammar. In the previous chapter our research questions concerned specific variables, but here they concerned the hypotheses about the history of Norwegian more generally. Through repeating a similar analysis across many changes, these methods allow us to illuminate broad tendencies in the history of a language and thus answer such sweeping questions. In the next chapter we will take this insight further, and look at how such trends and patterns across the history of the language can speak to more general features of the operation of language change.

7

SPATIAL MODELS OF DIFFUSION

7.1. Background

An important question at the intersection of historical linguistics, dialectology, language contact and sociolinguistics concerns the mechanisms by which linguistic innovations spread between localities and the spatial patterns that result. The earliest model of language change in space was the tree model (Stammbaumtheorie, Schleicher 1853). In this model, languages are conceived of as discrete entities and changes as discrete events: once a change has happened within a language, all subsequent speakers of the language have the change. Only in exceptional cases is this idealised picture violated, with later speakers in one region having the change and those in another region lacking it, and this defines the moment at which a split has occurred; there are now two languages, one with the change and one without it, one in one region and one in another. Thus this type of idealised model ignores the possibility of horizontal transfer of material between non-identical languages, ignores internal variation, and minimises consideration of space as much as possible.

This way of thinking has much utility for dealing with comparative reconstruction and the languages of deep prehistory where our data is extremely sparse and where, as a result of Occam's Razor, a maximally simplified picture is the best we can hope to achieve. It is, however, difficult to square with the data of synchronic dialectology and the historical linguistics of the more recent past, where internal variation and contact effects are hard to ignore. The wave model (Wellentheorie, Schmidt 1872; Bloomfield 1933: 317) responds to this difficulty. In this model, changes are conceived of as occurring first at some specific point in space before being spread outwards by contact between speakers. Since speakers are in closer contact with people living near to them, an innovation in this model will always spread between adjacent localities: to reach distant localities, it must first spread to all those in between. From the point of view of dialectology, this will produce innovations in single, contiguous domains, whereas it allows for the possibility that conservative features will be used in non-contiguous domains where the later diffusion of an innovation has divided the space. Crucially, the wave model doesn't impose discrete boundaries on languages: changes are more likely to spread between structurally similar varieties, but there is no hard-and-fast cut-off. As a result, the set of features that can be shared by any two varieties is arbitrary, and the difference between two 'languages' is a continuous space where any number of points can be populated with real dialects (i.e. a dialect continuum). To unify our terminology with that of other fields, we might refer to the kind of spatially continuous spread of change that the wave model predicts as contagion diffusion.

The wave model has had much success, especially in explaining the distributions mapped in the dialectology of traditional European varieties. Nevertheless, it too makes important idealisations and simplifications, and there are data it struggles to account for. In terms of the underlying mechanism by which change spreads, the model of speaker mobility and language contact is very simple, and does not account for long-distance movement and contact, or for a greater frequency of movement in some particular direction. This means that the model cannot produce non-contiguous domains of innovation, and such domains have been found, especially in modern sociolinguistic data. Peter Trudgill, drawing on the work of earlier geographers (particularly Hägerstrand 1952; also Olsson 1965; Haggett 1965), proposed the gravity model (Trudgill 1974; Chambers & Trudgill 1980) to account for these deficits. In the gravity model, the linguistic influence of any population centre on any other is a function of their relative populations (larger places have greater influence on smaller places) and their distances (nearer places have greater influence than distant places). The mechanism behind this is, again, primarily mobility and contact: speakers have more motivation to travel into larger population centres and so the varieties spoken in such centres are necessarily in contact with a larger region; even if this is not the case, speakers may be more likely to come into contact with speakers from more populous places simply because there are more of them. In terms of spatial patterns, this should produce an identifiable point of innovation, with uptake of the change falling off with distance from this point, but also a series of discontinuous zones around larger towns and cities. This was found to fit sociolinguistic data from the south of England, with changes spreading out from London, and innovations in Modern Norwegian as spoken in the Brunlanes peninsula. A simpler variation on this was later put forward by Labov, labelled the cascade model (Labov 2001). In the cascade model change diffuses down a hierarchy of urban settlements by size, with little reference to their relative distances. This can better explain sociolinguistic data where we have discontinuous regions of change around major population centres but cannot identify a single most innovative location that could have been the point of innovation. Regardless which of these two models is preferred, we might refer to this kind of spread in which changes 'jump' between centres of population density before reaching intervening regions and in which urban locations are ahead of rural ones as hierarchy diffusion.

The opposite spatial pattern has also been observed, that of an innovation adopted preferentially in rural regions, with urban centres lagging behind. This 'contra-hierarchy' patterning was first identified by Bailey et al. (1993) and Wikle & Bailey (1997) for innovations in English dialects of Oklahoma, but has also been observed for *l*-vocalisation in Swiss German dialects (Leemann et al. 2014). It is generally explained by scholars as resulting from identity factors, whereby particular innovative features become markers of rural identity and so are rejected by urbanites (Bailey et al. 1993; Wolfram & Schilling-Estes 2003), rather than with reference to mobility and contact. Fagyal et al. (2010) explain it as resulting from the ability of dense but isolated clusters in social networks to converge on new variants through stochastic processes alone, where this would be highly unlikely for the larger network: this would suggest it might be easier for innovations (of all sorts) to succeed in rural areas, if we accept the assumption that social networks in such areas are more likely to form relatively isolated clusters.

I have so far described these as different models of language change, implying that each model is trying to explain the same real-world phenomena and infer the same real-world mechanisms of change. Under this way of thinking, finding discontinuous spread of innovations with cities leading a change (hierarchy diffusion) is counterevidence for the wave model, and finding a single continuous innovative area with no effect of population density (contagion diffusion) is counterevidence for the cascade and gravity models; finding contra-hierarchy diffusion is counterevidence for all three models. However, if we instead conceive of the three observed patterns of diffusion as three separate and robustly observed phenomena then the different models are not necessarily in conflict, but are simply attempting to explain different things: the wave model attempts to explain contagion diffusion; the cascade model attempts to explain hierarchy diffusion; and the gravity model attempts to explain both.

Burridge (2017; 2018) and Burridge & Blaxter (2020; 2021) propose models for linguistic diffusion adapted from statistical physics which have the capacity to generate all three types of pattern. Variation and change is driven by acquisition from nearby speakers and 'conformity', a bias for the plurality variant in the input. Speakers have an interaction kernel which determines their likelihood of coming into contact with other speakers as a function of distance: the further away, the lower the likelihood of contact. These elements alone will generate dialect regions with isoglosses, and contagion diffusion through the movement of those isoglosses. Population density also plays a role in the model: because the likelihood of contact between any two speakers is a function of their distance, if there are more speakers at a given locality then speakers at nearby low-density localities will have a disproportionate amount of contact with that locality and be more likely to adopt its usage. As a result, an isogloss that runs through a population density gradient of this type will tend to move away from the high density location: isoglosses will tend to form and be stable around cities. Given this, if an innovation starts in a rural area, we might expect the result to be contra-hierarchy diffusion, and if an innovation starts in an urban area, that area will tend to remain in a leading position. Finally, adding long-distance migration to the model allows for changes to spread discontinuously. Again, the simple fact of there being more speakers in higher-density areas, with the possibility of discontinuous spread and the repelling effect of population density gradients, will generate hierarchy diffusion. In short, then, the Burridge model can generate all three patterns we have discussed depending on the locations of innovations, rates of mobility and patterns of population density.

Whether it is right to conclude that all three spatial patterns are real and so the job of our models is to explain all of them, or whether the cascade or wave model alone might offer a complete picture already, is an empirical matter. Much of the data used in dialectological, historical linguistic and sociolinguistic research on these topics shares certain (sometimes unavoidable) weaknesses: datasets are typically too small, and patterns are not often subjected to rigorous statistical testing; datasets are often synchronic, or data treated as synchronic, which necessitates an extra analytical step to infer diachronic processes of change. In principle, it might turn out to be the case that one or more of our three observed types of diffusion is rare or non-existent with good enough data and statistical measures. Perhaps, for example, cities always have an influence on change and all spread is by hierarchy diffusion, but a tendency to treat rural and urban varieties separately in traditional dialectology combined with the difficulty of inferring dynamics from later stable states has created the illusion of contagion diffusion? Conversely, perhaps something about how we collect data for modern sociolinguistics has created hierarchy-type patterns artificially in our data?

More plausibly, it might seem conceivable that the different phenomena are associated with different periods of history. Since the wave model was largely a response to dialectological data explored in the nineteenth century – mapping the outcomes of linguistic changes which had happened in the Late Medieval and Early Modern periods – it might be that contagion diffusion was the norm at an earlier stage in the history of European languages and cultures. Since the gravity model was a response to sociolinguistic data gathered in the late-twentieth century from living languages, hierarchy diffusion might only have become the norm in the Late Modern period. This would seem entirely consonant with mechanisms centred on mobility and contact: as mobility, and particularly long-distance mobility, increased (due to changes in transport technology, increasing wealth, and changes in subsistence patterns following the industrial revolution), the relevance of immediate proximity should have declined and other factors could have come to play a greater role. As cities expanded and so population density gradients increased, the possibility that city dialects would behave differently to rural dialects might have come to the fore.

This could be supported if when examining rich, diachronic data for historical varieties we found primarily contagion diffusion, in contrast to commonly finding hierarchy diffusion in the richest modern sociolinguistic datasets. This is a hypothesis I will test on medieval Norwegian data in this chapter – although the reader will have noticed that it is already undermined by the evidence of chapters 5 and 6. The alternative possibility is that two or even all three types of diffusion process can be robustly observed in the medieval Norwegian data. This would offer support for the approach represented by the gravity model and the Burridge model, which assume that multiple spatial phenomena exist and that a good model of language change must therefore be able to reproduce multiple different kinds of spatial pattern.

To go further still, the models make predictions about the contexts in which different diffusion patterns should arise which we can test against the data. Both the Burridge model and the gravity model suggest that population density and migration patterns are relevant to this question, with hierarchy diffusion more likely with sharper population density gradients (i.e. bigger, denser cities) and more migration; the Burridge model suggests that point of innovation is also relevant, with innovations that begin in urban varieties more likely to undergo hierarchy diffusion and those which begin in rural varieties more likely to undergo contra-hierarchy diffusion.

What, then, was the demographic situation over the period covered? It is clear from a variety of types of evidence (most strikingly documentary records of abandoned farms) that the population reached a peak around the end of the thirteenth century and had declined substantially by the mid-sixteenth (Brothen 1996: 144; Orrman 2003b: 264; Antonson 2009). The general assumption in earlier scholarship had been that this was due to the plague in 1349 (which has been estimated by some historians as killing over 50 per cent of the population in Norway; Vahtola 2003) and the many smaller repetitions of this epidemic in the subsequent decades. However, more recent work has shown that the decline started earlier, likely around 1300. No doubt the plague hastened the process of depopulation, but climate change and resulting agricultural crisis and famine seem to have been central; Norwegian subsistence agriculture was highly labour-intensive, and there may have been a negative feedback loop in the viability of farming settlements so that once the population started to decrease, agricultural failure and resulting famine became increasingly more likely (Brothen 1996; Dybdahl 2012; Thun & Svarva 2018).

In principle, changes in the absolute size of the population alone do not play any role in these models of language diffusion – however, changes in relative population density or changes in migration patterns could have an effect. The plague probably hit worst in the most densely populated areas, particularly towns, where transmission was easiest (Holmsen 1984). This would have the effect of decreasing the sharpness of population density gradients and so lessening the likelihood of hierarchy or contra-hierarchy diffusion. However, rapid in-migration (partly from rural areas made uninhabitable by the degree of depopulation) is thought to have balanced out this effect to a significant degree (Dahlbäck 2003: 616), and overall urbanisation in Scandinavia largely stood still over the period covered, having reached a peak with something like 5 per cent of the population living in towns in 1300 in Denmark, 3 per cent in Sweden and Norway (Benedictow 2003: 237, 248). Thus we might not expect any changes in the overall propensity for (contra-)hierarchy vs. contagion diffusion as a direct consequence of the plague, but might expect an increase in the speed of changes triggered by a brief increase in the rate of long-distance communication of variants due to migration. On the other hand, it has been suggested that the depopulation was unevenly distributed across the country when the period is taken as a whole, with the effects worst in the north and west, and least dramatic in the south-east (Brothen 1996). This would imply a long-term, gradual increase in the tendency towards hierarchy effects, since the south-east was already the most densely populated area in which urbanisation had progressed the furthest.

As an aside, it is worth noting that Scandinavian towns were small by European standards of the time, and Norwegian towns small by Scandinavian standards (Dahlbäck 2003: 615). This might lead one to expect to see little evidence of hierarchy diffusion, if a certain threshold of urbanisation is needed to trigger this phenomenon; of course, we already have strong indications that this expectation would be wrong.

It is also worth considering what other factors might influence the spatial patterns we see when innovations diffuse. Anything which affects the learnability of an innovation – especially if it does so differentially for different kinds of speakers, or for speakers of different varieties – might exert some influence over its diffusion pathway. At its simplest, we might see effects associated with the linguistic domain of a variable. Types of variable more easily acquirable by adults and so more subject to adult change might be more shaped by long-distance migration: such variables might undergo more rapid change (cf. Nevalainen et al. 2011) and be more likely to diffuse discontinuously, showing hierarchy-type patterning. The most obvious candidates here would be lexical variables, surface phonetic variables, and any other variables which are easily available to conscious awareness (Sankoff 2013). Relatedly, since it has been observed that adults can change the relative frequencies of variants more easily than they can acquire new variants (Nahkola & Saanilahti 2004; Sankoff & Blondeau 2007; Raumolin-Brunberg 2009), we might expect re-organisations of existing systems of stable variation to be particularly subject to rapid, hierarchical change. On the other hand, complex variants, and variables deeply embedded in the grammar, seem less accessible for adult change (Labov 2007; Meyerhoff & Walker 2007; Sankoff & Blondeau 2007: 581). These, then, might be expected to change more slowly, with patterns determined by local rather than long-distance contacts. This most obviously implies contra-hierarchical or contagion diffusion, but it could also result in a leading position for a city with a clear isogloss around it but without discontinuous spread to other urban centres, if the innovation in question arose in an urban variety.

7.2. Methods

7.2.1. Approach

I will consider three approaches to exploring hierarchicality in these data; the first two of these I have already put to use in chapter 5. Firstly, we could simply use the kernel smoothing method to visualise the spatial distributions of variants over the course of changes and judge impressionistically how well what we see matches the different possible patterns. We would expect multiple urban centres to stand out as leading localities in the kernel smoothed estimates of a variable undergoing hierarchy diffusion; we would expect to see a single, continuous and expanding region of change in a variable undergoing contagion diffusion; and we would expect to see cities visibly lagging behind for a variable undergoing contra-hierarchy diffusion.

Secondly, again using kernel smoothing, we can set bandwidths to allow the comparison of estimates and error margins for particular localities, and thereby compare cities to individual smaller locations in their immediate vicinity. For both hierarchy and contra-hierarchy diffusion we would then expect to see significant differences in such comparisons, given the right moment in the change and a sufficiently large dataset.

Thirdly, instead of looking at specific localities, we can devise a test for hierarchy effects across the entire map and entire trajectory of a change. At any given moment, for a change undergoing hierarchy diffusion, urban centres should be ahead of the overall average for the language area and rural areas should be behind: in other words, there should be a positive correlation between innovativeness and population density. By contrast, for contra-hierarchy diffusion there should be a negative correlation and for contagion diffusion we might expect no correlation.

There are problems with all three of these approaches. Impressionistically identifying spatial patterns in kernel smoothed estimates tells us nothing about whether those patterns are large enough and supported by enough data that we should have confidence in them; we cannot know by this approach alone that such patterns are not the accidental effects of noise. Testing for differences between specific localities at specific times partially solves this problem, but is not without its own issues. Because we have to select specific locations to test, this could be subject to the criticism of p-hacking: we use an impressionistic measure to identify where the sharpest differences in the dataset are and only test those. This method also underutilises the data. Because the kernel functions work on the basis of distances from a specified point, we are not testing for a difference between the estimate in the city and estimates in *all* neighbouring rural locations, but just a single rural location. Where (as is always the case) we are faced with a paucity of data from such rural locations, we may end up concluding that we do not have enough data to come to any firm conclusion, in spite of the fact that we could have a much larger sample if we treated all rural locations together. Testing for hierarchy effects across an entire map by looking for correlations between innovativeness and population density solves these problems, but introduces new ones. Macro-scale patterns resulting from the place of innovation interacting with the uneven placement of cities could interfere with expected correlations. For example, a change spreading by contra-hierarchy diffusion which arose in south-eastern Norway might still show a positive correlation between innovativeness and population density overall, since even rural areas in south-eastern Norway had greater population density than much of the rest of the country. Conversely a change spreading by contagion diffusion but starting in a very low population-density region might show a negative correlation overall.

For these reasons, it is helpful to use all three methods together. If we can identify hierarchy effects impressionistically in the kernel smoothed estimates and these can be confirmed by one or both of our statistical tests, this can be taken as much stronger evidence than we could glean from any one of these approaches alone.[33] Conversely if our methods conflict, this suggests we need to look more closely at the data before coming to any strong conclusion.

---

[33] Another issue with the statistical approach to measuring hierarchicality proposed here is that it requires us to define the innovative variant in each instance. For this reason and those discussed above it is also worth exploring other statistical measures of hierarchicality that are insensitive to direction of change, and this is done in Blaxter et al. (forthcoming).

7.2.2. Hierarchicality measure

Kernel smoothed estimates in time (here labelled N) were calculated for each innovative variant of each variable; these are used as overall reference values for the extent of the change across the whole language area for each point in time. For each charter 1. . .b, we can also calculate its degree of change (i.e. the relative frequency of the innovative variant in that document) which we will label C. The reference value for national degree of change for the date of publication of a document n_y is then subtracted from its degree of change c_b to give its deviation from the expected degree of change d_b. For example, a document b with two tokens, one of the innovative variant and one of the conservative variant, would have a degree of change $c_b = 0.5$. If the document is dated at a point when the country as a whole has an estimated average degree of change $n_y = 0.3$, then the deviation would be $d_b = 0.2$: this document is 20 per cent ahead of the point we might expect a document to be at this date. On the other hand, if it were dated at a point when the country as a whole had an estimated average degree of change of $n_y = 0.9$, the deviation would be $d_b = -0.4$: this document represents a point in the change 40 per cent behind what we might expect given its date.

For population density estimates, I have used purely spatial kernel smoothed estimates for all original documents in the corpus: these were calculated with a Gaussian kernel with a 20km bandwidth.[34, 35] There are advantages and disadvantages to this approach. Of course, it is likely that rates of document production per head of population were not static across the country – this measure likely overestimates the density of the cities and underestimates the density of rural areas. As a partial correction for this, the measure has been scaled to realistic

---

[34] This bandwidth was determined by checking the density distributions we see with a series of different bandwidths and comparing them to the distribution of recognised towns in the period from Andersson (2003: 331). Higher bandwidths tended to merge multiple towns in the south-east into a single undifferentiated peak, whilst lower bandwidths create a very noisy distribution with many peaks of density that do not reflect known large settlements but simply clusters of related documents preserved together.

[35] Of course, as already discussed, relative population density probably changed across the period covered and it could be argued that we should instead be using a measure of population density that reflects this: in other words, using a temporal kernel as well as a spatial one for estimating population density from charter localisations. This was not done for two reasons. Firstly, there are simply not enough data. Such an approach would result in a very noisy measure, and this would undermine the meaningfulness of any correlations calculated with it. Secondly, there are substantial changes in the frequency of document localisations to particular areas over time that do *not* reflect changes in population density. For example, in the very latest period covered when most writing in Norway had shifted to Danish, we find relatively more documents in the corpus from Telemark. This is not because the population increased in Telemark but a product of drafting traditions and decisions made by the editors of the DN series about which documents were worthy of inclusion: the very latest documents represent those which show some sign of continuing earlier drafting traditions rather than being written entirely within the Danish tradition, and these earlier traditions seem to have been maintained for somewhat longer in Telemark. To take another example, the archives of the Catholic bishop Olav Engelbrektsson were preserved unusually fully due to his exile during the Reformation, creating a spike of documents to and from high-status individuals in the church in the 1520s and 1530s in our corpus, and these are disproportionately localised to cities. A time-sensitive measure of population density from these data would give the false impression that the population of the cities rose hugely in these two decades before falling again.

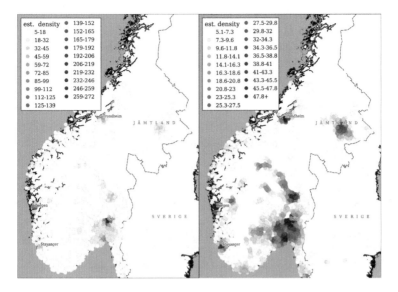

Figure 91. Estimated population density on the basis of charter localisations [Colour figure can be viewed at wileyonlinelibrary.com]

estimates of the maximum and minimum population density for the locations under study (of course, this has no effect on correlations, but gives a useful real-world interpretation of the values).[36] It will also generate spikes of apparent density at localities which were hubs of document production but not urban centres, such as monasteries. This density measure we will label P, with the density for the set of localisations for each document denoted p_b; these are visualised in Figure 91. The left-hand panel shows the raw densities; the right-hand panel shows the densities capped at 50 people/km², in order to better see how the smaller variations in density are distributed. As can be seen from the figure, this density measure clearly allows us to distinguish the cities of Oslo, Bergen, Hamar, Trondheim, Stavanger and Tønsberg from their surroundings; however, smaller cities like Stavanger are not actually much denser than rural parts of the populated south-east, and Oslo in

---

[36] The maximum population density was determined on the basis of Bergen, the most populous city. The area of the modern Bergenhus district, roughly equivalent to the old town, is 25.41km, and Dahlbäck (2003: 615) estimates the population of the city in 1500 as 7000; this implies a maximum local population density for Norway of 275.4821/km². For the minimum density, the parish of Valle, a parish far inland in Setesdal, was examined. On the basis of articles in Rygh et al. (1898–1936) this was estimated to have 33 medieval farms (i.e. there are 33 farms attested on or before 1600); given Benedictow's (2003: 240) estimate of 4.5 persons per farm, this implies a population of 148.5 people. A minimum convex hull was drawn around the co-ordinates of those of these farms that occur in our corpus to estimate the area of the parish at 29.2808km². This suggests a minimum population density of 5.0716/km². Note that this is far higher than estimates like Benedictow's for Jämtland of 0.15/km², but this reflects our particular goal: we are interested in the population density *in populated areas*, since this is the population density relevant to the question of how and when speakers would come into contact with each other. Very low estimates like Benedictow's reflect the inclusion of the enormous uninhabited regions which characterise the Scandinavian landscape.

particular is far denser than any other locality. When we look at variation at the lower end of the scale, we find that some rural regions are, by this measure, far more densely populated than others: the whole of Viken, but especially Eiker, northern Østfold and central Akershus; Frösön in Jämtland; parts of Gudbrandsdal; and parts of Telemark all stand out. Whether these variations really reflect differences in the medieval population density or not is a question beyond the scope of this chapter, but they should be borne in mind in interpreting our results. Of course, the handful of Swedish localities to which documents in the corpus are localised get extremely low estimates of population density; this is simply a product of the fact that this is largely a corpus of Norwegian.

We then define our measure of hierarchicality ι as the Pearson's correlation coefficient of document innovativeness $D_{1...b}$ and estimated population density at document localisation $P_{1...b}$ across all documents:

$$\iota = \frac{\text{cov}(D_{1...b}, \ P_{1...b})}{\sigma_D \sigma_P}.$$

In practice, weighted Pearson's correlation coefficients are needed to take into account the multiple and differently weighted localisations for each text. Thus weighted Pearson's correlation coefficients were calculated for each innovation using the R package *weights* (Pasek 2020). This was done with bootstrapping of standard errors and p-values with 10,000 bootstraps. The results of these calculations are given in Table 39.

Note that documents were included in these calculations only if they were dated in a period when the innovation was increasing and the estimated national

Table 39. Correlations (ι) between local population density (P) and document innovativeness relative to nationwide degree of change (D)

Innovation	Correlation ι	Bootstrapped correlation	Standard error	t value	p value
1sg -(V)r	0.1511	0.1513	0.0375	4.0313	0.0000
verða>blífa	0.0301	0.0301	0.0143	2.1138	0.0372
svarabhakti vowels	—0.0641	−0.0642	0.0091	−7.0573	0.0000
loss of [ð]	0.0120	0.0120	0.0119	1.0092	0.3172
loss of [θ]	0.0011	0.0010	0.0158	0.0661	0.9428
loss of genitives	0.1240	0.1239	0.0143	8.6377	0.0000
1pl -V (VS)	−0.0078	−0.0077	0.0079	−0.9661	0.3300
1pl -V (SV)	0.1948	0.1949	0.0103	18.8992	0.0000
1pl -(V)r	−0.0250	−0.0247	0.0204	−1.2097	0.2222
1pl -Vz	0.0259	0.0260	0.0217	1.1960	0.2320
1pl vér>mér	−0.0283	−0.0284	0.0207	−1.3758	0.1706
1pl mér>vi	0.1289	0.1288	0.0125	10.2612	0.0000
1pl mér>mit	−0.1350	−0.1349	0.0113	-11.8978	0.0000
1du vit>mit	−0.0127	−0.0126	0.0309	−0.4090	0.6868
1du mit>mér	−0.0053	−0.0054	0.0172	−0.3159	0.7510
1du mit>vi	0.1462	0.1460	0.0151	9.6617	0.0000

rate of the innovation was between 5 and 95 per cent. These restrictions were put on the data for three reasons. Firstly, the rates of variants can fluctuate in their early stages and their late stages for very long periods of time without showing any consistent direction of change; since there is no overall trajectory, it does not make sense to talk of hierarchy vs. contra-hierarchy vs. contagion diffusion, which describe processes of expansion of an innovation. If included, these data might overwhelm the signal from the period of rapid change. Second, these are models of *innovation* diffusion; for variants which both expand and recede in the period covered, only during the period of expansion should they be classed as innovations, and so the data from periods of decline are excluded. Thirdly, if we are using this method to help interpretation of the visualisations of the kernel smoothed estimates in earlier chapters, we should restrict ourselves to roughly the periods covered by those visualisations.

Another consideration I have not yet mentioned concerns overall changes in the relative proportion of documents localised to cities over the period covered by the corpus. If the proportion of documents localised to cities (or to high population density regions generally) is increasing over the course of a change, then data from cities will tend to be dated later than data from rural areas; as a result, a larger proportion of data showing the change will come from cities, and the kernel smoothed estimates will show artefactual pattern of cities leading. The converse effect will apply if the proportion of documents localised to cities is trending down. These artefacts will not influence ι, however, since individual documents are compared to a national average calculated without reference to spatial variation.

To check whether this effect might be a problem for any of the specific datasets investigated here, kernel smoothed estimates of the local population

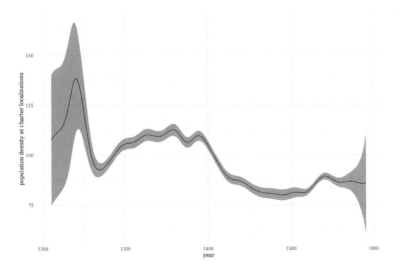

Figure 92. Kernel smoothed estimates of average population density at charter localisations by year [Colour figure can be viewed at wileyonlinelibrary.com]

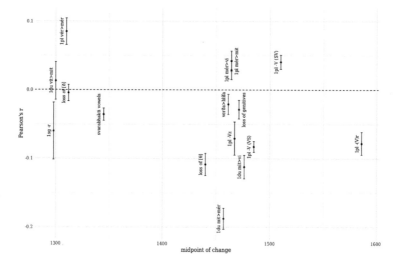

Figure 93. Correlations between local population density and document date by change mid-year, excluding data outside the 5-95 per cent rate for each change

density for locations to which charters were localised by charter date were calculated and are visualised in Figure 92: using this, we can see impressionistically whether the proportion of documents coming from high-density regions is increasing or decreasing at a given moment in time. Over the entire period covered by the corpus there is a gradual decrease in the average estimated population density at the locations to which charters are localised; this may reflect that the chances of document survival gradually increase with younger documents, and so a greater proportion of low-status documents from rural areas are extant among later charters. It could alternatively be taken to imply a real process of deurbanisation. Either way, this trend is slow enough that it is unlikely to influence any of the individual changes we are studying here, and is swamped in a number of individual periods by more rapid changes: a very sharp decrease in average population density at localisations in the second half of the thirteenth century; a more gradual increase going into the fourteenth century; and a steady decrease from the late fourteenth to the late fifteenth centuries. Figure 93 then shows the correlation between document date[37] and estimated population density at document localisations for each individual dataset including only documents when the overall rate of the change in question is estimated at between 5 and 95 per cent. These two figures thus provide us with a way to check whether changing trends in document localisations could have artificially produced an impression of cities leading or lagging in kernel smoothed estimates.

---

[37] Since document date is known in most cases down to the day, we can reasonably think of it as a continuous variable.

7.3. *Variables*

Only two new variables are introduced here: the spread of the reanalysed 1pl pronoun *mér*, replacing earlier *vér*, and the spread of the reanalysed 1du. pronoun *mit*, replacing earlier *vit*. These two are discussed below, and temporal and spatial-temporal kernel smoothed estimates are given (these two changes are also discussed in more detail in Blaxter 2019). The other changes included in our analysis have already been explored in chapters 5 and 6; the reader is referred back to those chapters for summaries and visualisations.

7.3.1. *Replacement of 1pl vér by reanalysed mér*

The replacement of the Old Norse 1pl nominative pronoun *vér* with the reanalysed form *mér* took place in the late thirteenth and early fourteenth centuries, at the early edge of the period we can reasonably investigate with this corpus, and so as with the levelling of 1sg. agreement and loss of voiced dental fricatives we are hampered by scarce and unbalanced data. The kernel smoothed estimates of different variants of this pronoun over time are visualised in Figure 94 (note that this is repeated from Figure 65) and the spatial kernel smoothed estimates of the innovative variant *mér* mapped in Figure 95.

We can see from these figures that there is no hint of a hierarchy effect in the spread of *mér*: the most innovative region for the whole course of the change is Oppland, particularly Gudbrandsdalen, Valdres and Hallingdal[38], and there might be some indication of a contra-hierarchy effect with cities lagging behind (particularly note the position of Oslo in 1320). Due to the nature of the dataset, this effect would be very difficult to demonstrate by direct comparisons of adjacent localities. However, looking at the map as a whole, we can demonstrate that there are meaningful regional differences: Figure 96 shows estimates and error margins for the three major cities, demonstrating that the east-west difference we see in Figure 95 is statistically significant, with Oslo leading; Figure 97 shows the estimates and error margins for Oslo compared with Sør-Fron in Gudbrandsdal, and we can see that the rural area is substantially ahead for the entirety of the period covered.

---

[38] Note that in spite of the fact that the most innovative region in the kernel smoothed estimates is Oppland, all of the very earliest individual examples of the change are from Vestlandet (cf. discussion in Blaxter 2019): two in a text from Ullensvang (DN IV.6), two others from elsewhere in Hordaland (I.98, II.81), one from Bergen itself (IV.82), and one from Stavanger (IV.72). However, there are so few tokens from rural inner Østlandet before 1310, with or without the change, that this is hardly evidence that the change had progressed further in the rural west than the rural east, and the next earliest token of *mér* I have localised to Gol in Hallingdal (V.54; although note that the editors of the DN did not venture a localisation). After this time, the data suggest the change is more advanced in the east. We should trust the statistics here rather than being swayed by individual data points.

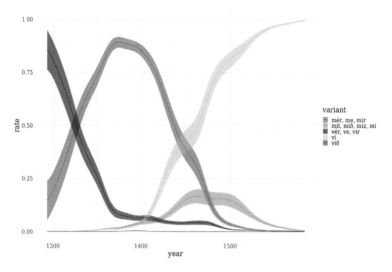

Figure 94. Kernel smoothed estimates of rates of morphological and lexical variants of the 1du./pl subject pronoun referring to more than two referents [Colour figure can be viewed at wileyonlinelibrary.com]

7.3.2. Replacement of 1du. vit by reanalysed mit

As with its plural counterpart, the replacement of the Old Norse 1du. nominative pronoun *vit* by the reanalysed form *mit* took place in the latter decades of the thirteenth and first half of the fourteenth centuries. The relative frequencies over time of different variants for the 1st person subject pronoun with two referents were estimated using kernel smoothing; these are given in Figure 98 (note that this is repeated from Figure 62). Spatial kernel smoothed estimates for the period 1300-1360 are visualised in Figure 99. Note that the change we are interested in here happens very early in the period covered by the corpus, at a point when the dataset is small and poorly distributed in space: this limits what we can say about spatial patterns.

Here, we see a relatively similar picture to that seen in section 7.3.1 for plural contexts, although the change is a little more advanced at the earliest point for which we can make estimates, and the differentiation of localities within the country is a little sharper. The whole of Østlandet is consistently innovative throughout the change; there is no sign of a hierarchy effect, although there is perhaps some contra-hierarchicality, with Oslo and Tønsberg lagging behind the rest of Viken. Of the rest of the country, the change takes longest to reach the south-west. At an earlier point, Stavanger stands out as the most conservative locality, but by the end of the change Bergen has swapped places with it to take this title. Comparison of individual localities is difficult with a dataset this small, but comparison of the three major cities (Figure 100) at least demonstrates that the difference between Oslo in the east and Bergen in the west is larger than the error margins.

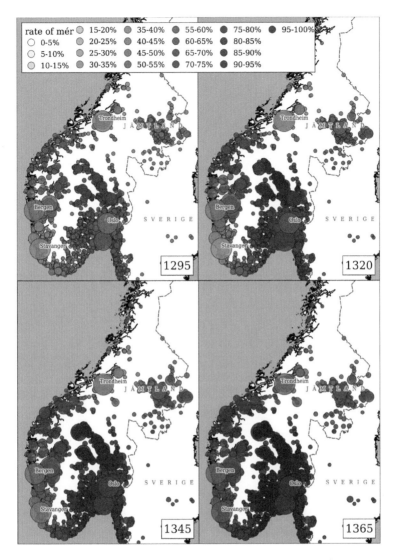

Figure 95. Spatial kernel smoothed estimates for the occurrence of reanalysed *mér* for plural referents for 1295-1365 [Colour figure can be viewed at wileyonlinelibrary.com]

7.4. *Results*

The correlations ι between estimated population density and innovativeness for each change, first given in Table 39, are visualised against the time at which the change crosses its midpoint in Figure 101. Table 40 summarises the results of each method for each change (changes are ordered by ι from low to high).

For certain changes, the results of our different methods reinforce each other, with the consequence that we can be reasonably confident in identifying a given

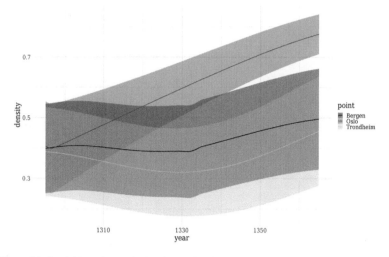

Figure 96. Spatial kernel smoothed estimates for the occurrence of reanalysed *mér* for plural referents for Bergen, Oslo and Trondheim [Colour figure can be viewed at wileyonlinelibrary.com]

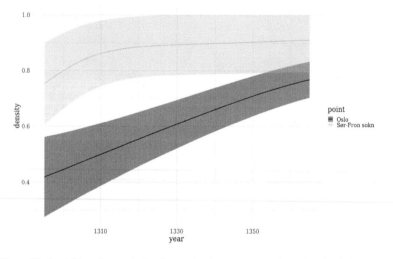

Figure 97. Spatial kernel smoothed estimates for the occurrence of reanalysed *mér* for plural referents for Oslo and Sør-Fron [Colour figure can be viewed at wileyonlinelibrary.com]

pattern. For the replacement of *mér* by *mit* for 1pl subjects, we can identify the cities lagging in visualisations of the kernel smoothed estimates (the change begins and spreads from a rural area but seems to skirt the cities when it reaches the south-east), this is confirmed as significant by comparisons of specific localities, and ι is negative (i.e. there is a significant negative correlation between document innovativeness and population density at localisation). There is a

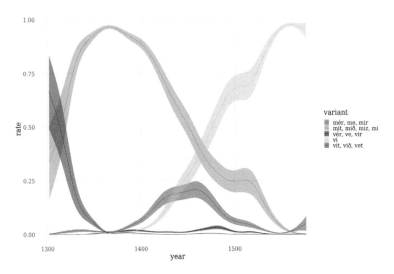

Figure 98. Kernel smoothed estimates of rates of morphological and lexical variants of the 1du./pl subject pronoun referring to two referents [Colour figure can be viewed at wileyonlinelibrary.com]

slight positive correlation between charter date and population density at localisation for this dataset, which would have the *opposite* effect on the kernel smoothed estimates to the one we see, making cities look more innovative and rural areas more conservative. Thus we can be very confident that this is a real example of contra-hierarchy diffusion.

For the shift from -*Vm* to -*V* on 1pl verbs in SUBJECT-VERB order, the opposite situation holds. Impressionistic examination of the kernel smoothed estimates shows the cities leading by a dramatic margin, and this is confirmed by comparisons between specific localities. There is a positive correlation between population density at localisation and document date, which might tend to generate such an appearance of innovative cities artificially, but it is very weak and so unlikely to be responsible for the strong effect we see in the kernel smoothed estimates. This is confirmed by a strong, positive ι, which cannot be a product of changing localisation population density. Therefore we can be clear that this is a real example of hierarchy diffusion.

At times, we find that our different methods clash. For the loss of genitive objects of *millum* and for the levelling of 1sg -*(V)* to -*(V)r*, inspection of the kernel smoothed estimates seems to show cities leading, but comparison of specific localities suggested that we did not have enough data to support this. For both of these variables, however, ι is strongly positive. An obvious way of understanding this is that although we do not have enough data from the specific localities compared to demonstrate the hierarchy diffusion pattern there, we *do* have enough data when all localities are taken together. These, then, should be considered solid examples of hierarchy diffusion. The same observations could

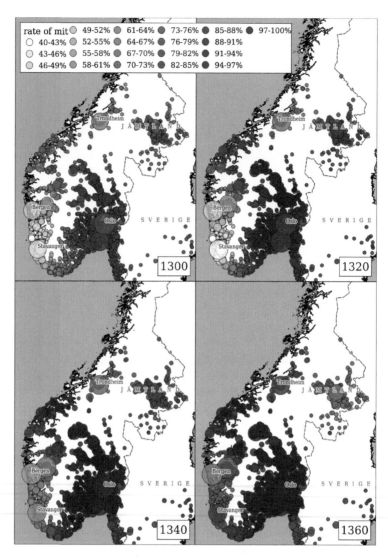

Figure 99. Spatial kernel smoothed estimates for the occurrence of reanalysed *mit* for dual referents for 1300-1360 [Colour figure can be viewed at wileyonlinelibrary.com]

be made concerning the replacement of 1pl *mér* by borrowed *vi*, but here both the correlation and the visible trend of leading cities are much weaker, so we should be more cautious. The appearance in the kernel smoothed estimates of cities leading here could also be a product of upward trending localisation population density.

A parallel case of contra-hierarchy diffusion can be seen in the replacement of 1pl *vér* by reanalysed *mér*: we do not have enough data to demonstrate contrasts

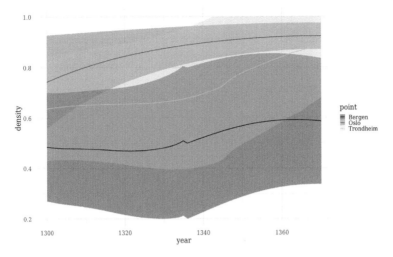

Figure 100. Spatial kernel smoothed estimates for the occurrence of reanalysed *mit* for dual referents for Bergen, Oslo and Trondheim [Colour figure can be viewed at wileyonlinelibrary.com]

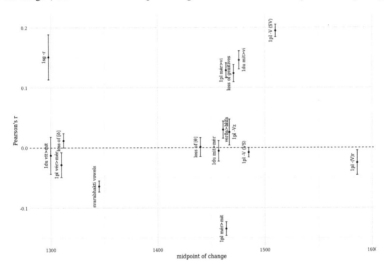

Figure 101. Correlations (*ι*) between local population density (P$_{1...b}$) and document innovativeness relative to nationwide degree of change (D$_{1...b}$) by change mid-year

between individual adjacent localities but we can demonstrate that some of the large-scale differences we see are significant by contrasting more distant localities; the impression of the overall pattern combined with the negative *ι*, especially in the context of countervailing trends in overall document localisation population density, means that we should probably conclude that this is an example of contra-hierarchy diffusion. Another parallel is found in the levelling to *-(V)r* for the present 1pl (i.e. loss of verb-subject agreement for

Table 40. Summary of results of different methods for assessing diffusion patterns for each change

Innovation	Impression of diffusion type	Locality contrasts significant	ι (correlation between innovativeness and pop. density)	Pop. density trend
1pl *mér>mit*	contra-hierarchy	yes	negative	↑
svarabhakti vowels	contagion		negative	↓
1pl *vér>mér*	slight contra-hierarchy	yes	marginally negative	↑
present 1pl *-(V)r*	slight contra-hierarchy	no	marginally negative	↓
1du *vit>mit*	contagion	yes	none	-
1pl *-V* (VS)	slight hierarchy	yes	none	↓
1du *mit>mér*	contagion		none	↓
loss of [θ]	contagion		none	↓
loss of [ð]	contagion		marginally positive	-
1pl *-Vz*	contagion		marginally positive	↓
verða>blífa	little pattern		marginally positive	↓
loss of genitives	hierarchy	no	positive	↓
1pl *mér>vi*	slight hierarchy	no	positive	↑
1du *mit>vi*	contagion		positive	↓
1sg *-(V)r*	hierarchy	no	positive	↓
1pl *-V* (SV)	hierarchy	yes	positive	↑

number). Examination of the kernel smoothed estimates for this variable indicated a marginal tendency for cities to lag behind at the edge of the innovative region, but this might have been a product of the downward trending localisation population density during this period in the corpus; certainly, it could not be confirmed by comparison of individual localities. However, ι is slightly negative, suggesting that we are seeing a contra-hierarchy effect here, albeit a very weak(ly evidenced) one.

Other clashes demand more nuanced interpretation. The rise of svarabhakti vowels shows the second largest negative ι value, strongly implying a change spreading by contra-hierarchy diffusion, and yet the change overall was judged as an example of contagion diffusion by examination of the kernel smoothed estimates (Figure 60). Population density at localisations is trending down across this dataset, which should reinforce an appearance of cities lagging behind, so this does not explain the mismatch. Closer examination of the kernel smoothed estimates shows that Oslo does lag slightly behind surrounding rural areas at the very beginning of the period covered: this might suggest a contra-hierarchy pattern that applied only during the early decades of the change. However, it is also notable that due to the pathway the diffusion of the innovation follows (reaching Vestlandet only via Gundbrandsdal and Romsdal), two of the largest cities, Bergen and Trondheim, are very late to change; this could create or reinforce a negative ι value, but is not contra-hierarchy diffusion. Thus although we might speculate about the change being spread by contra-hierarchy diffusion in its early stages, for the main period for which we have evidence we should conclude this is an example of contagion diffusion.

The replacement of dual *mit* by borrowed *vi* is a partial parallel. Here the overall impression is equivocal or of contagion diffusion, but ι is positive, suggesting hierarchy diffusion. A closer reading of the kernel smoothed estimates (Figure 73) shows that the most conservative region that remains in the tail end of the change is inland, rural Telemark; this could be responsible for an overall negative correlation between innovativeness and population density, but would not fall under the definition of hierarchy diffusion, since it is not a product of change spreading outwards from the cities. However, also note that the most innovative region at the beginning of the change is Jämtland, an area with no cities – this might be expected to have the opposite effect on ι. If we then take seriously this leading position of Jämtland, it might imply that what we see here is contagion diffusion, with a change spreading from the north-east. However, there is little evidence for this in the rest of Norway, and given the status of Jämtland in the period in question it is likely to be a consequence of Swedish literary norms that tells us little about speech. With such equivocal results it is safest to simply label this change as showing no clear diffusion pattern.

The levelling of 1pl -*Vm* to -*V* in VERB-SUBJECT order is another particularly difficult example. Here, an impressionistic examination of the results of the kernel smoothing suggested an (admittedly slight) tendency for cities to lead the change; certainly this would rather be expected given that the parallel change in the other syntactic context, the levelling of 1pl -*Vm* to -*V* in SUBJECT-VERB order, shows a strong hierarchy effect. What is more, this tendency was confirmed as greater than the margins of error for at least one specific pair of locations, and localisation population density is trending down across this dataset, which would have the effect of minimising the appearance of cities leading. However, ι is non-significant for this dataset, failing to offer confirmation that there is a real tendency for cities to lead the change here overall.

Returning to the visualisation of the kernel smoothed estimates for this change (Figure 45), we may see a clue to what is happening. The observation that the cities lead compared with rural regions primarily refers to Bergen and Trondheim; crucially, Oslo does not show any effect, or shows it only extremely weakly, having roughly the same rate as the surrounding rural south east. The problem here, then, may be generated by the unique position of Oslo and of Viken in our dataset. Viken represents 46.71 per cent of localisations within Norway, 44.33 per cent if Bohuslän is excluded. The next best represented region is Vestlandet, a rather larger area but comprising 16.72 per cent of localisations. On top of this, Oslo itself has the highest estimated population density of any location by some margin. Given this, it may be difficult for the method to detect a hierarchy effect in other cities in Viken if Oslo itself is not innovative, and if there is no hierarchy effect within Viken then this may subsume a signal from the rest of the country. Further exploration of the data confirms this hypothesis. If we calculate ι only on the subset of data outside Viken, we find that $\iota = 0.1533$ ($p{\approx}0$); we find an even higher value of $\iota = 0.1729$ ($p{\approx}0$) if we restrict ourselves to mainland Norway. Conversely, if we look *only* at the data within Viken (53.73 per cent of the data for this change), we find that $\iota = -0.0473$ ($p{\approx}0$). In other words, there is evidence of a strong hierarchy effect outside Viken, but this is counterbalanced by a weak countervailing pattern within Viken. This latter is not obviously confirmed from the kernel smoothed estimates, so we should be cautious of labelling it an example of contra-hierarchy diffusion, but we can be confident in our identification of hierarchy diffusion in the rest of the country.

We can largely conclude that other variables reflect contagion diffusion or show no interpretable pattern. The loss of [θ] and of [ð], the replacement of 1du. *vit* with reanalysed *mit*, the levelling of 1du. *mit* to *mér*, and the levelling of 1pl middle *-Vmz* to *-Vz* all appeared on inspection to show no particular effect of cities and have marginal or no correlation between localisation population density and document innovativeness. All of them do, however, show spatial effects, with coherent innovative regions which expand over time. These, then, are clear examples of contagion diffusion.

The replacement of native *verða* with borrowed *blífa* has a marginally positive ι value, but examination of the kernel smoothed estimates shows little evidence of the cities leading, and indeed minimal spatial effects at all: there is no clear expanding innovative region which could lead us to label this contagion diffusion, and instead the innovation seems to rise everywhere simultaneously. We could label this as an example of a very weak hierarchy effect, or as having no determinable diffusion pattern at all. It is interesting to look together at the three changes that we can be absolutely confident are the results of contact since they involve borrowed material: the rise of *blífa* and the rise of *vi* for plural and dual contexts. Comparing the kernel smoothed estimates (Figures 18, 69 and 73) and the ι values for these three, we find that they all show the same pattern: very small spatial effects are visible in the kernel smoothed estimates compared with other variables, but ι is positive, suggesting a hierarchy effect. This slight hierarchy effect with little differentiation among regions of the country is perhaps the geospatial signal of a superstrate effect in the Norwegian of this period.

Table 41 and Figure 102 summarise the conclusions of these analyses. Six changes have been identified as examples of contagion diffusion, three as contra-hierarchy diffusion (one very tentatively), five as hierarchy diffusion (one very tentatively) and two as showing no clear pattern. In Figure 102, changes are given solid lines during the period in which the innovation is estimated at between 15 and 85 per cent nationally and dotted lines from 5 to 15 and 85 to 95 per cent; this is done to highlight when each change is in its period of rapid diffusion. In Table 41, notes about place of innovation and possible contact sources, summarised from the preceding chapters, have also been added.

7.5. *Discussion*

What patterns have we seen across the results explored here and what bearing do they have on the theoretical background discussed in section 7.1? Firstly, and most trivially, these data clearly speak in favour of the idea that all three spatial patterns

Table 41. Summary of change diffusion types

Innovation	Diffusion type	Likely place of innovation in Norway	Contact
loss of [θ]	contagion	north-east	Swedish(?)
loss of [ð]	contagion	south-east	no
1du *vit>mit*	contagion	south-east	no
svarabhakti vowels	contagion	south-east	Swedish(?)
1pl *-Vz*	contagion	south-west	no evidence
1du *mit>mér*	contagion	Sørlandet	no
present 1pl *-(V)r*	contra-hierarchy(?)	Sørlandet	no(?)
1pl *mér>mit*	contra-hierarchy	Sørlandet	no
1pl *vér>mér*	contra-hierarchy	central Norway	no
1sg. *-(V)r*	hierarchy	south-east	no evidence
1pl *-V* (SV)	hierarchy	Bergen, Trondheim	Danish(?)
loss of genitives	hierarchy	Oslo	Swedish(?)
1pl *-V* (VS)	hierarchy (outside Viken)	no evidence	Danish(?)
1pl *mér>vi*	hierarchy(?)	no evidence	East Nordic
verða>blífa	no pattern	no evidence	East Nordic/Low German
1du *mit>vi*	no pattern	no evidence	East Nordic

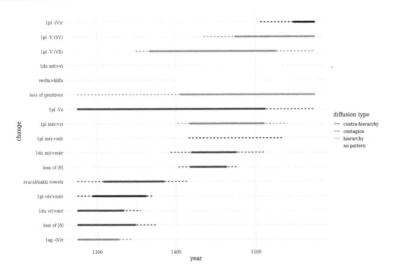

Figure 102. Summary of change diffusion types [Colour figure can be viewed at wileyonlinelibrary. com]

by which innovations can spread, hierarchy, contra-hierarchy and contagion diffusion, are real and occurred in the medieval period. Demonstrating all three types with the same methodology on the same corpus makes it seem much less likely that one or two of them are products of some unforeseen artefact of data collection or analytical tools (although, of course, this can never be excluded). Assuming that some degree of urbanisation (whether in terms of absolute or relative population density, absolute size of the cities, or the relative proportion of the population living in cities) must be reached for the differentiation of urban areas seen in hierarchy and contra-hierarchy diffusion, these data clearly demonstrate that that degree had been reached in Norway by 1300. Assuming that some frequency of long-distance movement must be passed to enable the discontinuous spread of innovations that is a feature of hierarchy diffusion, this frequency had clearly been passed in Norway by 1300. We should go on, then, to thinking about when and why the different modes of spread occur.

No extremely obvious and exceptionless patterns hold across the changes investigated when considering language-internal factors. Our three phonological changes (the rise of svarabhakti vowels and the loss of the two dental fricatives) all spread by contagion diffusion, but we also find morphological changes (the loss of number agreement on 1pl middle verbs (1pl -Vz), and 1du. *mit>mér*) and lexical changes (1du. *vit>mit*) spreading by contagion diffusion. Hierarchy diffusion seems to be associated with morphosyntactic changes, but not all morphological changes spread by hierarchy diffusion. We have only investigated structurally simplifying and structure-neutral changes here, so we cannot make a strong contrast between the modes of diffusion for rising and falling complexity. None of our structure-neutral changes showed a hierarchy effect, so we might tentatively suggest an association between structurally simplifying change and hierarchy diffusion, but in the case of the replacement of *verða* by *blífa*, we cannot confirm contra-hierarchy or contagion diffusion either: it is possible that this could be more confidently identified as a counter-example (that is, as a structure-neutral change spreading by hierarchy diffusion) if we had more data.

Looking at the times at which our changes occurred, there is, again, the suggestion of a pattern, but it is far from exceptionless even in this small dataset. Hierarchy diffusion seems to be more typical of changes in the fifteenth and early sixteenth century than previous centuries. However, there are examples of non-hierarchy diffusion in the fifteenth century (the two different levellings of *mit/mér* and the loss of [θ]) and, conversely, one early example of hierarchy diffusion, the levelling of 1sg. -(V) to -$(V)r$ around the turn of the fourteenth century. It might be tempting to see this as evidence that during the major period of population decline (the fourteenth through to the mid-fifteenth century) we see less hierarchy diffusion, but this would be extremely speculative on such thin data.

The most convincing patterns are perhaps those concerning place. The two changes which appear from the kernel smoothed estimates to have begun in cities (the levelling of 1pl -Vm to -V in SUBJECT-VERB order and the loss of genitives with *millum*) proceed to spread by hierarchy diffusion. Of the other three instances of hierarchy diffusion, the levelling of 1sg. -(V) to -$(V)r$ certainly began in the south-east, but our first evidence for the change comes too late on to be able to be more specific than that: certainly it is possible that within Norway it started in Oslo, or that it began in Swedish cities and jumped from there into Norwegian cities. The levelling of 1pl -Vm to -V in VERB-SUBJECT order and the replacement of 1pl *mér* by borrowed *vi* are both difficult to identify a place of innovation for since the latter seems to arise all across the country at once, whereas for the former our data starts at a point of stable variation in all regions; certainly we cannot say, however, that they were innovated in rural regions.

On the other hand, all of the changes which spread by contra-hierarchy diffusion began in truly rural areas: the south west or Sørlandet, mountainous inner Norway. The remaining changes which spread by contagion diffusion also all started in rural areas, although some in the relatively denser region of Viken.

The suggestion that the main factor driving the type of diffusion we see is simply where the change arises is very consistent with the Burridge model discussed above (section 7.1). Under this model, upward population density gradients act as barriers to diffusion. Thus, a change which starts in a low-population density area may spread to other low-density areas, but it will be harder for it to enter cities, creating the contra-hierarchy effect. By the same effect it is possible for a city to maintain a distinctive dialect compared with the area around it: if a change is innovated in a city, it is possible for usage of the innovative variant to be maintained in the city before or without it being spread elsewhere. These effects will hold as long as there are population density gradients and be stronger where the gradients are sharper. Thus we tend to see more dramatic hierarchy effects in Vestlandet, where Bergen represents the largest city in Norway but which is otherwise a relatively low-density region, than in more uniformly populous Viken. Finally, if there is enough long-distance population movement, this will allow non-contiguous spread of innovations, an effect which is most likely between cities simply as a consequence of their larger populations (an effect which might be exaggerated if cultural and economic phenomena generate an even greater frequency of contacts between cities than would be expected from density alone). This generates the other component of the hierarchy diffusion pattern: when a change starts in a city, and is maintained as a feature of the city dialect, it can also 'jump' to other distant cities, even before it has spread much locally.

The other three models of diffusion discussed above each fail to explain one or more of the patterns we have seen in these data. The wave model can account for the changes we have concluded spread by contagion diffusion but cannot explain discontinuous spread or differential behaviour of cities. The cascade model can explain the cases of hierarchy diffusion but not contagion diffusion, and certainly not contra-hierarchy diffusion. The gravity model can explain hierarchy diffusion and contagion diffusion (at least for the initial periods of changes which arise in rural areas) but offers no account of contra-hierarchy diffusion.

Thus in this chapter I have demonstrated how the kernel smoothing method – here supported by other statistical tools – can throw light on larger questions of how language change functions in space. I have offered strong evidence for one particular model of linguistic diffusion and shown deficits in others, and have provided robust examples of all three known types of linguistic diffusion from the late medieval period. I have also shown how the kernel smoothing method can complement other statistical methods. It would have been possible to look for hierarchy and contra-hierarchy patterns in the data using the correlation method without ever visualising the actual distributions involved, but combining this with the kernel smoothing method allows us to get a much more complete understanding of these data.

8

CONCLUSIONS

Over the course of this monograph I have tried to weave together three different strands. The first is methodological. I have argued that historical dialectology – in the broadest sense of any work exploring the spatial dimension of historical language data – has suffered from a lack of widely-used statistical tools for finding spatial and temporal patterns in noisy data. Historical texts are very difficult sources to work with: doubts about provenance, complex production histories, interacting writing standards, idiosyncratic orthographic practices, and lost information about writers can all contribute to create so much noise as to obscure spatial patterns in language use from the casual observer. As a result, I believe that a great deal of the historical language data we have has not been explored in a rigorous, reproducible or thorough way from a spatial standpoint: given the right methods, the field of historical dialectology may be one with many low-hanging fruits.

In this monograph, I have argued that kernel smoothing methods can answer our methodological requirements very well. These are conceptually straightforward methods that should be easy for scholars without a sophisticated statistical training to understand – the simplest version is simply a moving average – but they are flexible and can be well-suited to our research goals. In chapter 2 I discussed these methods in the context of some other ways we might try to explore spatial variation in historical linguistic data, and worked through some ideas on how best to select function parameters. However, my intention with this book is not only to argue in favour of a particular approach for the sake of those who already have the tools to follow it, but to disseminate these tools more widely. Accordingly, I have published the code I used in this book as an R package, and chapter 9 offers a step-by-step guide to undertaking this kind of research on your own data using this code. I am not a computer scientist and make no claim that this is the fastest or most elegant implementation of kernel smoothing out there. Instead, what I have aimed to do is offer a set of functions specifically designed with the data of historical linguistics and philology in mind.

The second strand in the book is a series of pieces of research into language variation and change in Middle Norwegian. Much of this work was first undertaken during my PhD, although all of it I have repeated and updated since as my understanding of the best analytical tools improved. In the first half of chapter 3 I discussed the non-linguistic and external-linguistic background to help in reading this linguistic work, primarily focusing on the broad political situation in Norway in this period and the nature and extent of contact between Norwegian and other languages. In the second half of this chapter I described the set of texts on which my work has been based, the *Diplomatarium Norvegicum*, and the annotated corpus I have developed from these texts, the *DN online*. This too was necessary context for the reader to fully assess the linguistic research that followed, but I also hope it may be useful to future scholars working on variation and change in the history of Norwegian. The *DN online* is freely available for use, and I invite others to explore it and use it in their work.

Chapter 4 then presented the linguistic variables that would be investigated and how the dataset for each had been collected; the subsequent three chapters were each structured around a specific research question we can ask of these data. In chapter 5 I asked whether the loss of the voiced and voiceless dental fricatives of Old Norwegian – by any conventional analysis a single phoneme in Old Norwegian – could be seen as constituting a single change, and argued that they could not: timing and spatial evidence strongly suggests these were two, entirely independent changes. I also asked whether the shift of the 1pl ending from distinctive -*Vm* to -*V* (often syncretic with the 3pl) should be considered a single change or not, and found that this, too, should be characterised as multiple. At the very least, we have a separate change in two different syntactic contexts, but this also interacts with tense. We can also separate out the innovation of the new morphological form (that is, endings in -*V* with a 1pl subject) from later changes that removed restrictions on its occurrence and transformed it from a stable minority variant into a new, rapidly spreading innovation.

In chapter 6, I assessed how the Middle Norwegian evidence bears on what I have labelled the 'Trudgill conjecture'; this was the focus of my PhD work, but I believe the analysis I put forward here is far more rigorous. In Trudgill's theory of sociolinguistic typology, language change can be classified according to its structural effect on system complexity: change can increase or decrease the complexity of the language, defined as the language becoming harder or easier for adult second-language learners. These different types of change are predictably associated with specific socio-historical contexts. Intensive contact between languages, with situations involving widespread adult second-language learning, will result in simplificatory change. By contrast, both isolation, and long-term, stable contact involving primarily child multilingualism will result in complex-ificatory change, although by different mechanisms. The history of the Nordic family for the last millennium appears to be an excellent case study for this theory. The Continental branch languages have undergone intensive contact and thoroughgoing morphological simplification; the Insular languages have been (relatively) isolated, and have preserved much more of the grammatical complexity of Old Norse. In this chapter, I used spatial and chronological evidence to assess how well this implied causal link between contact and simplificatory change fits the data from the Old and Middle Norwegian periods. I also compared the Trudgill conjecture to related, less tightly structured and narrowly focused hypotheses about the relationships between social context and types of language change.

The findings here were complex, reflecting the sophisticated nature of the theory and the complexity and size of the dataset. In its simplest form, the Trudgill conjecture might be taken to predict that simplificatory changes in the history of Norwegian were mostly innovated in Bergen, the most significant locus of intensive language contact – I can say with confidence that I have demonstrated that this was not the case. However, a fairer reading of the theory leads us to a rather wider set of predicted scenarios, and some of these are far more consistent with the data. In particular, I found that in many cases, simplificatory innovations may have spread from Swedish or Danish, languages for which intensive language contact was more widespread than for Norwegian. I found recurring patterns by which cities, and to a lesser extent coastal settlements, played a particular role in the spreading of simplificatory innovations, in keeping both with the Trudgill conjecture and other related theories. Overall, I argued that although these results are consistent with the Trudgill conjecture, our most important takeaway should be broader than this: in these changes we see repeated chronological and spatial patterns which speak strongly to *some* important role for external factors in answering Weinreich, Labov and Herzog's actuation problem, whether or not Trudgill's theory in particular is found to be the strongest such account. It appears from these data that the answer to the vexed question of why particular changes take hold in particular times and speech communities must in significant part be answered with reference to the social conditions in those speech communities.

In chapter 7, I then explored these data alongside data for two additional changes to explore a different research topic, that of the patterns by which innovative variants spread through a spatially distributed population. The existing historical linguistics and sociolinguistics literature offers us a number of models and points us towards three distinct patterns: continuous outward spread from a point of innovation (contagion diffusion); discontinuous spread in which urban areas lead compared with rural areas (hierarchy diffusion); and spread in which rural areas lead compared to urban areas (contra-hierarchy diffusion). I showed in this chapter that all three patterns seem to have occurred for different instances of language change in Middle Norwegian. There was no obvious relationship between known changes in population density and mobility patterns and the occurrence of these different types of diffusion, undermining an idea that changing urbanisation and mobility might have favoured or disfavoured hierarchy diffusion. However the data was consistent with a prediction taken from the Burridge model of linguistic diffusion that, given a certain degree of urbanisation, the pattern by which a change can spread is a function of where it starts relative to cities and the edge of the language area. This work thus offers a substantial piece of evidence to further our understanding of the operation of linguistic diffusion.

The third strand in the book, like the first, is methodological. As I presented the case studies described above, I returned each time to an argument about the purpose and potential of spatial analysis of historical linguistic texts. The label 'dialectology' may prompt some scholars to dismiss work as atheoretical, myopic, and of interest only to scholars of the history of a specific language. I believe that this is mistaken. As well as being a great source of fascination in its own right, information concerning how particular features of historical languages were distributed in space can help us answer a great many questions from other areas of historical linguistics. Many theories about how and why individual changes took place imply predictions about when and where we should first see evidence for them, and using historical dialectological techniques like those presented in this book allows us to test these predictions. The same can often be said for theories about the broad patterns of change across entire language histories, and even about how language change operates in the abstract, although here we will have to marshal spatial evidence for many instances of language change to look for consistent patterns. I hope that through the three chapters on case studies I have offered the reader convincing evidence of this wider utility for spatial analysis in historical linguistics.

In short, I have thought of this book not only as a report on the data, methods and results of a set of research projects of my own, but as an invitation to other researchers to follow a similar path in future work. In the case studies I have offered a detailed set of examples of the courses one might take through research projects of this sort, and the ways in which the results might be presented and related back to wider research questions. In the presentation of the method itself, however, and the arguments about the broad set of uses to which it may be put, I hope to have gone further, and offered the reader both means and motive to undertake spatial analyses of historical linguistic datasets of their own.

9

ANNEX: A STEP-BY-STEP GUIDE TO KERNEL SMOOTHING FOR HISTORICAL
DIALECTOLOGY

9.1. *Introduction*

The methods presented in this book are conceptually simple and widely used across many fields. However, statistics training is not always a component of a linguistics education, and many historical linguists do not have the tools to undertake quantitative data analysis easily available at their fingertips. With this in mind, this chapter will present a step-by-step guide to applying these methods to a new dataset. No attempt will be made here to explain the underlying statistics, which have already been covered in chapter 2. Rather, the focus will be on practical steps involved and the decisions that may arise while exploring a dataset. There are a great many implementations of methods in the kernel smoothing family in most statistical programming environments a researcher might be working (Python, R, etc.), and a more experienced data analyst should review these and identify the tool best suited to their particular problem. However, with the beginner in mind, this chapter will assume the use of R and specifically the package written for this book, with QGIS for visualisation.

9.2. *Software and dependencies*

Assuming the user has already installed R (R Core Team 2020), they should download and install the package kernelPhil from the CRAN repository:

```
install.packages("kernelPhil");
```

This should also install all the packages on which kernelPhil depends. Alternatively, the user could add these manually:

```
install.packages(c("benchmarkme", "directlabels", "dplyr", "ggplot2", "gridExtra", "Hmisc",
    "pbapply", "rgdal", "reshape2", "wordspace"));
```

For visualisation, the user should download and install QGIS (QGIS.org 2021), following the directions on the QGIS website.

9.3. *Preparing your data*

kernelPhil assumes data in one of two formats: a table in which each row represents a document or speaker, with a column for each variant recording a count of uses per document/speaker; or a table in which each row represents an observation of a token, with a column recording which variant the token was. We can describe these as 'count' or 'factor' formats, or as 'wide' and 'long' formats. These are exemplified in Tables 42 and 43 (note that for this chapter, we will be using an

Table 42. Example data in count/wide format

Document.id	Bjorn	Bjørn
III.1156.	1	2
IV.156.	2	0
XII.225.	0	1
XXI.998.	2	1
...		

Table 43. Example data in factor/long format

Token.id	Document.id	Dependent.variable
1	III.1156.	Bjorn
2	III.1156.	Bjørn
3	III.1156.	Bjørn
4	IV.156.	Bjorn
5	IV.156.	Bjorn
6	XII.225.	Bjørn
7	XXI.998.	Bjorn
8	XXI.998.	Bjørn
9	XXI.998.	Bjorn

example dataset take from the *DN online* corpus concerning whether the vowel in the Old Norse name *Bjǫrn* is written back – <biorn>, <byorn>, etc. – or front – <biœrn>, <bjørn>, etc.).

If undertaking smoothing in time, then a column with some numeric measurement of time should be present. If also undertaking smoothing in space, there should be two columns with the numeric spatial co-ordinates of each measurement. These can be as projected co-ordinates or unprojected longitude/latitude pairs (Table 44).

If we have multiple tokens per document/speaker and are using long format, we will need to weight each token by the number of tokens that document/speaker has produced. This can be done using a document id column, or manually by adding a weight column (Table 45).

Table 44. Example data in long format with year and co-ordinates

Token.id	Document.id	Year	Longitude	latitude	Dependent.variable
1	III.1156.	1540.145	59.38344	9.200896	Bjorn
2	III.1156.	1540.145	59.38344	9.200896	Bjørn
3	III.1156.	1540.145	59.38344	9.200896	Bjørn
4	IV.156.	1322.537	59.65072	6.354143	Bjorn
5	IV.156.	1322.537	59.65072	6.354143	Bjorn
6	XII.225.	1457.282	59.62552	9.716533	Bjørn
7	XXI.998.	1554.395	60.04606	9.632606	Bjorn
8	XXI.998.	1554.395	60.04606	9.632606	Bjørn
9	XXI.998.	1554.395	60.04606	9.632606	Bjorn

Table 45. Example data in long format with metadata and weights to normalise by document

Token.id	Document.id	year	Longitude	latitude	Dependent.variable	Weight
1	III.1156.	1540.145	59.38344	9.200896	Bjorn	1/3
2	III.1156.	1540.145	59.38344	9.200896	Bjørn	1/3
3	III.1156.	1540.145	59.38344	9.200896	Bjørn	1/3
4	IV.156.	1322.537	59.65072	6.354143	Bjorn	1/2
5	IV.156.	1322.537	59.65072	6.354143	Bjorn	1/2
6	XII.225.	1457.282	59.62552	9.716533	Bjørn	1
7	XXI.998.	1554.395	60.04606	9.632606	Bjørn	1/3
8	XXI.998.	1554.395	60.04606	9.632606	Bjørn	1/3
9	XXI.998.	1554.395	60.04606	9.632606	Bjorn	1/3

Adding a weight column can also allow us to deal with multiple localisation by repeating the data associated with a given document for each localisation, but weighting the document by the number of localisations (Table 46),

We could also aggregate this for the sake of saving storage (Table 47).

The data in this format should be loaded into R as a data frame – the easiest way of doing this is probably to prepare the dataset in a spreadsheet or database package, export it as a .csv, and read it into R:

```
df <- read.csv("path to your data.csv", header = TRUE, encoding = "UTF-8");
```

9.4. *Preliminary exploration*

Since the time-span of the changes you are studying has a bearing on choosing bandwidths, the first stage in analysing your data should be to gain an overall

Table 46. Example data in long format with metadata and weights with multiple locations per text

Localised. token.id	Token.id	Document.id	Year	Longitude	Latitude	Dependent. variable	Weight
1	1	III.1156.	1540.145	59.38344	9.200896	Bjorn	1/6
2	1	III.1156.	1540.145	59.69761	9.104760	Bjorn	1/6
3	2	III.1156.	1540.145	59.38344	9.200896	Bjørn	1/6
4	2	III.1156.	1540.145	59.69761	9.104760	Bjørn	1/6
5	3	III.1156.	1540.145	59.38344	9.200896	Bjørn	1/6
6	3	III.1156.	1540.145	59.69761	9.104760	Bjørn	1/6
7	4	IV.156.	1322.537	59.65072	6.354143	Bjorn	1/4
8	4	IV.156.	1322.537	59.48384	6.254299	Bjorn	1/4
9	5	IV.156.	1322.537	59.65072	6.354143	Bjorn	1/4
10	5	IV.156.	1322.537	59.48384	6.254299	Bjorn	1/4
11	6	XII.225.	1457.282	59.62552	9.716533	Bjørn	1
12	7	XXI.998.	1554.395	60.04606	9.632606	Bjørn	1/3
13	8	XXI.998.	1554.395	60.04606	9.632606	Bjørn	1/3
14	9	XXI.998.	1554.395	60.04606	9.632606	Bjorn	1/3

Table 47. Example aggregated data in long format with metadata and weights
with multiple locations per text

Datum.id	Document.id	Year	Longitude	Latitude	Dependent.variable	Weight
	III.1156.	1540.145	59.38344	9.200896	Bjorn	1/6
	III.1156.	1540.145	59.69761	9.104760	Bjorn	1/6
	III.1156.	1540.145	59.38344	9.200896	Bjørn	1/3
	III.1156.	1540.145	59.69761	9.104760	Bjørn	1/3
	IV.156.	1322.537	59.65072	6.354143	Bjorn	1/2
	IV.156.	1322.537	59.48384	6.254299	Bjorn	1/2
	XII.225.	1457.282	59.62552	9.716533	Bjorn	1
	XXI.998.	1554.395	60.04606	9.632606	Bjorn	2/3
	XXI.998.	1554.395	60.04606	9.632606	Bjørn	1/3

impression of its distribution in time. Load the package and generate a one-
dimensional kernel smooth of your data in time:

```
library(kernelPhil);
ks.in.time <- kernel.smooth.in.time(dataset = df);
ks.in.time$plot;
```

You can modify this function call by specifying different column names for
your dependent variable, time, and weight (dependent.variable = "your variable column here",
time = "your time column here", weight="your weight column here").

You can modify the bandwidth to a value that makes sense for your data: since
the goal here is just to get an impressionistic overview and not make precise
estimates, the choice of bandwidth is not especially important, but since over-
smoothed data may be less useful than under-smoothed data you should
probably choose a relatively low bandwidth (the default is 10). If your dataset is
relatively small, you may get an error message stating that the data never exceeds
the sample density threshold; if so, try a higher bandwidth or lower sample
density threshold. For example, your modified function call might look like:

```
ks.in.time <- kernel.smooth.in.time(
        dataset = df,
        dependent.variable = "changed",
        time = "datestamp",
        weight = "weighting",
        bandwidth = 50,
        sample.density.threshold=0.1);
ks.in.time$plot;
```

This will give you a plot of your variable over time. You then need to use
this to delimit the period of the change(s) you are investigating. The function
nearest.point() can help you to do this, specifying the variant and threshold rate
you are interested in:

```
nearest.point(
    kernel.smooths = ks.in.time,
    density = 0.15,
    variant = "your variant");
nearest.point(kernel.smooths = ks.in.time,
    density = 0.85,
    variant = "your variant");
```

This will return the points in time in your data when this variant is closest to 15 per cent and closest to 85 per cent, but you could set whatever threshold points are most relevant to the change you see in your data. With these you can define the range of your change:

```
change.range <- nearest.point(kernel.smooths = ks.in.time, density = 0.85, variant = "your
    variant") - nearest.point(kernel.smooths = ks.in.time, density = 0.15, variant = "your
    variant");
```

9.5. *Determining bandwidths*

Having installed the needed software, prepared your data, and got an overall impression of its distribution in time, the first analytical task is to determine bandwidths. You can set an upper and lower bound for your temporal bandwidth by reference to real-world priors: for example, taking the approach described in section 2.3.1, you might set your lower bound as 6.08 years and your upper bound as the range of your change divided by 1.6449. To determine a more precise value, you must set it in concert with your spatial bandwidth.

There are two ways of doing this, and both are dependent on first defining the spatial resolution, margin of error and significance level you are aiming for. In practice, a reasonable starting point might be to assume margin $= 0.1$, $\alpha = 0.05$, although you may have to increase the margin or accept a higher value of α if your dataset is not large. You can then set the minimum acceptable resolution in terms of the number of discrete cells that could be distinguished if the data were perfectly evenly distributed in space. To do this, the function calculate.bandwidths.by.resolution() can be used. For example, your function call might look like:

```
bw.by.resolution <- calculate.bandwidths.by.resolution(
    dataset = df,
    temporal.bandwidth.limits = c(6.08, change.range/qnorm(0.95)),
    temporal.bandwidth.n.levels = 100,
    minimum.spatial.resolution = 5);
bw.by.resolution$plot;
```

As before, you can set the names of your weight, dependent variable and time columns if they differ from the defaults. This will return the minimum temporal bandwidth and a plot of spatial resolution by temporal bandwidth and time (as well as summary plots if you set summary.plots = TRUE). You may get a warning stating: 'it is not possible to achieve this spatial resolution with these settings'. In this case, you do not have enough data to achieve the spatial resolution requested with this power level and within these temporal bandwidth limits – try rerunning the function with wider margins, a lower minimum spatial resolution, or a higher maximum temporal bandwidth.

In practice, this may not be the best way to identify bandwidths for your data. If your data are unevenly distributed in space, then this will hugely overestimate the real spatial resolution that can be achieved for a given temporal bandwidth. In such cases, a better approach may be to define a series of points for which you want estimates to be largely non-overlapping, and determine the temporal bandwidth needed to achieve this. For example, you might want to use the co-ordinates of the major cities of the region you are studying. Create a data.frame in R with the names and co-ordinates of your points in the same format as your data (again, if you're not used to using R then the easiest way to do this might be to create a .csv file in another package and read it into R with read.csv(). For example, your separated points table might look something like Table 48.

You can then determine your temporal bandwidth with the function calculate.bandwidths.by.separated.points(). Many of the arguments of this function are similar to those we have already seen, but you will now have the option of setting the names of your x and y co-ordinate columns (the default values are 'x' and 'y') and must pass the co-ordinates (and optionally the names) of your separated points. Because we are now dealing with the spatial component of our data, you also have the option of specifying a projection, if your co-ordinates are unprojected latitude/longitude pairs. Projections should be given in the form of a proj4 string, and for details of how to format these the reader should refer to the PROJ manual (PROJ contributors 2020)[39]. An example function call might look something like:

Table 48. Example separated points table

Id	Name	Longitude	Latitude
1	Oslo	10.752245	59.91387
2	Bergen	5.322054	60.39126
3	Trondheim	10.395053	63.43051
4	Hamar	11.056114	60.79916
5	Stavanger	5.733107	58.96998

[39] Note that PROJ.4 is deprecated as of February 2018 – as of writing this book, the current version is 7.2.1, and all version from 5.0 onwards are known simply as PROJ – but we are reliant here on existing R packages which still use PROJ.4, which was current from 1994 until 2018.

```
bw.by.separated.points <- calculate.bandwidths.by.separated.points(
        dataset = df,
        x = "longitude",
        y = "latitude",
        temporal.bandwidth.limits = c(6.08, change.range/qnorm(0.95)),
        separated.points = separated.points[, c("longitude", "latitude")],
        projection = "+proj=tmerc",
        include.visualisation = TRUE,
        separated.points.labels = separated.points$name);
bw.by.separated.points$plot;
```

As before, if it is impossible to attain non-overlapping estimates at your points given the settings you have used, you may have to try rerunning the function with wider margins or a higher maximum temporal bandwidth. You could also try a different set of points, selecting locations that are more dispersed, fewer in number, or better represented in your data.

9.6. *Temporal kernel smoothing*

Before moving on to running the spatial-temporal kernel smoothing, you may want to rerun the kernel smooth in time alone with the optimal bandwidth for spatial-temporal smoothing that you have just identified. Although this might not be the most effective visualisation of the overall trajectory of the change you are studying because it is likely to be very oversmoothed for analysing the data in time alone, it can be useful for understanding the results of your spatial-temporal visualisations. Simply repeat the function call you used in 9.2, now with the new bandwidth:

```
ks.in.time <- kernel.smooth.in.time(
        dataset = df,
        dependent.variable = "changed",
        time = "datestamp",
        weight = "weighting",
        bandwidth = your.numerical.bandwidth.here,
        sample.density.threshold = 0.1);
ks.in.time$plot;
```

9.7. *Spatial-temporal kernel smoothing*

Now that you have calculated the temporal bandwidth you will use for your analysis, you can move on to the analysis in space and time. To calculate kernel smooths in space and time, use the function kernel.smooth.in.space.and.time(). Most of the possible arguments should be familiar from the functions you have used so far. An example function call might look like:

```
ks.in.space.and.time <- kernel.smooth.in.space.and.time(
    dataset = df,
    x = "longitude",
    y = "latitude",
    margin = 0.2,
    temporal.bandwidth = 60,
    projection = "+proj=tmerc");
```

This call would first weight your data with a Gaussian temporal kernel with the bandwidth you supplied (in our example, 60), and then with a Gaussian spatial kernel with bandwidth adapting such that the sample size is always high enough to ensure an error margin of 0.2 on either side of the estimate with significance level 0.05. The function returns a list with the main parameters of your of function call (under return$parameters) and a list of data frames of the results (under return$results). Each data frame contains the results for a specific point in time, and within the data frames, each row contains the results for a specific locality at that point in time. For example, continuing with the example given above, to see the first few results at the first point in time, call:

```
head(ks.in.space.and.time$results[[1]])
```

And you might see something like Table 49.

The default settings will generate kernel smooths at five points in time, distributed evenly over the period covered by the dataset. This is unlikely to be optimal, and the user is advised to determine what points in time they are likely to need visualisations for and specify these with measure.times = c(time1, time2, ... It may be best to calculate smooths at a great many points in time to better explore the changing distribution of your data (and this will be needed if you are going to render video of the change), in which case a setting like measure.times = seq(from = 1300, to = 1550, by = 5) may be appropriate. However, the user should be aware that these functions may take a very long time to run.

Table 49. Example output of the kernel.smooth.in.space.and.time() function

	Longitude	Latitude	bw	Relative_ density_ Bjorn	Relative_ density_ Bjørn	Effective_ sample_ size	Weight_ at_point	Best
1	−1.235660	60.34696	208549.4	0.8487594	0.1512406	17.41702	0.40113293	Bjorn
2	−1.233531	60.00108	208547.0	0.8501339	0.1498661	17.41703	0.40113293	Bjorn
3	−1.345449	60.12106	210886.6	0.8497484	0.1502516	17.41703	1.12985386	Bjorn
4	−1.377505	60.21356	211567.5	0.8493974	0.1506026	17.41703	0.37874837	Bjorn
5	0.000000	0.00000	2468177.7	0.7818869	0.2181131	17.41703	0.09267169	Bjorn
6	18.068581	59.32932	157185.2	0.6468292	0.3531708	17.41702	0.84599286	Bjorn

Once you have generated your kernel smooths, you can save them to a directory with save.kernel.smooths(). This takes the output of kernel.smooth.in.space.and.time() (or kernel.smooth.in.space.and.time. with.margins()), the parent directory to which they should be saved, and the name of the variable as its three arguments. For example, your function call might look like:

```
save.kernel.smooths(
    kernel.smooth = ks.in.space.and.time,
    location = "./",
    variable.name = "your variable name here");
```

This will create a directory containing a .txt file with parameters and .csv files with the smoothed results for individual years (which can then be loaded again into R with load.kernel.smooths()).

9.8. *Spatial visualisation*

Having calculated your kernel smooths, you can now move on to visualising them. There are a great many GIS tools available that could be used for this purpose. For an experienced user it may be faster and easier to generate visualisations directly in R using rgdal and ggplot2 or similar packages. However, I assume here that the beginner user may benefit from the easy usability of a GIS package with a graphical user interface like QGIS, and indeed, the wide functionality and flexibility of such tools should recommend them even to the expert.

You will need to set up a background map on which to display your kernel smoothed data. This could be an existing map served from a tile server, or a map of your own based on freely available GIS data (administrative boundary shapefiles, elevation data, or similar). You will need to decide on projection, and visualise any specific points of interest to help your audience orient themselves on the map. There are numerous guides and tutorials online to doing these general tasks in QGIS, so I will not go through them here, and will instead focus only on how to visualise the kernel smooths.

The kernel smooths should be loaded into QGIS as 'Delimited text layers' (Layer > Add Layer > Add Delimited Text Layer ...). The file format is CSV and the geometry type is 'Point co-ordinates'. If the columns containing your co-ordinates have relatively self-explanatory names ('x' and 'y', or 'longitude' and 'latitude') then QGIS will select them automatically; if not, you should select the X and Y fields from the dropdowns. Make sure that the correct CRS is selected in the 'Geometry CRS' dropdown, matching the projection of your data. When you've added your new layer to the map, you should see points appear in a block colour: this is shown for our example data in the top left panel of Figure 103. You then have a number of options of which variables to visualise and how to visualise them; the variables you should find in the saved kernel smooths are listed in Table 50.

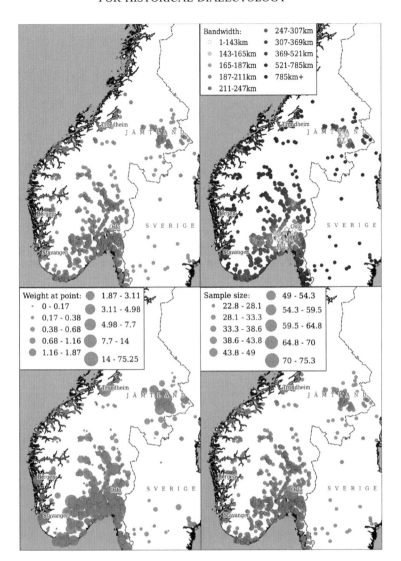

Figure 103. Raw points, bandwidths, weights and sample sizes [Colour figure can be viewed at wileyonlinelibrary.com]

Table 50. Variables in the saved kernel smooth files

Variable	Description
bw	the bandwidth used at this point
effective_sample_size	the effective sample size used to calculate this estimate
weight_at_point	the weight at this point after the application of the temporal kernel
relative_density_variant	the estimate for each variant
best	the variant with the highest estimate

The column 'bw' gives the spatial bandwidth used at each point and 'effective_sample_size' the sum of all weights after the application of both kernels at each point: these are visualised for example data in the top right and bottom right panels of Figure 103. Note that if using an adaptive spatial kernel then effective sample size will be almost spatially invariant, whereas if using a static spatial kernel then the spatial bandwidth will be invariant. In the case of our example, an adaptive kernel was used and so there is very little variation in the sample size across points[40]. These two are important numbers to have available (you want to be able to check that the bandwidths and sample sizes used fit your expectations) but are unlikely to be things you want to include in your final visualisation (although both can be useful means of indicating local sample density). The other three columns are the ones you are most likely to use for visualisation. The column 'weight_at_point' gives the weight of data at this point after the application of the temporal kernel: in other words, this can be used as a measure of how good the data is for this specific point in time and space; the higher this value, the better evidenced we should consider this estimate. This is visualised for the example data in the bottom left panel of Figure 103. The columns 'relative_density_...' report the actual estimate for each variant.

You can visualise these variables as a set of points, a series of polygons (such as Voronoi polygons), or an interpolated, continuous field – for this tutorial, I will only discuss the first of these, since I believe that for many datasets, especially where the population is quite unevenly distributed in the region being studied, interpolated visualisations can be misleading. When creating set of points, there are several visual properties you can manipulate to express different variables: colour (within which, hue, brightness and saturation can to some extent be treated separately); opacity; size; and symbol. I would not recommend using opacity to express a variable unless colour is *not* being used. Even then, it can be relatively difficult to read opacity with any precision – consider the bottom right panel of Figure 104. Using point size to express a numeric variable can create a very striking visualisation (consider the example in the bottom left panel of Figure 104) and has been used in much synchronic dialectology (for example, consider the maps in Anderson 1987). However, I would argue that it is often a misleading choice for the smoothed estimates for these kinds of data, since readers tend to assume that point size must reflect some 'size' variable (such as sample size). Point hue (for which consider the top left panel of Figure 104) and brightness (the top right panel of Figure 104) alone can also be very effective ways of visualising a numeric variable but also have their disadvantages. Using hue alone means that the visualisation will be difficult or impossible to read for readers with certain types of colour blindness (depending on the exact colours you select), and will be impossible to read if your

---

[40] The only point with a sample size different to the overall average is Oslo, the point with the most data. This is a result of there being more data at this single point than needed to achieve the required power: even with the lowest possible bandwidth, the sample size here is still bigger than everywhere else.

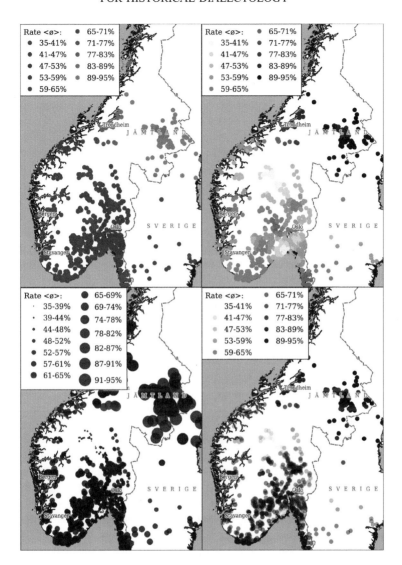

Figure 104. Visualising with hue, brightness, size and opacity [Colour figure can be viewed at wileyonlinelibrary.com]

work is read in greyscale (as is the case with hardcopies of this monograph). It is often better to use a gradient incorporating both hue and brightness together to express a numeric variable, as has been done in most of the maps in this book, allowing them to be read in greyscale while taking advantage of the expressiveness of colour where colour is available. However, it should be noted that this means the visualisation is not truly optimised for reading in either greyscale or colour. Another possibility, especially useful for multi-variant systems, is to use hue for the plurality variant and brightness for the proportion of the data it reflects; for examples of this, see Blaxter (2019). You can potentially also use point size to indicate one variable and some features of colour to indicate another.

To do all of this in QGIS, open the properties dialogue of your point layer and go to the 'Symbology' tab. Most of these effects can be achieved by selecting 'Graduated' from the symbology type dropdown at the top of this tab. Select the variable you wish to visualise in the 'Value' dropdown (you also have the option of entering an expression here: the most common thing you may wish to do is multiply a variable by 100 so as to visualise percentages). The 'Method' dropdown allows you to choose between colour and size as the property to be modified: if you select size, you will then have to enter the minimum and maximum sizes between which points will be scaled, and if colour, you will have to select a gradient from the 'Color ramp' menu. Once you have set up these visual properties, you can select the number of classes and classify your continuous numeric scale into these discrete classes. Note that there are different approaches to this discretisation too. QGIS will default to scaling the colour spectrum or size progression to the *observed* limits of your numeric variable (cf. the top left panel of Figure 105) but it may be more appropriate to use a real value scale such as a 0–100 per cent scale (the top right panel of Figure 105) or a scale based on round numbers (the bottom left panel). All of these have been done with equal-interval categorisations, but various uneven discretisations are possible – these are listed in the 'Mode' dropdown. Generally, the option that will create the most dramatic visual contrast will be the 'Equal count' mode scaled to the limits of your observed variable, whereas equal-interval categories scaled to the real limits of the variable may be the truest (least misleading) representation.

If you wish to have size and colour changing independently to reflect different variables (such as weight at point and the estimate of the dependent variable, as has been done in the maps throughout this book), the easiest way to do this is by using a graduated style for colour as described above, but setting symbol size dynamically. Open the 'Symbol' dialogue and then open the 'Data defined override' menu at the far right of 'Size'. From this, select 'Assistant'. This dialogue will allow you to set point size dynamically from one variable (or an expression including one or more variables), while the graduated symbology determines colour on the basis of another variable; an example of this is given in the bottom right panel of Figure 105.

There are an enormous range of options for visualising map data and most of these can be achieved one way or another in both graphical packages like QGIS and in R itself. It is also possible to create animated visualisations, and these can be especially appropriate when what you are trying to visualise is change over continuous time. To see examples of these, the reader is referred to the supplementary materials to Blaxter (2019). It is beyond the scope of this book to offer a fuller manual on GIS, but hopefully the approaches described so far will be enough to get the beginner digital cartographer started.

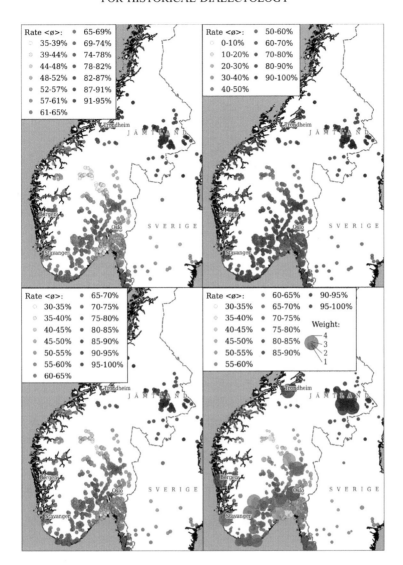

Figure 105. Scaling the dependent variable [Colour figure can be viewed at wileyonlinelibrary.com]

10

APPENDIX

Table 51. Parameters for kernel smooths by map or figure number

Innovation	Map/figure	Temporal bandwidth	Error margin	Contrasted localities
loss of [ð]	Figure 32	46.51 years	10%	Bergen, Oslo, Trondheim, Stavanger
loss of [θ]	Figure 33	18.08 years	15%	Bergen, Oslo, Trondheim, Hamar, Stavanger
loss of [ð]	Figure 34	46.51 years	10%	Bergen, Oslo, Trondheim, Stavanger
loss of [θ]	Figure 34	18.08 years	15%	Bergen, Oslo, Trondheim, Hamar, Stavanger
1pl -*V* (VS)	Figure 45	28.07 years	10%	Bergen, Oslo, Trondheim, Hamar, Stavanger
1pl -*V* (SV)	Figure 46	28.92 years	10%	Bergen, Oslo, Trondheim, Hamar, Stavanger
1pl -*V* (VS)	Figure 47	28.07 years	10%	Bergen, Oslo, Trondheim, Hamar, Stavanger
1pl -*V* (SV)	Figure 47	28.92 years	10%	Bergen, Oslo, Trondheim, Hamar, Stavanger
1pl -*V* (VS)	Figure 48	68.18 years	12.5%	Bergen, Vossevangen, Hamar, Fåberg, Oslo,
	Figure 49			Haug sokn, Hobøl sokn
	Figure 50			
1pl -*V* (SV)	Figure 51	63.24 years	12.5%	Bergen, Vossevangen, Hamar, Fåberg, Oslo,
	Figure 52			Haug sokn, Hobøl sokn
	Figure 53			
	Figure 54	28.92 years	10%	Bergen, Hamar, Oslo, Stavanger, Trondheim
1sg -*(V)r*	Figure 56	44.69 years	17.5%	Bergen, Oslo, Trondheim
	Figure 57			
	Figure 58	46.79 years	15%	Bergen, Gausdal sokn, Oslo, Stavanger
svarabhakti	Figure 60	36.87 years	17.5%	Bergen, Hamar, Oslo, Stavanger, Trondheim
vowels	Figure 61			
1du	Figure 63	51.18 years	12.5%	Hedenstad sokn, Hol sokn, Tønsberg, Vanse
mit>mér	Figure 64			sokn
1pl *mér>mit*	Figure 66	41.81 years	10%	Tønsberg, Vanse sokn, Vinje sokn
	Figure 67			
	Figure 68	41.59 years	17.5%	Hol sokn, Tønsberg, Vanse sokn, Vinje sokn
1pl *mér>vi*	Figure 69	40.47 years	7%	Bergen, Oslo, Trondheim
	Figure 70	46.56 years	17.5%	Bergen, Fåberg, Hamar, Haug sokn, Hobøl
	Figure 71			sokn, Oslo, sokn, Vossevangen
	Figure 72			
1du *mit>vi*	Figure 73	31.04 years	10%	Bergen, Oslo, Trondheim
1pl middle -	Figure 75	58.48 years	17.5%	Bergen, Hamar, Oslo, Trondheim
Vz	Figure 76	58.48 years	17.5%	Bergen, Frösön, Hamar, Oslo, Trondheim
loss of	Figure 78	48.37 years	15%	Bergen, Hamar, Oslo, Trondheim
genitives	Figure 81			
	Figure 82	65.31 years	22.5%	Bergen, Vossevangen
	Figure 83	85.61 years	22.5%	Fåberg sokn, Hamar
	Figure 84	72.52 years	25%	Haug sokn, Hobøl sokn, Oslo
1pl -*V* (VS)	Figure 85	28.07 years	10%	Bergen, Hamar, Oslo, Stavanger, Trondheim
1pl -*V* (SV)	Figure 86	28.92 years	10%	Bergen, Hamar, Oslo, Stavanger, Trondheim
present 1pl -	Figure 88	30.50 years	12.5%	Bergen, Oslo, Stavanger, Trondheim
(V)r	Figure 89			
	Figure 90			
1pl *vér>mér*	Figure 95	28.19 years	15%	Bergen, Oslo, Trondheim
	Figure 96			
	Figure 97	30.31 years	17%	Oslo, Sør-Fron sokn
1du *vit>mit*	Figure 99	27.64 years	20%	Bergen, Oslo, Trondheim
	Figure 100			

Table 52. Sizes of datasets

Variable	Context	Texts	Variants
status of /θ/	voiceless	5359	<þ> <th> <t> 7737 2643 7592
	voiced	9959	<ð> <d> <dh> <th> 8813 97186 26887 11567
svarabhakti vowels		6456	<a> <æ> <e> <i> <o> <ø> <u> Ø 1709 1601 27216 300 61 2 98 6630
1sg. agreement		301	-(V) -(V)r 98 793
1pl active agreement	VERB-SUBJECT	5773	-Vm -V -Ø -(V)r 9701 8292 304 659
	SUBJECT-VERB	5746	-Vm -V -Ø -(V)r 17241 6017 357 6017
1pl middle agreement		886	-Vmz -(V)z 413 1625
1pl subject pronoun		3113	vér vit mér mit vi 1505 3 5473 969 10919
1du. subject pronoun		2292	vér vit mér mit vi 133 208 729 4755 3830
lexical genitives	object of *millum*	1441	genitives no genitives 687 754

ACKNOWLEDGEMENTS

Writing this book has been a much longer, rockier road than expected – or at least, longer and rockier than I planned. Perhaps that's true of all books. As is also true of all books, this work could not have been written without help and counsel from many people around me along the way. My thanks to my PhD supervisor, David Willis, who offered vital guidance in the early years of this project; to my PhD examiners, Peter Trudgill and George Walkden, for their helpful feedback and encouragement; to Thomas Marge, whose insights into the problems of parameter setting were invaluable; to Francis Nolan and an anonymous reader who reviewed the proposal and manuscript for the Philological Society and offered essential advice in reshaping my initial plan; and to Susan Fitzmaurice and Melanie Green at the Philological Society, who gave the project their blessing and guided me through the publication process. All of this help was gratefully received and without it the book would have had a quite different – and much inferior – form. Needless to say, all remaining errors of fact, analysis or judgement are my own.

Correspondence
tamsin@icge.co.uk

REFERENCES

AASEN, IVAR, 1965. *Norsk grammatik.* Omarbeidet udgave af 'Det Norske Folkesprogs Grammatik', tredie uforandrede udgave. Oslo: Universitetsforlaget.

ADAMS, JONATHAN, 2015. *The revelations of St Birgitta: A study and edition of the Birgittine-Norwegian texts, Swedish National Archives, E 8902* (Studies in Medieval and Reformation Traditions. Texts & Sources 194 7). Leiden: Brill.

AKMAJIAN, ANDRIAN & RICHARD A. DEMERS, 2010. *An introduction to language and communication*, 2nd edn. Cambridge, MA: MIT Press.

ANDERSON, PETER M., 1987. *A structural atlas of the English dialects.* London; New York: Croom Helm.

ANDERSSON, HANS, 2003. 'Urbanisation', in Knut Helle (ed.), *The Cambridge history of Scandinavia.* Cambridge: Cambridge University Press. 312–342.

ÅNEMAN, CLAES, 1989. 'Runbelägget *til sihtunum*', in Lena Peterson & Svante Strandberg (eds.), *Studia onomastica. Festskrift till Thorsten Andersson.* Stockholm: Almqvist & Wiksell. 441–445.

ANTONSON, HANS, 2009. 'The extent of farm desertion in central Sweden during the late medieval agrarian crisis: Landscape as a source', *Journal of Historical Geography* 35(4). 619–641.

ATKINSON, QUENTIN D., 2011. 'Phonemic diversity supports a serial founder effect model of language expansion from Africa', *Science* 332(6027). 346–349.

BAILEY, GUY, TOM WIKLE, JAN TILLERY & LORI SAND, 1993. 'Some patterns of linguistic diffusion', *Language Variation and Change* 5(3). 359–390.

BENEDICTOW, OLE JØRGEN, 2003. 'Demographic conditions', in Knut Helle (ed.), *The Cambridge History of Scandinavia*, vol. 1. Cambridge: Cambridge University Press. 237–249.

BENSKIN, MICHAEL, 2011. 'Present indicative plural concord in Brittonic and Early English1: Present indicative plural concord', *Transactions of the Philological Society* 109(2). 158–185.

BENTZ, CHRISTIAN & MORTEN H. CHRISTIANSEN, 2013. 'Linguistic adaptation: The trade-off between case marking and fixed word orders in Germanic and Romance languages', in Gang Peng & Feng Shi (eds.), *Eastward Flows the Great River: Festschrift in Honor of Prof. Wiliam S-Y. Wang on his 80th Birthday.* Hong Kong: City of Hong Kong Press. 45–61.

BENTZ, CHRISTIAN & BODO WINTER, 2012. 'The impact of L2 speakers on the evolution of case marking', in TC Scott-Philips, M Tamariz, EA Cartmill & JR Hurford (eds.), *Proceedings of the 9th International Conference on the Evolution of Language.* Hackensack, NJ: World Scientific. 58–63.

BENTZ, CHRISTIAN & BODO WINTER, 2013. 'Languages with more second language learners tend to lose nominal case', *Language Dynamics & Change* 3 (1). 1–27.

BERG, IVAR, 2013. *Eit seinmellomalderleg skrivemiljø: Nidaros erkesete 1458–1537.* Trondheim: NTNU Ph.D. dissertation.

BERG, IVAR, 2015a. 'Nokre sider ved det norske kasusbortfallet i seinmellomalderen', *Maal og minne* 1, 1–35.

BERG, IVAR, 2015b. 'Stages in deflexion and the Norwegian dative', in Dag T. T. Haug (ed.), *Historical linguistics 2013. Selected papers from the 21st International Conference on historical Linguistics, Oslo, 5–9 August 2013.* Amsterdam: John Benjamins. 179–194.

BERG, IVAR, 2016. 'A note on the relationship between Scandinavian and Low German', *Journal of Historical Sociolinguistics* 2(2). 189–210.

BERG, IVAR, 2017. 'Business writing in early sixteenth-century Norway', in Esther-Miriam Wagner, Bettina Beinhoff & Ben Outhwaite (eds.), *Merchants of innovation.* Studies in language change. Berlin: De Gruyter. 89–107.

BERG, IVAR, 2018. Reformasjonen og norsk språkhistorie. *Teologisk tidsskrift* 7 (03). 167–176. https://doi.org/10.18261/issn.1893-0271-2018-03-02.

BERGE, ALVDIS, 1974. *Genitiv av substantiv i mellomnorske diplom frå 1425-1426: Ei jamføring med norrønt.* Universitetet i Bergen MA dissertation.

BLAXTER, TAM T., 2017a. *Annotated DN online.* Cambridge. http://www.icge.co.uk/dn_online/ (10 May, 2021).

BLAXTER, TAM T. 2017b. *Speech in space and time: Contact, change and diffusion in medieval Norway.* Cambridge: University of Cambridge Ph.D. https://doi.org/10.17863/CAM.15576 (DATE).

BLAXTER, TAM T., 2019. '*Ther varom mid j hia*: Tracing linguistic diffusion in the history of Norwegian using kernel density estimation', *Dialectologia et Geolinguistica* 27(1). 5–34.

BLAXTER, TAMSIN, WILLIS DAVID & LEEMANN ADRIAN. forthcoming. 'Urbanisation and morphosyntactic variation in Twitter data', in Arne Ziegler, Stefanie Edler & Georg Oberdorfer (eds.), *Urban matters. Current approaches in variationist sociolinguistics.* Studies in language variation 27. Amsterdam: John Benjamins Publishing Company.

BLAXTER, TAM & KARI KINN, 2018. 'On *ek* and *jak* In Middle Norwegian: Mixed methods In historical sociolinguistics', *Transactions of the Philological Society* 116(3). 383–409. http://doi.wiley.com/10.1111/1467-968X.12126 (23 July, 2018).

BLAXTER, TAM T. & PETER TRUDGILL, 2019. On case loss and svarabhakti vowels: The sociolinguistic typology and geolinguistics of simplification in North Germanic, *Journal of Linguistic Geography* 7(1). 1–13. https://doi.org/10.1017/jlg.2019.3.

BLOMKVIST, NILS, 1979. 'Kalmars uppkomst och äldsta tid', in Ingrid Hammarström (ed.), *Kalmar stads historia I: Kalmarområdets forntid och stadens äldsta utveckling.* Kalmar: Kulturnämnden i Kalmar. 167–309.

BLOOMFIELD, LEONARD, 1933. *Language.* New York: Holt.

BÖRJARS, KERSTI, 2003. 'Morphological status and (de)grammaticalisation: The Swedish possessive', *Nordic Journal of Linguistics* 26(2). 133–163.

BRATTEGARD, OLAV, 1932. 'Über die organisation und die urkunden des hansischen kontors zu Bergen bis 1580', *Bergens historiske Forenings Skrifter* 38. 237–303.

BRAUNMÜLLER, KURT, 1989. 'Voraussetzungen für die Übernahme mittelniederdeutscher Sprachstrukturen in die skandinavischen Sprachen', in Karl Hyldgaard-Jensen, Kurt Erich Schöndorf, Vibeke Winge & Birgit Christensen (eds.), *Niederdeutsch in Skandinavien II : Akten des 2. nordischen Symposions 'Niederdeutsch in Skandinavien' in Kopenhagen, 18–20. Mai 1987*. Berlin: Erich Schmidt Verlag. 9–29.

BRAUNMÜLLER, KURT, 1995. Semikommunikation und semiotische Strategien. Bausteine zu einem Modell für die Verständigung im Norden zur Zeit der Hanse. In Kurt Braunmüller (ed.), *Niederdeutsch und die skandinavischen Sprachen II*, 35–70. Heidelberg: Universitätsverlag C. Winter.

BRAUNMÜLLER, KURT, 2007. 'Receptive multilingualism in Northern Europe in the Middle Ages. A description of the scenario', in Jan Derk ten Thije & Ludger Zeevaert (eds.), *Receptive multilingualism: Linguistic analyses, language policies and didactic concepts* (Hamburg Studies on Multilingualism 6). Amsterdam: Benjamins Publishing. 95–111.

BRAUNMÜLLER, KURT, 2012. 'Semi-communication and beyond: some results of the Hamburg Hanseatic Project (1990–1995)'. in Lennart Elmevik & Ernst Håkon Jahr (eds.), *Contact between Low German and Scandinavian in the Late Middle Ages: 25 years of research* (Acta Academiae Regiae Gustavi Adolphi CXXI). Uppsala: Kungl. Gustav Adolfs Akademien för svensk folkkultur. 95–111.

BREMMER, ROLF H., 2009. *An introduction to Old Frisian: History, grammar, reader, glossary*. Amsterdam: John Benjamins.

BRITAIN, DAVID, 2009. 'One foot in the grave? Dialect death, dialect contact, and dialect birth in England', *International Journal of the Sociology of Language* 2009(196/197). 121–155.

BROTHEN, JAMES A. 1996. 'Population decline and plague in late medieval Norway', *Annales de Démographie Historique* 1996. 137–149.

BRYLLA, EVA, 1987. *Singular ortnamnsböjning i fornsvenskan: starkt böjda namn med utgångspunkt från sörmländskt material* (Skrifter utgivna genom Ortnamnsarkivet i Uppsala 6). Uppsala: Stockholm.

BUCHSTALLER, ISABELLE & ALEXANDRA D'ARCY, 2009. 'Localized globalization: A multi-local, multivariate investigation of quotative be like', *Journal of Sociolinguistics* 13(3). 291–331.

BULL, TOVE, 1995. 'Language contact leading to language change: The case of Northern Norway', in Jan Fisiak (ed.), *Linguistic change under contact conditions*. Berlin: Mouton de Gruyter. 15–35.

BULL, TOVE, 2010. *Jurij Kusmenko: Der samische einfluss auf die skandinavischen sprachen*. Berliner Beiträge zur Skandinavistik (nr. 10). Berlin: Nordeuropa-Institut der Humboldt-Universität.

BULL, TOVE, 2011. 'Samisk påverknad på norsk språk', *NOA – Norsk som andrespråk* 27(1). 5–32.

BURKHARDT, MIKE, 2015. 'Kontors and outposts', in Donald J. Harreld (ed.), *A companion to the Hanseatic League* (Brill's Companions to European History, Vol. 8). Leiden: Brill. 128–161.

BURRIDGE, JAMES, 2017. 'Spatial evolution of human dialects', *Physical Review X* 7(3). 031008-01–031008-27. http://link.aps.org/doi/10.1103/PhysRevX.7.031008 (20 January 2018).

BURRIDGE, JAMES, 2018. 'Unifying models of dialect spread and extinction using surface tension dynamics', *Royal Society Open Science* 5(1). https://doi.org/10.1098/rsos.171446.

BURRIDGE, JAMES, & TAMSIN BLAXTER, 2020. 'Using spatial patterns of English folk speech to infer the universality class of linguistic copying', *Physical Review Research* 2(4).043053 https://doi.org/10.1103/PhysRevResearch.2.043053.

BURRIDGE, JAMES & TAMSIN BLAXTER, 2021. 'Inferring the drivers of language change using spatial models', *Journal of Physics Complexity* 2(3).035018. https://doi.org/10.1088/2632-072X/abfa82.

CHAMBERS, J. K. & PETER TRUDGILL, 1980. *Dialectology* (Cambridge Textbooks in Linguistics). Cambridge: Cambridge University Press.

CHRISTIANSEN, HALLFRID, 1956. Me - vi i nynorsk. In Svend Aakjær & Peter Skautrup (eds.), *Festskrift til Peter Skautrup 21. Januar 1956*, 175–181. Aarhus: Universitetsforlaget i Aarhus.

CIPOLLONE, NICK, STEVEN H. KEISER & SHRAVAN VASISHTH, 1998. *Language files: Materials for an introduction to language and linguistics* (7th edn). Columbus, OH: Ohio State University Press.

CLEASBY, RICHARD, GUÐBRANDUR VIGFÚSSON & GEORGE WEBBE DASENT, 1894. *An Icelandic-English dictionary, based on the ms. collections of the late Richard Cleasby*. Oxford: Clarendon Press.

DAHL, ÖSTEN, 2001. 'Complexification, erosion, and baroqueness', *Linguistic Typology* 5(2–3). 374–377.

DAHL, ÖSTEN, 2011. Are small languages more or less complex than big ones? *Linguistic Typology* 15(2). 171–175.

DAHLBÄCK, GÖRAN, 1998´. 'Invandring – säsrkilt tysk – till Sverige under medeltiden', in Lars Nilsson & Sven Lilja (eds.), *Invandrarna och lokalsamhället: Historiska aspekter på integrationen av invandrare i nordiska lokalsamhällen* (Studier i stads- och kommunhistoria 16). Stockholm: Stads- och Kommunhistoriska Institutet. 11–30.

DAHLBÄCK, GÖRAN, 2003. 'The towns', in Knut Helle (ed.), *The Cambridge history of Scandinavia*. Cambridge: Cambridge University Press. 611–634.

DAVIS, NORMAN, 1953. *Sweet's Anglo-Saxon primer* (9th edn). London: Oxford University Press.

DELSING, LARS-OLOF, 1999. 'Review essay: Muriel Norde: The history of the genitive in Swedish. A case study in degrammaticalization', *Nordic Journal of Linguistics* 22(1). 77–90.

DELSING, LARS-OLOF, 2001. 'The Swedish genitive: A reply to Norde', *Nordic Journal of Linguistics* 24(1). 119–120.

DELSING, LARS-OLOF, 2002. 'The morphology of Old Nordic II: Old Swedish and Old Danish', in Oskar Bandle, Ernst Håkon Jahr, Allan Karker, Hans-Peter Naumann, Ulf Teleman & Kurt Braunmüller (eds.), *The Nordic languages: An international handbook of the history of the North Germanic languages*. Berlin: Walter de Gruyter. 925–939.

DOKUMENTASJONSPROSJEKTET, 1997a. Ein kort introduksjon til Dokumentasjonsprosjektet. https://www.dokpro.uio.no/organisasjon/ Infobrosjyre.html (24 September 2021).

DOKUMENTASJONSPROSJEKTET, 1997b. Om den elektroniske utgaven av Diplomatarium Norvegicum. http://www.dokpro.uio.no/dipl_norv/diplom_ hjelp.html (24 September 2021).

DONOHUE, MARK & JOHANNA NICHOLS, 2011. 'Does phoneme inventory size correlate with population size?' *Linguistic Typology* 15(2). 161–170.

DYBDAHL, AUDUN, 2012. 'Climate and demographic crises in Norway in medieval and early modern times', *The Holocene* 22(10). 1159–1167.

ELMEVIK, LENNART & ERNST HÅKON JAHR, 2012. 'Twenty-five years of research on the contact between Low German and Scandinavian', in Lennart Elmevik & Ernst Håkon Jahr (eds.), *Contact between Low German and Scandinavian in the Late Middle Ages: 25 years of research* (Acta Academiae Regiae Gustavi Adolphi CXXI). Uppsala: Kungl. Gustav Adolfs Akademien för svensk folkkultur. 9–16.

ENGER, HANS-OLAV, 2011. 'Gender and contact – a natural morphology perspective on Scandinavian examples', in Peter Siemund (ed.), *Linguistic universals and language variation* (Trends in Linguistics: Studies and Monographs 231). Berlin: De Gruyter Mouton. 171–203.

ENGER, HANS-OLAV, 2013. 'Inflectional change, "sound laws" and the autonomy of morphology: The case of Scandinavian case and gender reduction', *Diachronica* 30(1). 1–26.

FAARLUND, JAN TERJE, 2004. *The syntax of Old Norse*. Oxford: Oxford University Press.

FAGYAL, ZSUZSANNA, SAMARTH SWARUP, ANNA MARÍA ESCOBAR, LES GASSER & KIRAN LAKKARAJU, 2010. 'Centers and peripheries: Network roles in language change', *Lingua* 120(8). 2061–2079.

FARSTAD, STEIN E. 1991. *Særtrekk ved vokalismen i brev fra Hedmark 1356-1420*. Oslo: Universitet i Oslo MA dissertation.

FOSSEN, ANDERS BJARNE, 1979. *Bergen bys historie*. Vol. II. Bergen-Oslo-Tromsø: Universitetsforlaget.

FOTHERINGHAM, STEWART, CHRIS BRUNSDON & MARTIN CHARLTON, 2003. *Geographically weighted regression*. Chichester: John Wiley & Sons.

GORDON, E. V. & A. R. TAYLOR, 1956. *An introduction to Old Norse* (2nd edn). Oxford: Oxford University Press.

GRØTVEDT, PER NYQUIST, 1939. *Lydverket i lovhåndskrifter fra Borgartingslag 1300–1350. Med et tillegg om sørøstnorske diplomer* (Skrifter udg. af Videnskabs-Selskabet i Christiania II. Hist.-Filos. Klasse, 1938. No. 7). Oslo: Jacob Dybwad.

GRØTVEDT, PER NYQUIST, 1949. *Studier over målet i lagmannsbrev fra Oslo 1350–1450* (Skrifter utgitt av Det Norske Videnskaps-Akademi i Oslo II. Hist.-Filos. Klasse, 1948. No. 2). Oslo: Jacob Dybwad.

GRØTVEDT, PER NYQUIST, 1970. *Skrift og tale i mellomnorske diplomer fra Folden-området 1350–1450 II. Vestre og Indre Folden* (Skrifter frå Norsk målførearkiv XXII). Oslo: Universitetsforlaget.

HÆGSTAD, MARIUS, 1902. *Maalet i dei gamle norske kongebrev* (Videnskabsselskabets Skrifter I. Historisk-filos. Klasse, 1902. No. 1). Kristiania: Jacob Dybwad.

HÆGSTAD, MARIUS, 1907. *Vestnorske maalføre fyre 1350* (Videnskapsselskapets Skrifter II. Hist.-Filos. Klasse 1907. no. 1. Vol. I.) Nordvestlandsk. Kristiania: Jacob Dybwad.

HÆGSTAD, MARIUS, 1915. *Vestnorske maalføre fyre 1350* (Videnskapsselskapets Skrifter II. Hist.-Filos. Klasse 1914. no. 5. Vol. II). Sudvestlandsk 1. Rygjamaal. Kristiania: Jacob Dybwad.

HÆGSTAD, MARIUS, 1916. *Vestnorske maalføre fyre 1350* (Videnskapsselskapets Skrifter II. Hist.-Filos. Klasse 1915. no. 3. Vol. II). Sudvestlandsk 2', indre sudvestlandsk. Færøymaal Islandsk. Kristiania: Jacob Dybwad.

HÆGSTAD, MARIUS & ALF TORP, 2015. In Leiv Heggstad, Finn Hødnebø & Erik Simensen (eds.), *Norrøn Ordbok* (5th edn). Oslo: Det Norske Samlaget.

HÄGERSTRAND, TORSTEN, 1952. *The propagation of innovation in waves* (Lund Studies in Geography B 44). Lund: Lund University Press.

HAGGETT, PETER, 1965. *Locational analysis in human geography*. London: Arnold.

HALL, ALARIC, 2013. Jón the Fleming: Low German in thirteenth-century Norway and fourteenth-century Iceland. *Leeds Working Papers Linguistics* 18. 1–33.

HAMMEL-KIESOW, ROLF, 2015. The early Hanses', in Donald J. Harreld (ed.), trans. Lore Schultheiss, *A companion to the Hanseatic League* (Brill's Companions to European History, Vol. 8). Leiden: Brill. 15–63.

HAUGEN, EINAR, 1976. *The Scandinavian languages: An introduction to their history* (The Great Languages). London: Faber and Faber.

HAY, JENNIFER & LAURIE BAUER, 2007. 'Phoneme inventory size and population size', *Language* 83(2). 388–400.

HELLBERG, LARS, 1960. *Plural form i äldre nordiskt ortnamnskick*. Uppsala: AS Lundequistska bokhandeln.

HELLE, KNUT, 1982. *Bergen bys historie*. Vol. I. Bergen-Oslo-Tromsø: Unversitetsforlaget.

HOCKETT, CHARLES F., 1958. *A course in modern linguistics*. New York: Macmillan.

Hødnebø, Finn, 1960. *Norske diplomer til og med år 1300* (Corpus Codicum Norvegicorum Medii Aevi Folio serie vol. II). Oslo: Selskapet til utgivelse av gamle norske håndskrifter.

Hødnebø, Finn, 1966. *Utvalg av norske diplomer 1350–1550* (Nordisk filologi. Texter och läroböcker för universitetsstudier. Ser. A: Texter 13). Oslo, København, Stockholm: Dreyer, Munksgaard, Svenska bokförlaget/Norstedta.

Holmsen, Andreas, 1984. *Den store manndauen*. Oslo: Universitetsforlaget.

Huitfeldt-Kaas, H. J. (ed.), 1901–1903. *Diplomatarium Norvegicum* (Vol. 16). Oslo: Christiania.

Huitfeldt-Kaas, H. J., Gustav Storm, Alexander Bugge, Christian Brinchmann & Oluf Kolsrud (eds.), 1902–1919. *Diplomatarium Norvegicum. Romerske oldbreve* (Vol. 17–18). Oslo: Christiania.

Huitfeldt-Kaas, HJ, Gustav Storm, Alexander Bugge, Christian Brinchmann & Oluf Kolsrud (eds.), 1910–1915. *Diplomatarium Norvegicum. Aktstykker vedrørende Norges forbindelse med De britiske øer* (Vol. 19–20). Oslo: Christiania.

Indrebø, Gustav, 1951. *Norsk målsoga*. Bergen: J. Griegs boktr.

Indrebø, Gustav, 1993. 'Litt um burtfallet av fleirtal i verbalbøygjingi i norsk', in Ernst Håkon Jahr & Ove Lorentz (eds.), *Historisk språkvitenskap/Historical linguistics* (Studier i norsk språkvitenskap/Studies in Norwegian linguistics 5). Oslo: Novus. 136–144.

Ingason, Anton Karl, Julie Anne Legate & Charles Yang, 2013. 'The evolutionary trajectory of the Icelandic new passive', *University of Pennsylvania Working Papers in Linguistics* 19(2). 91–100.

Jahr, Ernst Håkon (ed.), 1990. *Den Store dialektboka*. Oslo: Novus.

Jahr, Ernst Håkon, 1995. 'Niederdeutsch, Norwegisch und Nordisch. Sprachgemeinschaft und sprachkontakt in der Hansezeit', in Kurt Braunmüller (ed.), *Niederdeutsch und die skandinavischen sprachen II*. Heidelberg: Universitätsverlag C. Winter. 125–144.

Jahr, Ernst Håkon, 1999. 'Sociolinguistics in historical language contact: The Scandinavian languages and Low German during the Hanseatic period', in Ernst Håkon Jahr (ed.), *Language change: Advances in historical sociolinguistics*. Berlin: Mouton de Gruyter. 119–140.

Jansson, Valter, 1934. *Fornsvenska legendariet. Handskrifter och språk* (Nordiska texter och undersökningar 4). Stockholm: H. Geber.

Kauhanen, Henri, 2020. cre: Constant Rate Effects. R. https://github.com/hkauhanen/cre (1 March 2021).

Kauhanen, Henri & George Walkden, 2018. 'Deriving the constant rate effect', *Natural Language & Linguistic Theory* 36(2). 483–521.

Kinn, Kari, 2010. *Formelle subjekter i norsk – en diakron undersøkelse*, institutt for lingvistiske og nordiske studier, Oslo: Universitet i Oslo MA dissertation. http://urn.nb.no/URN: NBN: no-26842 (5 December, 2013).

Kinn, Kari, 2011. Overt non-referential subjects and subject-verb agreement in Middle Norwegian. *Working Papers in Scandinavian Syntax* 88, 21–50.

KINN, KARI, 2016. *Null Subjects in the History of Norwegian*. Oslo: University of Oslo Ph.D.

KLEVMARK, THOMAS, 1983. *Varom mer I hia I Haddingiadale: Særtrekk ved vokalismen i brev fra Hallingdal 1309–1463*. Oslo: Universitetet i Oslo MA dissertation.

KORTMANN, BERND & BENEDIKT SZMRECSANYI, 2009. 'World Englishes between simplification and complexification', in L Siebers & T Hoffmann (eds.), *World Englishes: Problems, properties and prospects*. Amsterdam: Benjamins. 265–285.

KROCH, ANTHONY S., 1989. 'Reflexes of grammar in patterns of language change', *Language Variation and Change* 1(3), 199–244.

KUSMENKO, JURIJ, 2008. *Der samische einfluss auf die skandinavischen sprachen: Ein beitrag zur skandinavischen sprachsgeschichte* (Berliner Beiträge Zur Skandinavistik Bd. 10). Berlin: Nordeuropa-Institut der Humboldt-Universität.

KUSTERS, WOUTER, 2008. 'Complexity in linguistic theory, language learning and language change', in Matti Miestamo, Kaius Sinnemäki & Fred Karlsson (eds.), *Language complexity: Typology, contact, change* (Studies in Language Companion Series 94). Amsterdam: John Benjamins Publishing. 3–22.

LABOV, WILLIAM, 1969. 'Contraction, deletion and inherent variability in the English copula', *Language* 45(4). 773–818.

LABOV, WILLIAM, 2001. *Principles of linguistic change*. Volume 2: Social factors. Oxford: Blackwell Publishers Ltd.

LABOV, WILLIAM, 2007. 'Transmission and diffusion', *Language* 83(2). 344–387.

LANDRØ, PER ROALD, 1975. *Jón Egilsson: Islending eller nordmann? En undersøkelse av språket hos Islands første publicus notarius*. Trondheim: NLHT Trondheim Ph.D. dissertation.

LANGER, CHRISTIAN C. A. & CARL R. UNGER (eds.), 1847–1861. *Diplomatarium Norvegicum* (Vols. 1–5). Oslo: Christiania.

LARSEN, AMUND B., 1993. 'Antegnelser om substantivbøiningen i middelnorsk', in Ernst Håkon Jahr & Ove Lorentz (eds.), *Historisk språkvitenskap/Historical linguistics* (Studier i norsk språkvitenskap/Studies in Norwegian linguistics 5). Oslo: Novus. 59–68.

LARSSON, GABRIELA BJARNE, 2012. 'Wives or widows and their representatives', *Scandinavian Journal of History* 37(1). 49–68.

LASCH, AGATHE, 1974. *Mittelniederdeutsche Grammatik* (Sammlung Kurzer Grammatiken Germanischer Dialekte Nr. 9). Tübingen: Niemeyer.

LEEMANN, ADRIAN, MARIE-JOSÉ KOLLY & VOLKER DELLWO, 2014. 'Crowdsourcing regional variation in speaking rate through the iOS app 'Dialäkt Äpp'', in *Proceedings of Speech Prosody 2014*, 217–221. https://www.zora.uzh.ch/105430/1/Leemann%2C%20Kolly%2C%20Dellwo%20%282014%29%20-%20Crowdsoucring%20regional%20variation%20in%20speaking%20rate%20through%20the%20the%20iOS%20app%20Dial%C3%A4kt%20%C3%84pp.pdf (24 September 2021).

LIGHTFOOT, DAVID, 1979. *Principles of diachronic syntax*. Cambridge: Cambridge University Press.

LIGHTFOOT, DAVID, 1991. *How to set parameters: Arguments from language change*. Cambridge, MA: MIT Press.

LUICK, KARL, 1922. 'Review of 1st edn of Wilhelm Horn's *Sprachkörper und sprachfunktion*', *Englishe Studien* 56. 185–203.

LUICK, KARL, 1924. 'Review of 2nd edn of Wilhelm Horn's *Sprachkörper und sprachfunktion*', *Englishe Studien* 58. 235–245.

LUPYAN, GARY & RICK DALE, 2010. 'Language structure is partly determined by social structure', *PLoS ONE* 5(1). e8559. https://doi.org/10.1371/journal.pone.0008559.

MADDIESON, IAN, 2006. 'Correlating phonological complexity: Data and validation', *Linguistic Typology* 10(1). 106–123.

MADDIESON, IAN, 2007. 'Issues of phonological complexity: Statistical analysis of the relationship between syllable structures, segment inventories and tone contrasts', in M-J Solé, P Beddor & M Ohala (eds.), *Experimental approaches to phonology*. Oxford: Oxford University Press, 93–103.

MADDIESON, IAN, TANMOY BHATTACHARYA, ERIC D. SMITH & WILLIAM CROFT, 2011. 'Geographical distribution of phonological complexity', *Linguistic Typology* 15(2). 267–279.

MAGERØY, HALLVARD (ed.), 1970–1976. *Diplomatarium Norvegicum* (Vol. 21). Oslo: Christiania.

MÄHL, STEFAN, 2012. 'Low German texts from Late Medieval Sweden', in Lennart Elmevik & Ernst Håkon Jahr (eds.), *Contact between Low German and Scandinavian in the Late Middle Ages: 25 years of research* (Acta Academiae Regiae Gustavi Adolphi CXXI). Uppsala: Kungl. Gustav Adolfs Akademien för svensk folkkultur. 113–122.

MCWHORTER, JOHN, 2001. 'The world's simplest grammars are creole grammars', *Linguistic Typology* 5(2–3). 125–166.

MCWHORTER, JOHN, 2011. *Linguistic simplicity and complexity: Why do languages undress?* (Language Contact and Bilingualism I). Berlin: Walter de Gruyter.

MEISEL, JÜRGEN M., 2011. 'Bilingual language acquisition and theories of diachronic change: Bilingualism as cause and effect of grammatical change', *Bilingualism: Language and Cognition* 14(2). 121–145.

MEYERHOFF, MIRIAM & JAMES A. WALKER, 2007. 'The persistence of variation in individual grammars: Copula absence in "urban sojourners" and their stay-at-home peers, Bequia (St Vincent and Grenadines)', *Journal of Sociolinguistics* 11(3). 346–366.

MORAN, STEVE, DANIEL MCCLOY & RICHARD WRIGHT, 2012. 'Revisiting population size vs. phoneme inventory size', *Language* 88(4). 877–893.

MØRCK, ENDRE, 1980. *Passiv i mellomnorske diplom*. Oslo: Universitet i Oslo MA dissertation.

MØRCK, ENDRE, 1999. 'Sociolinguistic studies on the basis of medieval Norwegian charters', in Ernst Håkon Jahr (ed.), *Language change: advances in historical sociolinguistics*. Berlin: Mouton de Gruyter. 263–290.

MØRCK, ENDRE, 2005. 'Morphological developments from Old Nordic to Early Modern Nordic: Inflexion and word formation', in Oskar Bandle, Ernst Håkon Jahr, Allan Karker, Hans-Peter Naumann, Ulf Teleman & Kurt Braunmüller (eds.), *The Nordic languages: An international handbook of the history of the North Germanic Languages*. Berlin: Walter de Gruyter. 1128–1148.

MØRCK, ENDRE, 2011. 'Mittelnorwegisch', in Odd Einar Haugen (ed.), trans. Astrid van Nahl, *Altnordische philologie* (De Gruyter Lexikon). Berlin: De Gruyter. 527–580.

NÆSHAGEN, FERDINAND LINTHOE (ed.), 1990–1995. *Diplomatarium Norvegicum* (Vol. 22). Oslo: Christiania.

NAHKOLA, KARI & MARJA SAANILAHTI, 2004. 'Mapping language changes in real time: A panel study on Finnish', *Language Variation and Change* 16(2). 75–91.

NEDKVITNE, ARNVED, 2012. 'A post-national perspective on the German Hansa in Scandinavia', in Lennart Elmevik & Ernst Håkon Jahr (eds.), *Contact between Low German and Scandinavian in the Late Middle Ages: 25 years of research* (Acta Academiae Regiae Gustavi Adolphi CXXI). Uppsala: Kungl. Gustav Adolfs Akademien för svensk folkkultur. 17–37.

NEDKVITNE, ARNVED, 2014. *The German Hansa and Bergen 1100–1600* (Quellen und Darstellungen zur Hansischen Geschichte neue Folge, Band 70). Cologne: Böhlau Verlag.

NEDREBØ, YNGVE, 1990. 'Bergen – frå Skandinavias største by til strilane sin hovudstad'. *Frå Fjon til Fusa: årbok for Nord- og Midhordland sogelag*. 35–67.

NERBONNE, JOHN, 2010. 'Measuring the diffusion of linguistic change', *Philosophical Transactions of the Royal Society B* 365(1559). 3821–3828.

NESSE, AGNETE, 2001. *Språkkontakt mellom norsk og tysk i hansatidens Bergen*. Tromsø: Universitet i Tromsø Ph.D. dissertation.

NESSE, AGNETE, 2002. *Språkkontakt mellom norsk og tysk i hansatidens Bergen* (Det Norske Videnskaps-Akademi II. Hist.-Filos. Klasse Skrifter og avhandlinger Nr. 2). Oslo: Novus Forlag.

NESSE, AGNETE, 2012a. 'Four languages, one text type: The neighbours' books of Bryggen 1529–1936', in Merja Stenroos, Martti Mäkinen & Inge Særheim (eds.), *Language contact and development around the North Sea*. Amsterdam: John Benjamins Publishing. 81–98.

NESSE, AGNETE, 2012b. 'Norwegian and German in Bergen', in Lennart Elmevik & Ernst Håkon Jahr (eds.), *Contact between Low German and Scandinavian in the Late Middle Ages: 25 years of research* (Acta Academiae Regiae Gustavi Adolphi CXXI). Uppsala: Kungl. Gustav Adolfs Akademien för svensk folkkultur. 75–94.

NEVALAINEN, TERTTU, HELENA RAUMOLIN-BRUNBERG & HEIKKI MANNILA, 2011. The diffusion of language change in real time: Progressive and conservative individuals and the time depth of change. *Language Variation and Change* 23 (1), 1–43. https://doi.org/10.1017/S0954394510000207.

NICHOLS, JOHANNA, 2009. 'Linguistic complexity: A comprehensive definition and survey', in Geoffrey Sampson, David Gil & Peter Trudgill (eds.), *Language complexity as an evolving variable*. Oxford: Oxford University Press. 110–125.

NIYOGI, PARTHA & ROBERT C. BERWICK, 1997. 'A dynamical systems model for language change', *Complex Systems* 11(3). 161–204.

NJÅSTAD, MAGNE, 2003. *Grenser for makt: konflikter og konfliktløsing mellom lokalsamfunn og øvrighet ca 1300–1540* (Skriftserie fra Institutt for Historie og Klassiske Fag 42). Trondheim: Inst. for Historie og Klassiske Fag, NTNU.

NORDE, MURIEL, 1997. *The history of the genitive in Swedish. A case study in degrammaticalization*. Amsterdam: Universiteit van Amsterdam Ph.D. dissertation.

NORDE, MURIEL, 2001. 'The history of the Swedish genitive: The full story. A reply to Delsing', *Nordic Journal of Linguistics* 24(1). 107–117.

NORDE, MURIEL, 2006. 'Demarcating degrammaticalization: The Swedish s-genitive revisited', *Nordic Journal of Linguistics* 29(2), 201–238.

NOREEN, ADOLF, 1970. *Altisländische und altnorwegische Grammatik: (Laut- und Flexionslehre); unter Brücksichtigung des Urnordischen* (Altnordische Grammatik von Adolf Noreen; 1). Halle: Niemeyer.

OLSSON, G., 1965. *Distance and human interaction*. Philadelphia, PA: Regional Science Institute.

O'NEIL, WAYNE, 1978. 'The evolution of Germanic inflectional systems: A study in the causes of language change', *Orbis* 28(2). 248–286.

ORRMAN, ELJAS, 2003a. 'Church and society', in Knut Helle (ed.), *The Cambridge History of Scandinavia* (Vol. 1). Cambridge: Cambridge University Press. 421–462.

ORRMAN, ELJAS, 2003b. 'Rural conditions', in Knut Helle (ed.), *The Cambridge History of Scandinavia* (Vol. 1). Cambridge: Cambridge University Press. 250–311.

OTTOSSON, KJARTAN, 2003. 'Utviklinga av person- og numerusbøyinga av verb i gammalnorsk og mellomnorsk', in Jan Terje Faarlund (ed.), *Språk i endring: indre norsk språkhistorie*. Oslo: Novus. 111–183.

PARKVALL, MIKAEL, 2008. 'The simplicity of creoles in a cross-linguistic perspective', in Matti Miestamo, Kaius Sinnemäki & Fred Karlsson (eds.), *Language complexity: Typology, contact, change* (Studies in Language Companion Series 94). Amsterdam: John Benjamins Publishing. 265–285.

PASEK, JOSH, 2020. *weights: Weighting and Weighted Statistics*. https://cran.r-project.org/package=weights.

PERRIDON, HARRY, 2013. 'The emergence of the s-genitive in Danish', *Language Sciences* 36. 134–146.

PETTERSEN, EGIL, 1991. *Språkbrytning i Vest-Norge 1450–1550 II*. Bergen: Alma Mater.

PINTZUK, SUSAN, 2003. 'Variationist approaches to syntactic change', in Brian D. Joseph & Richard D. Janda (eds.), *The handbook of historical linguistics*. Oxford: Blackwell. 509–528.

PROJ CONTRIBUTORS, 2020. PROJ coordinate transformation software library. Open Source Geospatial Foundation. https://proj.org/ (24 Feburary 2021).

QGIS.ORG, 2021. *QGIS Geographic Information System*. QGIS Association. http://www.qgis.org/ (26 July 2021).

R CORE TEAM, 2020. *R: A Language and Environment for Statistical Computing*. Vienna, Austria: R Foundation for Statistical Computing. https://www.R-project.org/ (8 March 2021).

RAMBØ, GRO-RENÉE, 2008. *Historiske og sosiale betingelse for språk-kontakt mellom nedertysk og skandinavisk i seinmiddelalderen – et bidrag til historisk språksosiologi.* Kristiansand: Universitet i Agder Ph.D. dissertation.

RAMBØ, GRO-RENÉE, 2012. 'Language contact, communication and change', in Lennart Elmevik & Ernst Håkon Jahr (eds.), *Contact between Low German and Scandinavian in the Late Middle Ages: 25 years of research* (Acta Academiae Regiae Gustavi Adolphi CXXI). Uppsala: Kungl. Gustav Adolfs Akademien för svensk folkkultur. 39–55.

RAUMOLIN-BRUNBERG, HELENA, 2009. 'Lifespan changes in the language of three early modern gentlemen', in Minna Nevala, Arja Nurmi & Minna Palander-Collin (eds.), *The language of daily life in England (1450–1800)*. Amsterdam: John Benjamins. 165–196.

REINHAMMER, MAJ, 1973. *Om dativ i svenska och norska dialekter. 1. Dativ vid verb.* Uppsala: Almqvist & Wiksell.

ROMAINE, SUZANNE, 1992. 'The evolution of linguistic complexity in Pidgin and Creole Languages', in John A. Hawkins & Murray Gell-Mann (eds.), *The evolution of human languages. Proceedings of The Workshop on the Evolution of Human Languages, August 1989, Santa Fe, New Mexico*, vol. XI. Santa Fe Institute: Addison-Wesley Publishing. 213–238.

RUMPF, JONAS, SIMON PICKL, STEPHAN ELSPASS & WERNER KÖNIG, 2009. 'Structural analysis of dialect maps using methods from spatial statistics', *Zeitschrift für Dialektologie und Linguistik* 76(3). 280–308.

RYGH, OLUF, JOHAN ALBERT KJÆR, HJALMAR FALK, AMUND B. LARSEN, MAGNUS BERNHARD OLSEN, KARL RYGH & J. QVIGSTAD, 1898–1936. *Norske gaardnavne: Oplysninger samlede til brug ved matrikelens revision.* Kristiania: W. C. Fabritius.

SANKOFF, GILLIAN, 2013. 'Longitudinal Studies', in Robert Bayley, Richard Cameron & Ceil Lucas (eds.), *The Oxford handbook of sociolinguistics*. Oxford: Oxford University Press. https://doi.org/10.1093/oxfordhb/9780199744084.013.0013.

SANKOFF, GILLIAN & HÉLÈNE BLONDEAU, 2007. 'Language change across the lifespan: /r/ in Montreal French', *Language* 83(3). 560–588.

SCHIMMELPFENNIG, GRO, 1985. *Lydverket i Vest-Agder-diplomer fra før 1450.* Universitet i Oslo: Universitet i Oslo. MA dissertation.

SCHLEICHER, AUGUST, 1853. 'Die ersten spaltungen des indogermanischen urvolkes', *Allgemeine Monatsschrift für Wissenschaft und Literatur* 3. 786–787.

SCHMIDT, JOHANNES, 1872. *Die verwandtschaftsverhältnisse der indogermanischen sprachen.* Weimar: Hermann Böhlau.

SCHREIER, DANIEL, 2009. 'Language in Isolation, and Its [sic] Implications for Variation and Change', *Language and Linguistics Compass* 3(2). 682–699.

SCHULTE, MICHAEL, 2005. 'Phonological developments from Old Nordic to Early Modern Nordic I: West Scandinavian', in Oskar Bandle, Ernst Håkon Jahr, Allan Karker, Hans-Peter Naumann, Ulf Teleman & Kurt Braunmüller (eds.), *The Nordic languages: An international handbook of the history of the North Germanic Languages*. Berlin: Walter de Gruyter. 1081–1096.

SÉGUY, J., 1973. 'La relation entre la distance spatiale et la distance lexicale', *Revue de Linguistique Romane* 35(1). 335–357.

SEIP, DIDRIK ARUP, 1934. *Studier i norsk språkhistorie*. Oslo: H. Aschehoug & Co. (W. Nygaard).

SEIP, DIDRIK ARUP, 1954. *Nye studier i norsk språkhistorie. [Festskrift på 70-års dagen]*. Oslo: Aschehoug.

SEIP, DIDRIK ARUP, 1955. *Norsk språkhistorie til omkring 1370* (2nd edn). Oslo: H. Aschehoug & Co.

SEIP, DIDRIK ARUP, 1993. 'Om vilkårene for nedertyskens innflytelse på nordisk', in Ernst Håkon Jahr & Ove Lorentz (eds.), *Historisk språkvitenskap/Historical linguistics* (Studier i norsk språkvitenskap/Studies in Norwegian linguistics 5). Oslo: Novus. 145–149.

SHOSTED, RYAN K., 2006. 'Correlating complexity: A typological approach', *Linguistic Typology* 10(1). 1–40.

SIBLER, PIUS, 2011. *Visualisierung und geostatistische analyse mit daten des syntaktischen atlas der Deutschen Schweiz (SADS)*. Zurich: Department of Geography, University of Zurich. Masters' thesis. https://www.dialektsyntax. uzh.ch/dam/jcr:4622fa3e-22a8-40f1-b8f5-2a7ccb69e892/glaser_bart_sibler_wei bel_2012.pdf (2 April 2021).

SINNEMÄKI, KAIUS, 2009. 'Complexity in core argument marking and population size', in Geoffrey Sampson, David Gil & Peter Trudgill (eds.), *Language complexity as an evolving variable*. Oxford: Oxford University Press. 126–140.

SKARD, VEMUND, 1973. *Norsk språkhistorie. Bind I – til 1523*. Oslo: Universitetsforlaget.

SKAUTRUP, PETER, 1968. *Det danske sprogs historie* (Vol. 2: Fra Unionsbrevet til Jyske Lov). København: Gyldendal.

SKJEKKELAND, MARTIN, 2005. *Dialektar i Noreg: tradisjon og fornying*. Kristiansand: Høyskoleforlaget.

SLUNGåRD, STAALE, 2015. *Staten og geistligheten: En undersøkelse av Jemtland 1571–1645*. NTNU MA. http://hdl.handle.net/11250/2388025.

TAGLIAMONTE, SALI A. & ALEXANDRA D'ARCY, 2007. Frequency and variation in the community grammar: Tracking a new change through the generations, *Language Variation and Change* 19(2). 1–19.

THOMASON, SARAH GREY & TERRENCE KAUFMAN, 1988. *Language contact, creolization, and genetic linguistics*. Berkeley, CA: University of California Press.

THUN, TERJE & HELENE SVARVA, 2018. Tree-ring growth shows that the significant population decline in Norway began decades before the Black Death. *Dendrochronologia* 47. 23–29.

THURSTON, WILLIAM R., 1987. *Processes of change in the languages of northwestern New Britain* (Pacific Linguistics B99). Canberra: The Australian National University.

THURSTON, WILLIAM R., 1988. 'How exoteric languages build a lexicon: Esoterogeny in West New Britain', in Ray Harlow & Robin Hooper (eds.), *VICAL 1: Oceanic languages. Papers from the Fifth International Conference on Austronesian Linguistics, Auckland, New Zealand, January 1988.* Auckland: Linguistic Society of New Zealand. 555–579.

THURSTON, WILLIAM R., 1994. 'Renovation and innovation in the languages of northwestern New Britain', in Tom Dutton & Darrell T Tyron (eds.), *Language contact and change in the Austronesian Wworld* (Trends in Linguistics: Studies and Monographs 77). Berlin: Mouton de Gruyter. 573–609.

TOFT, ELLEN HELLEBOSTAD, 2009. *Adnominal and adverbial genitive constructions in Old Norse.* Oslo: Universitet i Oslo Ph.D. dissertation.

TØNNESSEN, RAGNHILD, 1995. *Verbalbøying i eit utval Oslo-diplom 1450–1499.* Oslo: Universitetet i Oslo Hovudoppgåve.

TROSTERUD, TROND, 2001. 'The changes in Scandinavian morphology from 1100 to 1500', *Arkiv för nordisk filologi* 116. 153–191.

TROUSDALE, GRAEME & MURIEL NORDE, 2013. Degrammaticalization and constructionalization: Two case studies, *Language Sciences* 36. 32–46.

TRUDGILL, PETER, 1974. Linguistic change and diffusion: Description and explanation in sociolinguistic dialect geography, *Language in Society* 3(2). 215–246.

TRUDGILL, PETER, 2001. Contact and simplification: Historical baggage and directionality in linguistic change, *Linguistic Typology* 5(2/3). 372–374.

TRUDGILL, PETER, 2011. *Sociolinguistic typology: Social determinants of linguistic complexity.* Oxford: Oxford University Press.

TYLDEN, PER, 1944. *Me - vi: Ein studie frå det gamalnorske og mellomnorske brevriket* (Skrifter utgitt av Det norske videnskaps-akademi i Oslo. II, Hist.-filos. klasse 1944: 4). Oslo: Jacob Dybwad.

Unger, Carl R & HJ Huitfeldt-Kaas (eds.), 1863–1900. *Diplomatarium Norvegicum* (Vol. 6–15). Oslo: Christiania.

VAHTOLA, JOUKO, 2003. 'Population and settlement', in Knut Helle, *The Cambridge History of Scandinavia* (Vol. 1). Cambridge: Cambridge University Press. 559–580.

VERSLOOT, ARJEN P., 2008. *Mechanisms of language change: vowel reduction in 15th century West Frisian (LOT International Series 195).* Utrecht: Landelijke Onderzoekschool Taalwetenschap (LOT).

VERSLOOT, ARJEN, 2020. 'Historical dialectology: West Frisian in seven centuries', in Stanley D Brunn & Roland Kehrein (eds.), *Handbook of the changing world language map.* Cham: Springer International. 405–442.

WEINREICH, URIEL, 1953. *Languages in contact, findings and problems*. New York: Linguistic Circle of New York.

WEINREICH, URIEL, WILLIAM LABOV & MARVIN HERZOG, 1968. 'Empirical foundations for a theory of language change', in Winfred P Lehmann & Yakov Malkiel (eds.), *Directions for Historical Linguistics*. Austin/London: University of Texas Press, 97–195.

WERNER, OTMAR, 1984. 'Morphologische entwicklung in den Germanischen sprachen', in J Untermann & B Brogyany (eds.), *Das Germanische und die rekonstruktion der Indo-germanischen grundsprache*. Amsterdam: Benjamins. 181–226.

WESSÉN, ELIAS, 1954. *Om det tyska inflytandet på svenskt språk under medeltiden (Skrifter utgivna av Nämuden för svensk språkvård 12)*. Stockholm.

WESSÉN, ELIAS, 1968. *Svensk språkhistoria* (Vol. 1: Ljudlära och ordböjningslära, 8th edn). Lund: Almqvist & Wiksell.

WETÅS, ÅSE, 2003. 'Kan ein komparativ studie av namn og appellativisk materiale kasta lys over kasusbortfallet i mellomnorsk?' in Jan Terje Faarlund (ed.), *Språk i endring: Indre Norsk språkhistorie*. Oslo: Novus. 279–309.

WETÅS, ÅSE, 2008. *Kasusbortfallet i mellomnorsk*. Oslo: Universitet i Oslo Ph.D. dissertation.

WHEELER, DAVID & MICHAEL TIEFELSDORF, 2005. 'Multicollinearity and correlation among local regression coefficients in geographically weighted regression', *Journal of Geographical Systems* 7(2). 161–187.

WIKLE, THOMAS & GUY BAILEY, 1997. The spatial diffusion of linguistic features in Oklahoma. *Proceedings of the Oklahoma Academy of Science* 77. 1–15.

WILLIS, DAVID, 2017. 'Investigating geospatial models of the diffusion of morphosyntactic innovations: The Welsh strong second-person singular pronoun chdi', *Journal of Linguistic Geography* 5(1). 41–66.

WINFORD, DONALD, 2005. 'Contact-induced changes: Classification and processes', *Diachronica* 22(2). 373–427.

WOLFRAM, WALT & NATALIE SCHILLING-ESTES, 2003. 'Dialectology and linguistic diffusion', in Brian D Joseph & Richard D Janda (eds.), *The handbook of historical linguistics* (Blackwell Handbooks in Linguistics). Malden, MA: Blackwell. 713–735.

WRAY, ALISON & GEORGE W. GRACE, 2007. 'The consequences of talking to strangers: Evolutionary corollaries of socio-cultural influences on linguistic form', *Lingua* 117(3). 543–578.

WURZEL, WOLFGANG ULLRICH, 2001. 'Creoles, complexity and linguistic change', *Linguistic Typology* 5. 377–387.

YANG, CHARLES D., 2002. *Knowledge and learning in natural language* (Oxford Linguistics). Oxford; New York: Oxford University Press.

ZOËGA, GEIR T., 2004. *A concise dictionary of Old Icelandic* (Medieval Academy Reprints for Teaching 41). Toronto: University of Toronto Press.

Printed and bound by CPI Group (UK) Ltd, Croydon, CR0 4YY
22/04/2022
03121140-0001